ROUTLEDGE · ENGLISH · TEXTS

GENERAL EDITOR · JOHN DRAKAKIS

PERCY BYSSHE SHELLEY

Selected Poetry and Prose

ROUTLEDGE · ENGLISH · TEXTS

GENERAL   EDITOR · JOHN   DRAKAKIS

Forthcoming

PERCY BYSSHE SHELLEY

Selected Poetry and Prose

Edited by Alasdair D.F. Macrae

LONDON AND NEW YORK

First published in 1991
by Routledge
11 New Fetter Lane,
London EC4P 4EE

Simultaneously published in the USA and
Canada
by Routledge
a division of Routledge, Chapman and Hall
Inc.
29 West 35th Street, New York, NY 10001

Introduction, critical commentary and
notes © 1991 Alasdair D. F. Macrae

Printed in Great Britain by Clays Ltd,
St Ives plc

British Library Cataloguing in
Publication Data
Shelley, P. B. (Percy Bysshe) 1792–1822
Shelley: selected poetry and prose. –
(Routledge English texts).
I. Macrae, Alasdair D. F. II. Series
821.7

Library of Congress Cataloging in
Publication Data
Shelley, Percy Bysshe, 1792–1822.
[Selections. 1991]
Shelley, selected poetry and prose/
edited by Alasdair D. F. Macrae.
p. cm. – (Routledge English texts)
Includes bibliographical references and
index.
I. Macrae, Alasdair D. F.
II. Title. III. Series.
PR 5403.M25 1991
821'.7 – dc20   90–41096

ISBN 0415 01607X (pbk)

For Elise

Contents

Introduction

In his excellent book *The Age of Revolution 1789–1848*, E. J. Hobsbawm begins his Introduction with the following paragraph:

> Words are witnesses which often speak louder than documents. Let us consider a few English words which were invented, or gained their modern meanings, substantially in the period of sixty years with which this volume deals. They are such words as 'industry', 'industrialist', 'factory', 'middle class', 'capitalism', and 'socialism'. They include 'aristocracy' as well as 'railway', 'liberal' and 'conservative' as political terms, 'nationality', 'scientist', and 'engineer', 'proletariat' and (economic) 'crisis'. 'Utilitarian' and 'statistics', 'sociology', and several other names of modern sciences, 'journalism' and 'ideology', are coinages or adaptations of this period. So are 'strike' and 'pauperism'.

Most of these terms relate to social or political matters but, as Hobsbawm knew, the list of new vocabulary can be extended to demonstrate changes in many other areas of activity. The period into which Shelley was born in 1792 saw some of the most enormous and abrupt changes in the history of European civilization.

As the eighteenth century progressed, many social theorists concentrated their attention less on how human beings group together in societies and what the bonds are that hold a society together, and more on how the nature of a society can be transformed into a new kind of association. These theorists did not sit down and invent notions of a new society out of the air; they were pushed towards certain possibilities by their observations of what was happening around them in England or France or wherever. All

1

political shifts are in part a reaction to an existing situation and in part a pursuit of a vision of the future. Obviously, no one fixed situation prevailed across a century and different continents; certain characteristics, however, were apparent. What were these characteristics?

The bulk of the population lived in the country; even in industrialized England the urban population outnumbered the rural population only after 1850. Most people lived their whole lives without moving beyond the parish of their birth. The cycle of the seasons, the tending of crops and animals, provided the pattern for their lives. Because of poor roads and slow transport and a high level of illiteracy, the intrigues of the royal court, the deliberations of Parliament, and innovations in literature and science must have barely impinged on the consciousness of a fisherman in Cornwall or a farm labourer in Perthshire. The landowner and employer would have had almost absolute local power over their tenants and employees. Often, it seemed that the legal system was constructed so as to protect the wealth and privileges of those who inherited wealth and to prevent the poor from improving their condition. A person could be hanged or deported even for petty crimes. Recruits were found for the British navy by armed press-gangs kidnapping men in coastal areas; conditions on board ship were so bad that few could be persuaded to volunteer for service. In times of poor harvests, natural disasters and disease, the systems of community welfare were usually rudimentary, and ordinary working people living at subsistence level were very vulnerable. There was a high infant mortality rate and, moreover, child-bearing was a danger to the mother.

Notwithstanding these gloomy features of life for many people in Britain in the middle of the eighteenth century, there is another way of seeing the situation. People grew up belonging to a community, sharing pleasures and adversities, aware of a continuity beyond their individual lives, a tradition perpetuated in stories and song. There has been a temptation, and this was a tendency in the Romantic period, to carry this view into sentimentality. In the second half of the century there took place an increasing move of people from the countryside into the towns, partly as a result of Enclosure Acts (from 1760 on) which, in effect, excluded the peasantry from what had been communally worked land, and partly because the new factories, resulting from technical advances and inventions, created a demand for labourers. Oliver Goldsmith, in his poem *The Deserted Village* (published 1770), laments the changes he saw happening in rural England and Ireland:

Ill fares the land, to hastening ills a prey,
Where wealth accumulates, and men decay;

Princes and Lords may flourish, or may fade;
A breath can make them, as a breath has made;
But a bold peasantry, their country's pride,
When once destroyed, can never be supplied.
  A time there was, ere England's griefs began,
When every rood of ground maintained its man;
For him light labour spread her wholesome store,
Just gave what life required, but gave no more;
His best companions, innocence and health;
And his best riches, ignorance of wealth.

As the processes of industrialization accelerated, as the squalor and degradation in the towns became more obvious, and with the fears, political disturbances and social dislocations associated with the Napoleonic Wars, it became easier, perhaps even necessary, for people to cultivate an idealized and consolatory picture of Britain in an earlier generation. Also, in contrast to city life, the natural world was represented by poets as benign, healthy and even wise.

Alongside the mass of people who existed precariously, there were groups who enjoyed huge wealth. A hereditary aristocracy based on the ownership of land lived in leisure and luxury and at the top of the aristocracy was the hereditary monarchy. Notwithstanding the constitutional changes introduced during and after the temporary removal of the monarchy by the Puritans in the seventeenth century, the structure of power in England remained concentrated in the same class of people through much of the eighteenth century. True, the monarch's individual political wishes could be overruled by Parliament but a system of preferment and patronage perpetuated lines of advancement in the church, the armed forces, public institutions and the government itself. Furthermore, and this came to be the most vexing and insistent failure of Britain to modernize its political system, Parliament was totally unrepresentative of the country as a whole: not simply in terms of social class but also in terms of actual areas of the country. In 1815 a quarter of the seats in the Commons were returned by five shires in the south-west of England; London had a tiny representation and Birmingham and Manchester had none. In the north of England, the part most affected by industrialization and urbanization, the people had hardly any opportunity to make their opinions felt at a parliamentary level. What we would now call trade unionism was disapproved of and often banned by successive governments; even after 1825, when the

Combination Act (1799) against unions was repealed, associations of working people had to operate with great care. The development of the gap between the rich and the poor was to be explored in *Sybil, or the Two Nations* (1845), a novel by Benjamin Disraeli, who, when he later became Tory Prime Minister, was responsible for some enlightened legislation to help the disadvantaged areas of society.

What was the attitude of organized religion to these obvious inequalities and injustices? The Church of England, as the state religion of England, operated as an arm of the state and tended to confirm and justify the political values. There were, certainly, individuals of piety, humaneness and reforming zeal in the church, but, as an institution, it lacked conviction and saw little reason to question its privileged status in the country. Oxford and Cambridge, the only universities in England, refused entry to Roman Catholics and Nonconformists until as late as 1871 and retained a strong clerical basis; in the period at the end of the eighteenth century and the beginning of the nineteenth they were not particularly distinguished for their intellectual ferment. The very complacency and spiritual dullness of the Church of England prompted John Wesley (1703–91) to look elsewhere for his religious inspiration and his quest led to the development of Methodism, not formally separated from the Church of England till four years after his death. In his ministry of about fifty years, Wesley preached over 40,000 sermons and, covering thousands of miles each year mainly on horseback, he took his gospel of salvation to every corner of England and Wales, but particularly to areas without churches, to new towns and slums. His emotional brand of Christianity was the largest manifestation of revivalist, sometimes hysterical, religion, which catered for a need felt by many people, for whom the more conventional forms of religion were moribund, but also aroused the concern of some observers who saw such religious enthusiasm as irrational, dangerously subjective and socially anarchic. Whether Methodism and other Dissenting sects helped to neutralize, contain and buy off what could have issued as revolution in working-class and middle-class people in the 1790s, or whether the idealism of these sects was part of a gradual reformist movement in English society, is a question still energetically debated by historians. Alongside these religious changes, a considerable secularization took place in British society, and a number of the leading thinkers at the end of the eighteenth century took a positive stand against organized religion. Some held a deist position and argued that an

4

individual could apprehend some notion of a deity not in theological dogmas but in the planned character of the universe; others saw religious belief as a denial of human value and an obstacle to necessary social and intellectual development. Against the threat of what was seen as the irreligion of the French Revolution, some people turned back to religious orthodoxies.

Overall, looking back at the period leading up to the end of the eighteenth century, the observer is struck by an expansionist tendency in Britain. In the wars and treaties in Europe, the Americas and Asia in the middle of the century, Britain had secured a huge empire which was to provide the raw materials and the market for a vast increase in its manufacturing industries. Country houses and public buildings exhibited the trophies and works of art acquired around the world. (The national galleries and museums which manifested the economic and military power of Britain were established in the nineteenth century.) In this process, there were three happenings or sequences of events which provoked serious thought and shaped the nature of Britain's development.

In the midst of the imperialist expansion, the American colonies revolted and succeeded in gaining their independence from Britain. The war of 1775–83 was less significant for Britain in a military sense than as an ideological stimulus. The colonists succeeded, it seemed to European observers, partly because they had an ideal to fight for, and this political ideal came to be formulated in the Declaration of Independence of 1776. The first draft of the Declaration was written by Thomas Jefferson, later to be President of the United States, and its most famous sentence reads:

> We hold these truths to be self evident: that all men are created equal; that they are endowed by their Creator with certain ['inherent' in Jefferson's draft] inalienable rights; that among these are life, liberty, and the pursuit of happiness; that to secure these rights, governments are instituted among men, deriving their just powers from the consent of the governed; that whenever any form of government becomes destructive of these ends, it is the right of the people to alter or abolish it, and to institute new government, laying its foundation on such principles, and organizing its powers in such form, as to them shall seem most likely to effect their safety and happiness.

This unequivocal assertion of equality and the sovereignty of the people sent ripples across the Atlantic which provided impetus to the wave of revolution in France. What was most impressive was the success of the American revolt; such slogans as 'No taxation without representation' might have seemed naïve and premature but the victory of the Americans offered an example which could be repeated elsewhere.

In the period in France prior to 1789, the period which came to be called the *ancien régime*, changes did take place, reforms were happening, tentative moves were made to widen the process of government. Revolutions occur, it seems, not when oppression is at its maximum but when a certain release is allowed and when people are granted some measure of advancement but are ambitious for more power, more quickly. Some of the writers whose particular influence can be discerned in the Revolution will be discussed later. What helped to create an intellectual climate in France was the work of an assortment of thinkers, often collaborating in loose association with each other and collectively labelled *les philosophes*. Such major figures as Montesquieu, Voltaire, Buffon, d'Holbach and Rousseau contributed articles to the *Encyclopédie* edited by Diderot. The subtitle of the twenty-eight volumes was 'Dictionnaire raisonné des sciences, des arts et des métiers'; this vast project, eventually completed in 1772 after over twenty years' effort, often against official bans and disapproval, offered a comprehensive display of advanced knowledge and opinion on almost every aspect of life. Across the articles there is a prevailing attitude of rationalism which called into doubt conventional assumptions concerning religion and the social order.

Many of the *philosophes* expressed their admiration for an English way of doing things; they saw English society as less rigid, more tolerant of new ideas, more pragmatic. The events of the French Revolution, however, caused very extreme reactions in different minds across the Channel. To begin with, most radicals in Britain were wildly enthusiastic at the overthrow of the old order and the exciting possibilities for the future. Attitudes began to change, often to fear and hostility, as the events unfolded from the initial meeting of the Assembly of the States-General in May 1789 and the destruction of the old prison, the Bastille, in July, through the establishment of a more democratic state, to the arrest and execution of King Louis XVI in 1793, the Reign of Terror, 1793–4, the declaration of war by Britain on France and eventually the assumption of total power by Napoleon Bonaparte in 1799. Britain and France were at war for about twenty years till Napoleon was finally defeated at Waterloo in 1815. Debate raged in Britain, and some of the very freedoms so admired by the French *philosophes* were curtailed by a scared government. Distinctions between political parties became more pronounced from this period on (it is symptomatic that the modern terms Left and Right entered the vocabulary from seating arrangements in the French Assembly), and the word 'revolution' in politics came to be used exclusively for drastic, even violent, change. The states around France saw the Revolution as a highly contagious disease which had to be eradicated at its source; the further reactionary view saw an inevitable pattern in all revolution: if the legitimate (that is, existing) hierarchy of power and privilege is tampered with, a blood-bath (the Reign of Terror) must follow. We shall see later that one of Shelley's ambitions in his poetry was to rebut the false logic of this argument and present revolution in a more favourable light. He wished to avoid the example of Wordsworth (who was in France during the early part of the Revolution), for whom then

Bliss was it in that dawn to be alive,
And to be young was very Heaven!

but who, according to Shelley, lost all hope of human betterment and lapsed into a compliance with the forces of reactionary politics.

It was as a parallel to the momentous changes of the French Revolution that a Frenchman chose to describe this period in Britain as the Industrial Revolution. Why Britain should have led the world in industrialization is difficult to ascertain. Certainly through its own resources and those of its colonies it had access to raw materials and commercial wealth, and in the eighteenth century advances took place in agriculture which enabled a larger population in towns to be fed. What was crucial, however, and distinguished Britain from France was the tolerance to new ideas and the pragmatism so envied by the French *philosophes*. In France as well as Britain in the eighteenth century there was much talk of 'improvement'; the two strongest contributory countries to what has come to be called the Age of Enlightenment were France and Scotland, the *Encyclopédie* being matched by the *Encyclopaedia Britannica*, produced in Edinburgh (first edition 1768–71). In Britain ideas led to practical applications and advances. The most significant single invention, or rather development, was the Scotsman James Watt's steam-engine, which by the 1780s was being used in mines, in the new canals and in spinning mills. The making of roads and canals, the powering of vehicles on land and sea, mass production in factories – all were to change the nature of Britain irreversibly. Because coal now replaced water as the source of power, most of the new factories were sited near the coalmines in the northern half of England, south Wales and the central lowlands of Scotland. Little consideration was given to town planning or to the welfare of the workers, and horrific conditions at work and in housing developed quickly. The very advances in iron-working, printing, chemistry, medicine, engineering and the spectacular growth in trade and wealth highlighted the abject misery and exploitation of working people. In the years after Waterloo thousands of demobilized and maimed soldiers and families without husbands or fathers added to a sense of uprootedness (the word 'alienation', so common in later Marxist terminology, came into its modern use at this period). Until they were finally repealed in 1846, successive Corn Laws kept the price of grain high by regulating the amount of cheap imported grain, and the threat of starvation was used by employers to hold down wages.

INTELLECTUAL INFLUENCES ON SHELLEY

Events of 200 years ago may be given a significance, have causes and effects attached to them, be interpreted differently, by different historians, but, even allowing for such differences of focus, the events have a fixity which is much more difficult to claim for intellectual history. Some books and ideas may be so taken for granted in a particular period that people in that period can fail to mention or even notice their influence. Furthermore, when we look back over 200 years, we are most interested in the books that can still excite us and we may neglect or ignore books which enjoyed a fashion in that period but which are no longer immediately relevant to our tastes. For example, John Bunyan's *Pilgrim's Progress*, originally published 1678-84, was one of the most widely read books in Britain in Shelley's lifetime; E. P. Thompson in his authoritative work *The Making of the English Working Class* (1963) can claim: '*Pilgrim's Progress* is, with *Rights of Man* [by Thomas Paine], one of the two foundation texts of the English working-class movement.' How many people today, even those interested in the working-class movement, read Bunyan? And how many now read James MacPherson (1736-96), who claimed to have translated the ancient Gaelic poet Ossian and whose books were admired as immortal masterpieces across every country in Europe?

When we try to ascertain the influence of his reading on an individual writer, the problem is even more vexed: Shelley, who consistently attacked organized Christianity and challenged the morality implicit in much of the

Old Testament, was a regular reader of the Bible, and Jesus was one of his heroes. In fact, Shelley was immensely well read not just in literature but in science, history and, above all, philosophy. The lengthy notes to his long poem *Queen Mab*, published before he was twenty-one, display the width of his early reading, and he later translated poetry from Greek, Latin, German, Spanish and Italian. Theories on clouds, diet, geology, genetics, political economy, gases, magnetism, were all exciting to him and his reading on such subjects can be traced in his poetry. He wished poetry to include scientific knowledge rather than be in opposition to it; in this respect he is unusual among the main Romantic poets in English but anticipates the ambitions of such later poets as Walt Whitman (1819–92) and Hugh MacDiarmid (1892–1978). His travels in Europe allowed him to see the effects of different systems of government and in France he saw the ravages caused by the Napoleonic Wars. His mind was unparochial in both place and time; his knowledge of the cultures of ancient Greece and Rome was thorough and provided him with a perspective for his observations on his own surroundings.

Repeatedly he returned to the writings of Plato (*c*.428–*c*.348 BC). Because Socrates, Plato's teacher, did not write any books and Plato used Socrates as the central speaker in most of his books, it is difficult to distinguish the teachings of the two philosophers. Socrates emerges as a man dedicated to truth, the very pursuit of which led to a noble martyrdom when he was condemned to death by the ruling council of Athens for religious heresy and corrupting the youth of the city with his teachings. In his heroism and opposition to ignorance and hypocrisy, Socrates provided Shelley with one of his strongest models. Plato was considered by Shelley to be one of the finest poets: in his dialogues, where philosophical argument is conducted by characters who represent different positions, Plato writes with a strong dramatic sense and a cunning use of irony and devises memorable images to convey ideas. He saw the world around us as unreal, a distorted imitation of the real world of Ideal Forms; in *The Republic* he describes human beings as sitting in a cave with their backs to the light outside, and what they take to be real consists of shadows cast on the back wall of the cave. The philosopher's task, according to Plato, is to discard the shadows and learn to look towards the real. After all the eighteenth century's philosophical discussions on the nature and reliability of perception, Shelley found Plato's idea illuminating and the challenge implicit in it exciting. He grafted some of his political idealism on to this stem. What, according to Plato, urges some people to strive towards reality is their vision of a spiritual love; Shelley adapts this notion into his ideal of Intellectual Beauty. In Plato the poet is actually viewed with considerable ambivalence: he may be described as divinely inspired or as mad but Shelley accepts only the favourable view and fuses that with Plato's idea of the philosopher to create a quester after truth and beauty with a gift for expression.

The idealist and ethereal vision that he derived from Plato was countered by his reading of philosophers nearer his own time, particularly David Hume (1711–76). Although not a commercial or critical success when it was published in 1739–40, Hume's *A Treatise of Human Nature* has been seen by subsequent philosophers as one of the turning points in western thought. Hume queried the very basis of our thinking about the world and how our minds work. In an age when many thinkers considered that if only men would exert their rational powers all human problems could be solved, he challenged this faith in reason and argued that what we like to deem the results of reasoning are often merely convenient habits which make our lives simpler. On personal identity, religious beliefs, miracles and political hopes, he cast the same sceptical eye. A genial man himself, he seemed surprised at the shocked reaction to his reasoning. His emphasis on what makes people feel happy and his claim that moral arguments are based on feelings rather than reason helped to give substance and validity to cultivated sensations. Hume's demolition of reason might appear to lead to a condition of despair, but he insisted that the ordinary pleasures of life are sufficient for his happiness:

Most fortunately it happens that, since reason is incapable of dispelling these clouds, nature herself suffices to that purpose, and cures me of this philosophical melancholy and delirium, either by relaxing this bent of mind, or by some avocation, and lively impression of my senses, which obliterate all these chimeras. I dine, I play a game of backgammon, I converse, and am merry with my friends; and when, after three or four hours' amusement, I would return to these speculations, they appear so cold, and strained, and ridiculous, that I cannot find in my heart to enter into them any farther.

(*A Treatise of Human Nature*, Conclusion to Book I)

Our most cherished notions, including religious beliefs, are, according to him, imaginative constructs which render the world a more comprehensible and satisfactory situation for us. Hume usually seems, however, quite tolerant of other people's beliefs, so long as they are not imposed on, or at the expense of, someone else.

What Shelley saw in the work of Voltaire (1694–1778) was a much more abrasive mind, a sharper satirical edge. Throughout his long life, the French writer waged repeated campaigns against bigotry, the abuse of power, superstition and selfishness; he suffered imprisonment in the Bastille, exile from France, banishment from fashionable society in Paris, and condemnation by religious and political authorities. In *Candide* (1759) he mocks glib optimism, the belief that happy progress is inevitable; natural disasters and human greed force disillusionment on the idealist.

It was, however, Rousseau (1712–78), of all modern thinkers, who was most admired by Shelley, and such was the power of his writing that, for Shelley, he transcended mere prose and became one of the great poets. This quarrelsome, restless and often unhappy man introduced radical proposals for increasing human happiness. He argued that social development and culture of the sort advocated by his contemporaries made people less rather than more genuinely civilized. Society deprives individuals of freedom and he sets up nature as a surer instructor. The child is given a previously unheard-of prominence in Rousseau's scheme; the child should be brought up in rural surroundings and should learn not from books but from need and pleasure and practice. Recognizing that, whatever state of bliss may have prevailed in primitive times, we cannot go backwards, he outlines in *The Social Contract* (1762) how society could be realigned to allow the people to be the government with full equality of property and opportunity. Finally, as a seal of his plea for individualism, his *Confessions* was published after his death; it invites the reader to share in his description and analysis of intimate parts of his life. Any one of half a dozen of his books could be claimed as the most important contribution to the Romantic movement.

While acknowledging his own debt to Rousseau and Voltaire and the effect of their ideas on leaders in the French Revolution, Shelley had serious reservations about both men. In his essay 'Proposals for an Association of Philanthropists' (1812) he writes:

> Voltaire was the flatterer of kings, though in his heart he despised them – so far has he been instrumental in the present slavery of his country. Rousseau gave licence by his writings to passions that only incapacitate and contract the human heart. So far hath he prepared the necks of his fellow beings for that yoke of galling and dishonourable servitude which at this moment it bears.

Two years earlier, when he was eighteen, Shelley read *The Enquiry Concerning Political Justice* by William Godwin (1756–1836). Originally published in 1793, this book, which now seems rather dull, had a marked and prolonged influence on British radical thought. Godwin, later to be Shelley's father-in-law, believed that, if knowledge was expanded and people were appealed to rationally, then error would be eradicated, progress would be inevitable and human beings, in realizing their potential, would become perfect; the state with all its controls, laws and institutions (such as marriage) would wither away and individuals would live in benevolent harmony. Later, as his son-in-law, Shelley did not find him such a model of rationality and generosity but he continued to acknowledge Godwin as a courageous fighter for justice. Godwin's anarchist vision could not tolerate any authority imposed centrally or from above: he deplored religious orthodoxies, censorship in any form, systems of inherited wealth and power, national welfare and even any scheme of general education. Although his doctrines were as extreme as those of his friend Thomas Paine (1737–1809), he escaped imprisonment or banning because the Prime Minister, Pitt, decided that *Political Justice* was too expensive a book to cause much damage. Paine had been deeply involved in the struggle for American independence and his pamphlets were held in high regard by the leaders of the Revolution in France. Edmund Burke, who had supported the Americans' wish for autonomy but who was appalled at what took place in France in the name of freedom, published his *Reflections on the Revolution in France* in 1790. In it he argued passionately against change by violence, claiming that society is an organic entity and must reform itself at a pace the society can understand and accept. This classic defence of the conservative line enraged Thomas Paine, who felt that Burke's high-toned perspective ignored the cruel iniquities and suffering of the people in France. In order to avoid arrest for sedition, Paine had to flee England, between the publication of Part I of *The Rights of Man* in 1791 and Part II in 1792. Apart from being an attack on Burke and a defence of the Revolution in France, the book analyses the basis of society and outlines how Britain should learn from the examples of America and France and create a new system free from inherited privilege by providing equal opportunities and welfare for all its citizens. In France in 1792–3, while he was an elected member of the Convention, he denounced the executions taking place, including that of Louis XVI, and was imprisoned and threatened with execution himself. In 1793–5 he brought out his *Age of Reason* in which he castigated much of what was taught as Christianity: he deplored what he described as 'the obscene stories' of the Old Testament, and questioned the reliability of much of the New Testament, including the virgin birth of Jesus.

Shelley, born in 1792, read both Godwin and Paine when they were no longer so immediately and dangerously controversial but the ideas promulgated by both men were still deemed novel, seditious and heretical. The French Revolution, such a testing ground for ideas and ideals, remained the dominating event of Shelley's lifetime and, despite a gathering scepticism based on disappointments and experience, he remained very much a fellow promoter of the ideals of Godwin.

LITERARY BACKGROUND

When Shelley was young he read with relish quantities of garish Gothic novels creaking with tombs, ghosts, magic and macabre horrors. He himself wrote two puerile examples: *Zastrozzi* and *St Irvyne, or The Rosicrucian*, both published in 1810. Apart from Rousseau's *The New Héloise* and Goethe's *The Sorrows of Young Werther*, he expressed little interest in novels. Although he wrote some plays, he disliked what he knew of the contemporary London theatre. It would appear that he preferred to read plays, and the dramatists he liked most were Sophocles, Shakespeare, Calderón and Goethe.

Undoubtedly, his main literary interest was in poetry (although it must be remembered that he considered Plato, Francis Bacon and Rousseau as poets). Because of his competence in several languages, he was able to take equal delight in Homer and Milton, and in Tasso and Lucretius. His particular taste in poetry and his ideas on poetry will be examined later. At this point, I am more concerned with the processes in literature of which he was a part. 'Poets', writes Shelley, 'not otherwise than philosophers, painters, sculptors and musicians, are, in one sense, the creators, and, in another, the creations of their age. From this subjection the loftiest do not escape.' And, in the Preface to *The Revolt of Islam* (written in 1817), he accepts that

> There must be a resemblance, which does not depend upon their own will, between all the writers of any particular age. They cannot escape from subjection to a common influence which arises out of an infinite combination of circumstances belonging to the times in which they live; though each is in a degree the author of the very influence by which his being is thus pervaded.

The label most commonly used by literary historians to designate the age in which Shelley lived is 'Romantic', and, however vague, ambiguous and misleading the term is, it does point to some of the characteristics of him and his contemporaries.

The Romantic movement developed at the end of the eighteenth century and within a generation it affected the literature written in all the main languages of Europe. Part of its early impetus came from a growing disenchantment with some of the literary and social conventions evident in the poetry fashionable in eighteenth-century Britain. Too often poetry seemed narrowed and constrained by the poet's adherence to a poetic diction, a notion of decorum and an identification with a class interest. Discordant elements emerged in such poets as Christopher Smart (1722–71), William Cowper (1731–1800) and George Crabbe (1754–1832); and much more markedly in Robert Burns (1759–96) and William Blake (1757–1827). It would be misguided to suggest that these poets formed any kind of homogeneous group, but, in different ways, they anticipated some of the features to be found more fully developed in poets such as Wordsworth and Shelley.

One of these features is the prominence given to the poet's autobiographical self in his poetry. The earlier etiquette rationed the display of personal feelings; poetry was a social utterance and, therefore, at a discreet remove from the intimate details of the poet's private life. Rousseau at the opening of his *Confessions* (completed in 1765 and published in 1781) proclaims, 'My purpose is to display to my kind a portrait in every way true to nature and the man I shall portray will be myself.' Such an egocentric focus is very marked in Romantic poetry, and the bizarre, the eccentric, the nonconformist, the unsocialized are valued tokens of individualism. Also in tune with Rousseau's theories, the untutored child is credited with a spontaneity, a freshness of perception and a direct wisdom; the poet's childhood (although this is not particularly obvious in Shelley) becomes a subject and source of poems. Wordsworth's *The Prelude*, constantly revised between its inception in 1798 and the poet's death in 1850, is the most extreme and lengthy examination of self in the poetry of this period, but Wordsworth's description, a 'poem on the growth of my own mind', can be applied to many contemporary poems. What often emerges in such egocentric poems is the instability and even the unlocatability of any tidy entity called the self. Shelley was particularly aware of this insubstantiality and goes so far, in his 'Essay on Life', as to question the very notion of separate selves in different people or any distinction between an individual and the world around.

In the poetry of this period, 'the world around' is more commonly the

14

world of nature rather than the world of society found in Augustan poetry. Simultaneously with the movement of thousands of people from the countryside into the newly industrialized towns, there was a growing fascination among artists and writers with untamed nature. Wild places were sought out like sites of pilgrimage and in poetry the language of religion was conferred on the mysteries and powers of natural forces. In the painter J. M. W. Turner's work the same sense of awe is apparent as in the poetry of Wordsworth and Shelley. In 'Tintern Abbey' (1798) Wordsworth declares himself

> well pleased to recognise
> In nature and the language of the sense
> The anchor of my purest thoughts, the nurse,
> The guide, the guardian of my heart, and soul
> Of all my moral being.

Despite his admiration for Wordsworth, Shelley could not accept the older poet's view of nature as a moral guide, and his own poetry from *Alastor* (1815) onwards offers a critique of Wordsworth's philosophy.

According to many of the poets contemporary with Shelley – even Byron, who claimed to admire Pope above all recent writers – the poets of the eighteenth century were conformist and acquiescent in a prevailing social and moral order. Starting with Blake in the 1780s, the poets during the following forty years tried out in their work new idealisms and challenged or dismantled every aspect of previously accepted thought. Taboo subjects such as incest were explored, and extremes in rebelliousness, criminality and anarchism were entertained and given some sort of validity. The Byronic hero, driven by an often undisclosed passion into melancholy or exile, was related to that other Romantic figure possessed by nympholepsy, an obsession with an unattainable desire. Poets came to see themselves as being at odds with society and even with the circumstances of ordinary life, as prophetic figures, pointing to a promised land transformed by the power of the imagination.

In line with these subversive and visionary ambitions, the style of poetry had to move from the orthodoxy of eighteenth-century heroic couplets, and this is one of the most experimental phases in English poetry. Coleridge, following the German critic A. W. Schlegel, advanced a notion of organic as distinct from mechanical form. In his 'Lectures on Shakespeare' he claims:

The organic form . . . is innate; it shapes as it develops itself from within, and the fulness of its development is one and the same with the perfection of its outward form. Such is the life, such is the form. Nature, the prime genial artist, inexhaustible in diverse powers, is equally inexhaustible in forms. Each exterior is the physiognomy of the being within, its true image reflected and thrown out from the concave mirror. And even such is the appropriate excellence of her chosen poet, of our own Shakespeare, himself a nature humanized, a genial understanding directing self-consciously a power and an implicit wisdom deeper than consciousness.

This connection between nature and a 'wisdom deeper than consciousness' and art is central to a great deal of Romantic poetry; it is manifested in the increased use of mythical and symbolic motifs and in an openness of form to accommodate such large-scale and elusive material. Shelley's *Prometheus Unbound* is an obvious example, and his special admiration in contemporary writing was reserved for the potential of Byron revealed in *Don Juan* and the mastery of Goethe in *Faust*. In *Prometheus Unbound* and *Faust* a wide variety of verse forms is employed and Byron, although he adheres to ottava rima throughout *Don Juan*, performs such juggling acts with verse, syntax and register that the effect is one of irregularity and certainly not of mechanicalness. In a letter to his publisher, Byron boasted, 'I *have* no plan . . . the Soul of such writing is in its licence.' It is significant that in the case of each of the three poems its author had difficulty in deciding how or when to complete the work.

A NOTE ON THE TEXT

There is no authoritative and generally accepted text for Shelley's poetry and prose. The extensive work done recently on the materials available should, in the next few years, issue in more reliable editions. The first of three volumes of the complete poems edited by the late G. M. Matthews and K. Everest was published in 1989 by Longman.

The conventions of punctuation have not remained constant from Shelley's time to our time; and editors have had to strike some balance between what can be considered to be Shelley's intended punctuation and what makes sense to the editor. Moreover, in earlier times the publisher/printer was often responsible for such matters as punctuation and, certainly in Shelley's case, the poet did not always supervise the details of how his writings were printed. The texts in this volume have been edited with the main aim in mind of clarity for the reader. Square brackets are used in this selection to indicate a gap in Shelley's manuscript; in some cases a suggestion is made as to how the gap may be plausibly filled. The order of the poems is roughly chronological. With the exception of the Preface to *Prometheus Unbound*, which precedes the text of the poem, the selection of prose pieces follows the selection of poems.

Chief editions of Shelley's work:

Ingpen, R., and Peck, W. E., *The Complete Works of Percy Bysshe Shelley*, 10 vols, London, Benn, 1926–30.

Hutchinson, T., *The Complete Poetical Works of Percy Bysshe Shelley* (1904), revised by G. M. Matthews, London, Oxford University Press, 1970.

Clark, D. L., *Shelley's Prose: or, the Trumpet of a Prophecy*, Albuquerque, University of New Mexico Press, 1966.

Jones, F. L., *The Letters of Percy Bysshe Shelley*, 2 vols, Oxford, Clarendon Press, 1964.

Shelley's life and some contemporary events

	1789 Outbreak of the French Revolution.
	1790 Edmund Burke: *Reflections on the Revolution in France*.
	1791 Paine: *The Rights of Man* (Part I).
1792 Percy Bysshe Shelley born at Horsham, Sussex, the son of Timothy Shelley, landowner and Whig Member of Parliament.	1792 Mary Wollstonecraft: *A Vindication of the Rights of Woman*.
	1793 Louis XVI of France executed. Britain declared war on France. The Reign of Terror (till 1794). Godwin: *Enquiry Concerning Political Justice*. Paine: *The Age of Reason*.
	1794 Blake: *Songs of Experience*.
	1795 Thomas Carlyle born.
	1796 Robert Burns died.
	1798 Wordsworth and Coleridge: *Lyrical Ballads*. Rebellion in Ireland.
	1799 Robert Owen began his model factory at New Lanark, Scotland.

1804	To Eton (till 1810)	1804	Napoleon became emperor. Kant died.
		1808	Goethe: *Faust* (Part I).
		1809	Beethoven: Fifth Symphony. Tennyson born.
1810	Published two Gothic novels, *Zastrozzi* and *St Irvyne*; *Original Poetry by Victor and Cazire* (with his sister); *Posthumous Fragments of Margaret Nicholson*. Entered Oxford University.	1810	Wars for independence in South America began.
1811	Wrote *The Necessity of Atheism*. Sent down from Oxford. Eloped with Harriet Westbrook and married in Edinburgh. Met Southey.	1811	J. M. W. Turner lectured on landscape painting at the Royal Academy.
1812	Made speeches in Dublin and published *Address to the Irish People*, *Proposals for an Association of Philanthropists* and *Declaration of Rights*. Worked on establishing a model village in North Wales. Became a vegetarian. Met William Godwin and Thomas L. Peacock.	1812	Invasion of Russia by Napoleon and his retreat. Byron: *Childe Harold* (Canto One). Browning born.
1813	Returned briefly to Ireland. *Queen Mab* printed. Ianthe Shelley born.	1813	Jane Austen: *Pride and Prejudice*.
1814	*A Refutation of Deism* printed. Travelled to the	1814	Napoleon exiled to Elba.

continent with Mary Godwin and her stepsister Claire Clairmont. Charles Shelley born to estranged wife Harriet.

1815 Death of his grandfather gave Shelley a sizeable income. Death of Mary's first child. *Alastor* written.

1816 Son William born to Mary. Met Byron at Lake Geneva. Wrote 'Hymn to Intellectual Beauty' and 'Mont Blanc'. Suicide of Harriet. Married Mary.

1817 Met Keats. Developed friendship with Leigh Hunt. Denied custody of Harriet's children. Finished writing *Laon and Cythna*. Published *A Proposal for Putting Reform to the Vote*; *History of a Six Weeks' Tour*; *An Address to the People on the Death of the Princess Charlotte*. Clara Shelley born.

1818 *Laon and Cythna* published as *The Revolt of Islam*. Left for Italy (where he was to spend the remainder of his life). Translated Plato's *Symposium*. Met Byron in Venice. Began *Prometheus Unbound*; *Julian and Maddalo* and 'Lines Written among the Euganean Hills'. Daughter Clara died. Met the Gisbornes.

Sir Walter Scott: *Waverley*. Invention of steam printing machine.

1815 Battle of Waterloo. Congress of Vienna (opened 1814). Corn Laws passed.

1816 Spa Fields riots in London.

1817 Coleridge: *Biographia Literaria*. Death of Princess Charlotte. Execution of the leaders of riot at Derby. Habeus Corpus suspended.

1818 First steamship crossing of the Atlantic. Karl Marx born. Mary Shelley: *Frankenstein* (begun in 1815). Peacock: *Nightmare Abbey* (Shelley is caricatured as Scythrop Glowry). Keats: *Endymion*.

1819	Again moved about between several parts of Italy. Finished *Julian and Maddalo*; *Prometheus Unbound* (in two stages). Wrote *The Cenci*; *The Mask of Anarchy*; *Peter Bell the Third*; 'Ode to the West Wind'. Began *A Philosophical View of Reform*. Published *Rosalind and Helen*. Son William died, son Percy Florence born.	1819	Peterloo massacre at Manchester. The 'Six Acts' (repressive measures) passed by Parliament. Byron: *Don Juan* (first two Cantos).
1820	Settled in north-west of Italy, mainly in Pisa. Wrote 'The Sensitive Plant', 'Ode to Liberty', 'The Cloud', 'To a Skylark', 'Letter to Maria Gisborne', *The Witch of Atlas*, 'Ode to Naples', *Swellfoot the Tyrant*. Published *The Cenci*; *Prometheus Unbound*. Friendship with Emilia Viviani.	1820	Death of George III and accession of Prince Regent as George IV. Democratic uprisings in Spain and Italy. Cato Street Conspiracy to kill the Cabinet in London discovered. Keats: *Lamia and Other Poems*. John Clare: *Poems Descriptive of Rural Life and Scenery*.
1821	Jane and Edward Williams arrived in Pisa. Worked on 'A Defence of Poetry'. Wrote *Epipsychidion*; *Adonais*; *Hellas*. Byron arrived at Pisa.	1821	Napoleon died. Keats died in Rome. Greek War of Independence (from the Turks) began. Rising in Naples crushed.
1822	Worked on a play, *Charles the First*, and *The Triumph of Life*. Wrote poems to Jane Williams. Translated scenes from Goethe's *Faust* and from Calderón.	1822	Matthew Arnold born. Suicide of Castlereagh.

Drowned when sailing
back with Edward
Williams from Livorno
where he had welcomed
Leigh Hunt to Italy.

		1823	The Monroe Doctrine.
1824	Publication of *Posthumous*	1824	Death of Byron at
	Poems, edited by Mary		Missolonghi.
	Shelley.		
		1825	First railway ran from
			Stockton to Darlington.
			Foundation of University
			of London.
		1832	The Reform Bill.
			Death of Goethe and
			Scott.
			Mazzini founded 'Young
			Italy'.
1839	*The Poetical Works of*		
	P. B. S. in four volumes		
	published by Mary Shelley.		

PERCY BYSSHE SHELLEY

Selected Poetry and Prose

MUTABILITY

We are as clouds that veil the midnight moon;
  How restlessly they speed, and gleam, and quiver
Streaking the darkness radiantly! – yet soon
  Night closes round, and they are lost for ever;

Or like forgotten lyres, whose dissonant strings
  Give various response to each varying blast,
To whose frail frame no second motion brings
  One mood or modulation like the last.

We rest – a dream has power to poison sleep;
  We rise – one wandering thought pollutes the day: 10
We feel, conceive or reason, laugh or weep;
  Embrace fond woe, or cast our cares away:

It is the same! – For, be it joy or sorrow,
  The path of its departure still is free:
Man's yesterday may ne'er be like his morrow;
  Nought may endure but Mutability.

Composed 1814?
First published 1816

TO WORDSWORTH

Poet of Nature, thou hast wept to know
That things depart which never may return:
Childhood and youth, friendship and love's first glow,
Have fled like sweet dreams, leaving thee to mourn.
These common woes I feel. One loss is mine
Which thou too feel'st, yet I alone deplore:
Thou wert as a lone star, whose light did shine
On some frail bark in winter's midnight roar;
Thou hast like to a rock-built refuge stood
Above the blind and battling multitude;   10
In honoured poetry thy voice did weave
Songs consecrate to truth and liberty –
Deserting these, thou leavest me to grieve,
Thus having been, that thou shouldst cease to be.

Composed 1814?
First published 1816

* Numbers in square brackets refer to pages on which notes may be found.

HYMN TO INTELLECTUAL BEAUTY

I

The awful shadow of some unseen Power
  Floats though unseen amongst us, – visiting
  This various world with as inconstant wing
As summer winds that creep from flower to flower;
Like moonbeams that behind some piny mountain shower,
    It visits with inconstant glance
    Each human heart and countenance;
Like hues and harmonies of evening,
    Like clouds in starlight widely spread,
    Like memory of music fled, –   10
    Like aught that for its grace may be
Dear, and yet dearer for its mystery.

II

Spirit of BEAUTY, that doth consecrate
  With thine own hues all thou doest shine upon
  Of human thought or form, – where art thou gone?
Why dost thou pass away and leave our state,
This dim vast vale of tears, vacant and desolate?
    Ask why the sunlight not forever
    Weaves rainbows o'er yon mountain river,
Why aught should fail and fade that once is shown,   20
    Why fear and dream and death and birth
    Cast on the daylight of this earth
    Such gloom, why man has such a scope
For love and hate, despondency and hope?

III

No voice from some sublimer world hath ever
  To sage or poet these responses given;
  Therefore the name of God and ghosts and Heaven,
Remain the records of their vain endeavour,
Frail spells – whose uttered charm might not avail to sever,
    From all we hear and all we see,   30
    Doubt, chance, and mutability.

Thy light alone – like mist o'er mountains driven,
    Or music by the night wind sent
    Through strings of some still instrument,
    Or moonlight on a midnight stream,
Gives grace and truth to life's unquiet dream.

IV

Love, Hope, and Self-esteem, like clouds depart
  And come, for some uncertain moments lent.
  Man were immortal and omnipotent,
Didst thou, unknown and awful as thou art,   40
Keep with thy glorious train firm state within his heart.
    Thou messenger of sympathies,
    That wax and wane in lovers' eyes,
Thou, that to human thought art nourishment,
    Like darkness to a dying flame,
    Depart not as thy shadow came,
    Depart not – lest the grave should be,
Like life and fear, a dark reality.

V

While yet a boy I sought for ghosts, and sped
  Through many a listening chamber, cave and ruin,   50
  And starlight wood, with fearful steps pursuing
Hopes of high talk with the departed dead.
I called on poisonous names with which our youth is fed,
    I was not heard, I saw them not;
    When musing deeply on the lot
Of life, at that sweet time when winds are wooing
    All vital things that wake to bring
    News of buds and blossoming, –
    Sudden, thy shadow fell on me;
I shrieked, and clasped my hands in ecstasy!   60

VI

I vowed that I would dedicate my powers
  To thee and thine – have I not kept the vow?
  With beating heart and streaming eyes, even now

I call the phantoms of a thousand hours
Each from his voiceless grave: they have in visioned bowers
    Of studious zeal or love's delight
    Outwatched with me the envious night;
They know that never joy illumed my brow
    Unlinked with hope that thou wouldst free
    This world from its dark slavery,   70
    That thou, O awful LOVELINESS,
Wouldst give whate'er these words cannot express.

VII

The day becomes more solemn and serene
  When noon is past – there is a harmony
  In autumn, and a lustre in its sky,
Which through the summer is not heard or seen,
As if it could not be, as if it had not been.
    Thus let thy power, which like the truth
    Of nature on my passive youth
Descended, to my onward life supply   80
    Its calm – to one who worships thee,
    And every form containing thee,
    Whom, SPIRIT fair, thy spells did bind
To fear himself, and love all human kind.

Composed 1816
First published 1817

MONT BLANC

Lines written in the Vale of Chamouni

I

The everlasting universe of things
Flows through the mind, and rolls its rapid waves,
Now dark – now glittering – now reflecting gloom –
Now lending splendour, where from secret springs
The source of human thought its tribute brings
Of waters, – with a sound but half its own,
Such as a feeble brook will oft assume

In the wild woods, among the mountains lone,
Where waterfalls around it leap forever,
Where woods and winds contend, and a vast river   10
Over its rocks ceaselessly bursts and raves.

II

Thus thou, Ravine of Arve – dark, deep Ravine –
Thou many-coloured, many-voicèd vale,
Over whose pines, and crags, and caverns sail
Fast cloud-shadows and sunbeams: awful scene,
Where Power in likeness of the Arve comes down
From the ice-gulfs that gird his secret throne,
Bursting through these dark mountains like the flame
Of lightning through the tempest; – thou dost lie,
Thy giant brood of pines around thee clinging,   20
Children of elder time, in whose devotion
The chainless winds still come and ever came
To drink their odours, and their mighty swinging
To hear – an old and solemn harmony;
Thine earthly rainbows stretched across the sweep
Of the aethereal waterfall, whose veil
Robes some unsculptured image; the strange sleep
Which when the voices of the desert fail
Wraps all in its own deep eternity; –
Thy caverns echoing to the Arve's commotion,   30
A loud, lone sound no other sound can tame,
Thou art pervaded with that ceaseless motion,
Thou art the path of that unresting sound –
Dizzy Ravine! – and when I gaze on thee
I seem as in a trance sublime and strange
To muse on my own separate phantasy,
My own, my human mind, which passively
Now renders and receives fast influencings,
Holding an unremitting interchange
With the clear universe of things around;   40
One legion of wild thoughts, whose wandering wings
Now float above thy darkness, and now rest
Where that or thou art no unbidden guest,
In the still cave of the witch Poesy,

Seeking among the shadows that pass by,
Ghosts of all things that are, some shade of thee,
Some phantom, some faint image; till the breast
From which they fled recalls them, thou art there!

III

Some say that gleams of a remoter world
Visit the soul in sleep, – that death is slumber,   50
And that its shapes the busy thoughts outnumber
Of those who wake and live. – I look on high;
Has some unknown omnipotence unfurled
The veil of life and death? or do I lie
In dream, and does the mightier world of sleep
Spread far around and inaccessibly
Its circles? For the very spirit fails,
Driven like a homeless cloud from steep to steep
That vanishes among the viewless gales!
Far, far above, piercing the infinite sky,   60
Mont Blanc appears, – still, snowy, and serene;
Its subject mountains their unearthly forms
Pile round it, ice and rock; broad vales between
Of frozen floods, unfathomable deeps,
Blue as the overhanging heaven, that spread
And wind among the accumulated steeps;
A desert peopled by the storms alone,
Save when the eagle brings some hunter's bone,
And the wolf tracks her there – how hideously
Its shapes are heaped around! rude, bare, and high,   70
Ghastly, and scarred, and riven. – Is this the scene
Where the old Earthquake-daemon taught her young
Ruin? Were these their toys? or did a sea
Of fire envelop once this silent snow?
None can reply – all seems eternal now.
The wilderness has a mysterious tongue
Which teaches awful doubt, or faith so mild,
So solemn, so serene, that man may be,
In such a faith, with nature reconciled;
Thou hast a voice, great Mountain, to repeal   80
Large codes of fraud and woe; not understood

32

By all, but which the wise, and great, and good
Interpret, or make felt, or deeply feel.

IV

The fields, the lakes, the forests, and the streams,
Ocean, and all the living things that dwell
Within the daedal earth; lightning, and rain,
Earthquake, and fiery flood, and hurricane,
The torpor of the year when feeble dreams
Visit the hidden buds, or dreamless sleep
Holds every future leaf and flower; – the bound   90
With which from that detested trance they leap;
The works and ways of man, their death and birth,
And that of him and all that his may be;
All things that move and breathe with toil and sound
Are born and die; revolve, subside and swell.
Power dwells apart in its tranquillity
Remote, serene, and inaccessible:
And *this*, the naked countenance of earth,
On which I gaze, even these primeval mountains
Teach the adverting mind. The glaciers creep   100
Like snakes that watch their prey, from their far fountains,
Slow rolling on; there, many a precipice,
Frost and the Sun in scorn of mortal power
Have piled: dome, pyramid, and pinnacle,
A city of death, distinct with many a tower
And wall impregnable of beaming ice.
Yet not a city, but a flood of ruin
Is there, that from the boundaries of the sky
Rolls its perpetual stream; vast pines are strewing
Its destined path, or in the mangled soil   110
Branchless and shattered stand; the rocks, drawn down
From yon remotest waste, have overthrown
The limits of the dead and living world,
Never to be reclaimed. The dwelling-place
Of insects, beasts, and birds becomes its spoil;
Their food and their retreat forever gone,
So much of life and joy is lost. The race
Of man flies far in dread; his work and dwelling

Vanish, like smoke before the tempest's stream,
And their place is not known. Below, vast caves   120
Shine in the rushing torrents' restless gleam,
Which from those secret chasms in tumult welling
Meet in the vale, and one majestic River,
The breath and blood of distant lands, forever
Rolls its loud waters to the ocean waves,
Breathes its swift vapours to the circling air.

V

Mont Blanc yet gleams on high: – the power is there,
The still and solemn power of many sights,
And many sounds, and much of life and death.
In the calm darkness of the moonless nights,   130
In the lone glare of day, the snows descend
Upon that Mountain; none beholds them there,
Nor when the flakes burn in the sinking sun,
Or the star-beams dart through them. – Winds contend
Silently there, and heap the snow with breath
Rapid and strong, but silently! Its home
The voiceless lightning in these solitudes
Keeps innocently, and like vapour broods
Over the snow. The secret strength of things
Which governs thought, and to the infinite dome   140
Of heaven is as a law, inhabits thee!
And what were thou, and earth, and stars, and sea,
If to the human mind's imaginings
Silence and solitude were vacancy?

Composed 1816
First published 1817

OZYMANDIAS

I met a traveller from an antique land
Who said: 'Two vast and trunkless legs of stone
Stand in the desert. Near them, on the sand,
Half sunk, a shattered visage lies, whose frown,
And wrinkled lip, and sneer of cold command,

Tell that its sculptor well those passions read
Which yet survive, stamped on these lifeless things,
The hand that mocked them and the heart that fed;
And on the pedestal these words appear:
"My name is Ozymandias, king of kings: 10
Look on my works, ye Mighty, and despair!"
Nothing beside remains. Round the decay
Of that colossal wreck, boundless and bare
The lone and level sands stretch far away.'

Composed 1817
First published 1818

JULIAN AND MADDALO
A Conversation

I rode one evening with Count Maddalo
Upon the bank of land which breaks the flow
Of Adria towards Venice: a bare strand
Of hillocks, heaped from ever-shifting sand,
Matted with thistles and amphibious weeds,
Such as from earth's embrace the salt ooze breeds,
Is this; – an uninhabited sea-side,
Which the lone fisher, when his nets are dried,
Abandons; and no other object breaks
The waste, but one dwarf tree and some few stakes   10
Broken and unrepaired, and the tide makes
A narrow space of level sand thereon,
Where 'twas our wont to ride while day went down.
This ride was my delight. – I love all waste
And solitary places; where we taste
The pleasure of believing what we see
Is boundless, as we wish our souls to be:
And such was this wide ocean, and this shore
More barren than its billows; and yet more
Than all, with a remembered friend I love   20
To ride as then I rode; – for the winds drove
The living spray along the sunny air
Into our faces; the blue heavens were bare,

35

Stripped to their depths by the awakening North
And, from the waves, sound like delight broke forth
Harmonizing with solitude, and sent
Into our hearts aërial merriment.
So, as we rode, we talked; and the swift thought,
Winging itself with laughter, lingered not
But flew from brain to brain, – such glee was ours,   30
Charged with light memories of remembered hours,
None slow enough for sadness; till we came
Homeward, which always makes the spirit tame.
This day had been cheerful but cold, and now
The sun was sinking, and the wind also.
Our talk grew somewhat serious, as may be
Talk interrupted with such raillery
As mocks itself, because it cannot scorn
The thoughts it would extinguish: – 'twas forlorn
Yet pleasing, such as once, so poets tell,   40
The devils held within the dales of Hell
Concerning God, freewill and destiny:
Of all that earth had been or yet may be,
All that vain men imagine or believe,
Or hope can paint or suffering may achieve,
We descanted, and I (for ever still
Is it not wise to make the best of ill?)
Argued against despondency, but pride
Made my companion take the darker side.
The sense that he was greater than his kind   50
Had struck, methinks, his eagle spirit blind
By gazing on its own exceeding light.
Meanwhile the sun paused ere it should alight,
Over the horizon of the mountains; – Oh,
How beautiful is sunset, when the glow
Of Heaven descends upon a land like thee,
Thou Paradise of exiles, Italy!
Thy mountains, seas and vineyards and the towers
Of cities they encircle! – it was ours
To stand on thee, beholding it; and then   60
Just where we had dismounted, the Count's men
Were waiting for us with the gondola. –

As those who pause on some delightful way
Though bent on pleasant pilgrimage, we stood
Looking upon the evening and the flood
Which lay between the city and the shore
Paved with the image of the sky : . . the hoar
And aëry Alps towards the north appeared
Through mist, an heaven-sustaining bulkwark reared
Between the east and west; and half the sky   70
Was roofed with clouds of rich emblazonry
Dark purple at the zenith, which still grew
Down the steep west into a wondrous hue
Brighter than burning gold, even to the rent
Where the swift sun yet paused in his descent
Among the many-folded hills: they were
Those famous Euganean hills, which bear
As seen from Lido through the harbour piles
The likeness of a clump of peakèd isles –
And then – as if the Earth and Sea had been   80
Dissolved into one lake of fire, were seen
Those mountains towering as from waves of flame
Around the vaporous sun, from which there came
The inmost purple spirit of light, and made
Their very peaks transparent. 'Ere it fade,'
Said my companion, 'I will show you soon
A better station' – so, o'er the lagoon
We glided, and from that funereal bark
I leaned, and saw the city, and could mark
How from their many isles in evening's gleam   90
Its temples and its palaces did seem
Like fabrics of enchantment piled to Heaven.
I was about to speak, when – 'We are even
Now at the point I meant,' said Maddalo,
And bade the gondolieri cease to row.
'Look, Julian, on the West, and listen well
If you hear not a deep and heavy bell.'
I looked, and saw between us and the sun
A building on an island; such a one
As age to age might add, for uses vile,   100
A windowless, deformed and dreary pile;

And on the top an open tower, where hung
A bell, which in the radiance swayed and swung –
We could just hear its hoarse and iron tongue:
The broad sun sunk behind it, and it tolled
In strong and black relief. – 'What we behold
Shall be the madhouse and its belfry tower,'
Said Maddalo, 'and ever at this hour
Those who may cross the water, hear that bell
Which calls the maniacs each one from his cell   110
To vespers.' – 'As much skill as need to pray
In thanks or hope for their dark lot have they
To their stern maker,' I replied. 'O ho!
You talk as in years past,' said Maddalo.
' 'Tis strange men change not. You were ever still
Among Christ's flock a perilous infidel,
A wolf for the meek lambs – if you can't swim
Beware of Providence.' I looked on him,
But the gay smile had faded in his eye.
'And such,' – he cried, 'is our mortality,   120
And this must be the emblem and the sign
Of what should be eternal and divine! –
And like that black and dreary bell, the soul,
Hung in a heaven-illumined tower, must toll
Our thoughts and our desires to meet below
Round the rent heart and pray – as madmen do
For what? they know not, – till the night of death
As sunset that strange vision, severeth
Our memory from itself, and us from all
We sought and yet were baffled.' I recall   130
The sense of what he said, although I mar
The force of his expressions. The broad star
Of day meanwhile had sunk behind the hill,
And the black bell became invisible
And the red tower looked grey, and, all between,
The churches, ships and palaces were seen
Huddled in gloom; – into the purple sea
The orange hues of heaven sunk silently.
We hardly spoke, and soon the gondola
Conveyed me to my lodgings by the way.   140

The following morn was rainy, cold and dim:
Ere Maddalo arose, I called on him,
And whilst I waited with his child I played;
A lovelier toy sweet Nature never made,
A serious, subtle, wild, yet gentle being,
Graceful without design and unforeseeing,
With eyes – oh speak not of her eyes! – which seem
Twin mirrors of Italian Heaven, yet gleam
With such deep meaning, as we never see
But in the human countenance: with me   150
She was a special favourite: I had nursed
Her fine and feeble limbs when she came first
To this bleak world; and she yet seemed to know
On second sight her ancient playfellow,
Less changed than she was by six months or so;
For after her first shyness was worn out
We sate there, rolling billiard balls about,
When the Count entered. Salutations past –
'The words you spoke last night might well have cast
A darkness on my spirit – if man be   160
The passive thing you say, I should not see
Much harm in the religions and old saws
(Though I may never own such leaden laws)
Which break a teachless nature to the yoke:
Mine is another faith' – thus much I spoke,
And noting he replied not, added: 'See
This lovely child, blithe, innocent and free;
She spends a happy time with little care
While we to such sick thoughts subjected are
As came on you last night – it is our will   170
That thus enchains us to permitted ill –
We might be otherwise – we might be all
We dream of, happy, high, majestical.
Where is the love, beauty and truth we seek
But in our mind? and if we were not weak
Should we be less in deed than in desire?'
'Aye, if we were not weak – and we aspire
How vainly to be strong!' said Maddalo:
'You talk Utopia.' 'It remains to know,'

I then rejoined, 'and those who try may find   180
How strong the chains are which our spirit bind:
Brittle perchance as straw . . . We are assured
Much may be conquered, much may be endured,
Of what degrades and crushes us. We know
That we have power over ourselves to do
And suffer – what, we know not till we try;
But something nobler than to live and die –
So taught those kings of old philosophy
Who reigned, before Religion made men blind;
And those who suffer with their suffering kind   190
Yet feel their faith, religion.' 'My dear friend,'
Said Maddalo, 'my judgement will not bend
To your opinion, though I think you might
Make such a system refutation-tight
As far as words go. I knew one like you
Who to this city came some months ago,
With whom I argued in this sort, and he
Is now gone mad, – and so he answered me, –
Poor fellow! but if you would like to go
We'll visit him, and his wild talk will show   200
How vain are such aspiring theories.'
'I hope to prove the induction otherwise,
And that a want of that true theory, still
Which seeks a "soul of goodness" in things ill
Or in himself or others, has thus bowed
His being – there are some by nature proud,
Who patient in all else demand but this:
To love and be beloved with gentleness;
And being scorned, what wonder if they die
Some living death? this is not destiny   210
But man's own wilful ill.'

                              As thus I spoke,
Servants announced the gondola, and we
Through the fast-falling rain and high-wrought sea
Sailed to the island where the madhouse stands.
We disembarked. The clap of tortured hands,
Fierce yells and howlings and lamentings keen,
And laughter where complaint had merrier been,

Moans, shrieks and curses and blaspheming prayers
Accosted us. We climbed the oozy stairs
Into an old courtyard. I heard on high,   220
Then, fragments of most touching melody,
But looking up saw not the singer there –
Through the black bars in the tempestuous air
I saw, like weeds on a wrecked palace growing,
Long tangled locks flung wildly forth, and flowing,
Of those who on a sudden were beguiled
Into strange silence, and looked forth and smiled
Hearing sweet sounds. – Then I: 'Methinks there were
A cure of these with patience and kind care,
If music can thus move . . . but what is he   230
Whom we seek here?' 'Of his sad history
I know but this,' said Maddalo: 'he came
To Venice a dejected man, and fame
Said he was wealthy, or he had been so;
Some thought the loss of fortune wrought him woe;
But he was ever talking in such sort
As you do – far more sadly – he seemed hurt,
Even as a man with his peculiar wrong,
To hear but of the oppression of the strong,
Or those absurd deceits (I think with you   240
In some respects, you know) which carry through
The excellent impostors of this earth
When they outface detection – he had worth,
Poor fellow! but a humourist in his way' –
'Alas, what drove him mad?' 'I cannot say:
A lady came with him from France, and when
She left him and returned, he wandered then
About yon lonely isles of desert sand
Till he grew wild – he had no cash or land
Remaining, – the police had brought him here –   250
Some fancy took him and he would not bear
Removal; so I fitted up for him
Those rooms beside the sea, to please his whim,
And sent him busts and books and urns for flowers
Which had adorned his life in happier hours,
And instruments of music – you may guess

41

A stranger could do little more or less
For one so gentle and unfortunate;
And those are his sweet strains which charm the weight
From madmen's chains, and make this Hell appear   260
A heaven of sacred silence, hushed to hear.' –
'Nay, this was kind of you – he had no claim,
As the world says' – 'None – but the very same
Which I on all mankind were I as he
Fallen to such deep reverse; – his melody
Is interrupted – now we hear the din
Of madmen, shriek on shriek, again begin;
Let us now visit him; after this strain
He ever communes with himself again,
And sees nor hears not any.' Having said   270
These words, we called the keeper, and he led
To an apartment opening on the sea. –
There the poor wretch was sitting mournfully
Near a piano, his pale fingers twined
One with the other, and the ooze and wind
Rushed through an open casement, and did sway
His hair, and starred it with the brackish spray;
His head was leaning on a music book,
And he was muttering, and his lean limbs shook;
His lips were pressed against a folded leaf   280
In hue too beautiful for health, and grief
Smiled in their motions as they lay apart –
As one who wrought from his own fervid heart
The eloquence of passion, soon he raised
His sad meek face and eyes lustrous and glazed
And spoke – sometimes as one who wrote and thought
His words might move some heart that heeded not
If sent to distant lands; and then as one
Reproaching deeds never to be undone,
With wondering self-compassion; then his speech   290
Was lost in grief, and then his words came, each
Unmodulated, cold, expressionless, –
But that from one jarred accent you might guess
It was despair made them so uniform:
And all the while the loud and gusty storm

Hissed through the window, and we stood behind
Stealing his accents from the envious wind
Unseen. I yet remember what he said
Distinctly: such impression his words made.

'Month after month,' he cried, 'to bear this load   300
And as a jade urged by the whip and goad
To drag life on, which like a heavy chain
Lengthens behind with many a link of pain! –
And not to speak my grief – O not to dare
To give a human voice to my despair,
But live and move, and, wretched thing! smile on
As if I never went aside to groan,
And wear this mask of falsehood even to those
Who are most dear – not for my own repose –
Alas, no scorn or pain or hate could be   310
So heavy as that falsehood is to me –
But that I cannot bear more altered faces
That needs must be, more changed and cold embraces,
More misery, disappointment and mistrust
To own me for their father . . . Would the dust
Were covered in upon my body now!
That the life ceased to toil within my brow!
And then these thoughts would at the least be fled;
Let us not fear such pain can vex the dead.

'What Power delights to torture us? I know   320
That to myself I do not wholly owe
What now I suffer, though in part I may.
Alas, none strewed sweet flowers upon the way
Where, wandering heedlessly, I met pale Pain,
My shadow, which will leave me not again –
If I have erred, there was no joy in error,
But pain and insult and unrest and terror;
I have not, as some do, bought penitence
With pleasure, and a dark yet sweet offence,
For then, – if love and tenderness and truth   330
Had overlived hope's momentary youth,
My creed should have redeemed me from repenting;
But loathèd scorn and outrage unrelenting

43

Met love excited by far other seeming
Until the end was gained . . . as one from dreaming
Of sweetest peace, I woke, and found my state
Such as it is. –

        'O thou, my spirit's mate
Who, for thou art compassionate and wise,
Wouldst pity me from thy most gentle eyes
If this sad writing thou shouldst ever see –   340
My secret groans must be unheard by thee,
Thou wouldst weep tears bitter as blood to know
Thy lost friend's incommunicable woe.

  'Ye few by whom my nature has been weighed
In friendship, let me not that name degrade
By placing on your hearts the secret load
Which crushes mine to dust. There is one road
To peace and that is truth, which follow ye!
Love sometimes leads astray to misery.
Yet think not though subdued – and I may well   350
Say that I am subdued – that the full Hell
Within me would infect the untainted breast
Of sacred nature with its own unrest;
As some perverted beings think to find
In scorn or hate a medicine for the mind
Which scorn or hate have wounded – O how vain!
The dagger heals not but may rend again . . .
Believe that I am ever still the same
In creed as in resolve, and what may tame
My heart, must leave the understanding free,   360
Or all would sink in this keen agony –
Nor dream that I will join the vulgar cry,
Or with my silence sanction tyranny,
Or seek a moment's shelter from my pain
In any madness which the world calls gain,
Ambition or revenge or thoughts as stern
As those which make me what I am, or turn
To avarice or misanthropy or lust . . .
Heap on me soon, O grave, thy welcome dust!
Till then the dungeon may demand its prey,   370

And Poverty and Shame may meet and say –
Halting beside me on the public way –
"That love-devoted youth is ours – let's sit
Beside him – he may live some six months yet."
Or the red scaffold, as our country bends
May ask some willing victim, or ye friends
May fall under some sorrow which this heart
Or hand may share or vanquish or avert;
I am prepared – in truth with no proud joy –
To do or suffer aught, as when a boy   380
I did devote to justice and to love
My nature, worthless now! . . .

       'I must remove
A veil from my pent mind. 'Tis torn aside!
O, pallid as Death's dedicated bride,
Thou mockery which art sitting by my side,
Am I not wan like thee? at the grave's call
I haste, invited to thy wedding-ball
To greet the ghastly paramour, for whom
Thou has deserted me . . . and made the tomb
Thy bridal bed . . . But I beside your feet   390
Will lie and watch ye from my winding sheet –
Thus . . . wide awake though dead . . . yet stay, O stay!
Go not so soon – I know not what I say –
Hear but my reasons . . . I am mad, I fear,
My fancy is o'erwrought . . . thou art not here . . .
Pale art thou, 'tis most true . . . but thou art gone,
Thy work is finished . . . I am left alone! –

 'Nay, was it I who wooed thee to this breast
Which, like a serpent, thou envenomest
As in repayment of the warmth it lent?   400
Didst thou not seek me for thine own content?
Did not thy love awaken mine? I thought
That thou wert she who said, "You kiss me not
Ever, I fear you do not love me now" –
In truth I loved even to my overthrow
Her, who would fain forget these words; but they
Cling to her mind, and cannot pass away. –

'You say that I am proud – that when I speak
My lip is tortured with the wrongs which break
The spirit it expresses . . . Never one   410
Humbled himself before, as I have done!
Even the instinctive worm on which we tread
Turns, though it wound not – then with prostrate head
Sinks in the dust and writhes like me – and dies?
No: wears a living death of agonies!
As the slow shadows of the pointed grass
Mark the eternal periods, his pangs pass
Slow, ever-moving, – making moments be
As mine seem – each an immortality! –

'That you had never seen me – never heard   420
My voice, and more than all had ne'er endured
The deep pollution of my loathed embrace –
That your eyes ne'er had lied love in my face –
That, like some maniac monk, I had torn out
The nerves of manhood by their bleeding root
With mine own quivering fingers, so that ne'er
Our hearts had for a moment mingled there
To disunite in horror – these were not
With thee, like some suppressed and hideous thought
Which flits athwart our musings, but can find   430
No rest within a pure and gentle mind . . .
Thou sealedst them with many a bare broad word,
And cearedst my memory o'er them, – for I heard
And can forget not . . . they were ministered
One after one, those curses. Mix them up
Like self-destroying poisons in one cup,
And they will make one blessing which thou ne'er
Didst imprecate for, on me, – death. –

                                        'It were
A cruel punishment for one most cruel,
If such can love, to make that love the fuel   440
Of the mind's hell; hate, scorn, remorse, despair:
But *me* – whose heart a stranger's tear might wear
As water-drops the sandy fountain-stone,

Who loved and pitied all things, and could moan
For woes which others hear not, and could see
The absent with the glance of phantasy,
And with the poor and trampled sit and weep,
Following the captive to his dungeon deep;
Me – who am as a nerve o'er which do creep
The else unfelt oppressions of this earth,   450
And was to thee the flame upon thy hearth
When all beside was cold – that thou on me
Shouldst rain these plagues of blistering agony –
Such curses are from lips once eloquent
With love's too partial praise – let none relent
Who intend deeds too dreadful for a name
Henceforth, if an example for the same
They seek . . . for thou on me lookedst so, and so –
And didst speak thus . . . and thus . . . I live to show
How much men bear and die not! –

              'Thou wilt tell,   460
With the grimace of hate, how horrible
It was to meet my love when thine grew less;
Thou wilt admire how I could e'er address
Such features to love's work . . . this taunt, though true,
(For indeed Nature nor in form nor hue
Bestowed on me her choicest workmanship)
Shall not be thy defence . . . for since thy lip
Met mine first, years long past, since thine eye kindled
With soft fire under mine, I have not dwindled
Nor changed in mind or body, or in aught   470
But as love changes what it loveth not
After long years and many trials.

              'How vain
Are words! I thought never to speak again,
Not even in secret, – not to my own heart –
But from my lips the unwilling accents start,
And from my pen the words flow as I write,
Dazzling my eyes with scalding tears . . . my sight
Is dim to see that charactered in vain

On this unfeeling leaf which burns the brain
And eats into it . . . blotting all things fair   480
And wise and good which time had written there.

'Those who inflict must suffer, for they see
The work of their own hearts, and this must be
Our chastisement or recompense – O child!
I would that thine were like to be more mild
For both our wretched sakes . . . for thine the most
Who feelest already all that thou has lost
Without the power to wish it thine again;
And as slow years pass, a funereal train
Each with the ghost of some lost hope or friend   490
Following it like its shadow, wilt thou bend
No thought on my dead memory? –

                                        'Alas, love!
Fear me not . . . against thee I would not move
A finger in despite. Do I not live
That thou mayst have less bitter cause to grieve?
I give thee tears for scorn and love for hate;
And that thy lot may be less desolate
Than his on whom thou tramplest, I refrain
From that sweet sleep which medicines all pain.
Then, when thou speakest of me, never say   500
"He could forgive not." Here I cast away
All human passions, all revenge, all pride;
I think, speak, act no ill; I do but hide
Under these words, like embers, every spark
Of that which has consumed me – quick and dark
The grave is yawning . . . as its roof shall cover
My limbs with dust and worms under and over
So let Oblivion hide this grief . . . the air
Closes upon my accents, as despair
Upon my heart – let death upon despair!'   510

He ceased, and overcome leant back awhile,
Then rising, with a melancholy smile
Went to a sofa, and lay down, and slept
A heavy sleep, and in his dreams he wept

48

And muttered some familiar name, and we
Wept without shame in his society.
I think I never was impressed so much;
The man who were not, must have lacked a touch
Of human nature . . . then we lingered not,
Although our argument was quite forgot,   520
But calling the attendants, went to dine
At Maddalo's; yet neither cheer nor wine
Could give us spirits, for we talked of him
And nothing else, till daylight made stars dim;
And we agreed his was some dreadful ill
Wrought on him boldly, yet unspeakable,
By a dear friend; some deadly change in love
Of one vowed deeply which he dreamed not of;
For whose sake he, it seemed, had fixed a blot
Of falsehood on his mind which flourished not   530
But in the light of all-beholding truth;
And having stamped this canker on his youth
She had abandoned him – and how much more
Might be his woe, we guessed not – he had store
Of friends and fortune once, as we could guess
From his nice habits and his gentleness;
These were now lost . . . it were a grief indeed
If he had changed one unsustaining reed
For all that such a man might else adorn.
The colours of his mind seemed yet unworn;   540
For the wild language of his grief was high,
Such as in measure were called poetry;
And I remember one remark which then
Maddalo made. He said: 'Most wretched men
Are cradled into poetry by wrong,
They learn in suffering what they teach in song.'

If I had been an unconnected man
I, from this moment, should have formed some plan
Never to leave sweet Venice, – for to me
It was delight to ride by the lone sea;   550
And then, the town is silent – one may write
Or read in gondolas by day or night,
Having the little brazen lamp alight,

49

Unseen, uninterrupted; books are there,
Pictures, and casts from all those statues fair
Which were twin-born with poetry, and all
We seek in towns, with little to recall
Regrets for the green country. I might sit
In Maddalo's great palace, and his wit
And subtle talk would cheer the winter night   560
And make me know myself, and the firelight
Would flash upon our faces, till the day
Might dawn and make me wonder at my stay:
But I had friends in London too: the chief
Attraction here, was that I sought relief
From the deep tenderness that maniac wrought
Within me –'twas perhaps an idle thought –
But I imagined that if day by day
I watched him, and but seldom went away,
And studied all the beatings of his heart   570
With zeal, as men study some stubborn art
For their own good, and could by patience find
An entrance to the caverns of his mind,
I might reclaim him from his dark estate:
In friendships I had been most fortunate –
Yet never saw I one whom I would call
More willingly my friend; and this was all
Accomplished not; such dreams of baseless good
Oft come and go in crowds or solitude
And leave no trace – but what I now designed   580
Made for long years impression on my mind.
The following morning, urged by my affairs,
I left bright Venice.

           After many years
And many changes I returned; the name
Of Venice, and its aspect, was the same;
But Maddalo was travelling far away
Among the mountains of Armenia.
His dog was dead. His child had now become
A woman; such as it has been my doom
To meet with few, – a wonder of this earth   590
Where there is little of transcendent worth, –

Like one of Shakespeare's women: kindly she,
And with a manner beyond courtesy
Received her father's friend; and when I asked
Of the lorn maniac, she her memory tasked
And told as she had heard the mournful tale:
'That the poor sufferer's health began to fail
Two years from my departure, but that then
The lady who had left him, came again.
Her mien had been imperious, but she now   600
Looked meek – perhaps remorse had brought her low.
Her coming made him better, and they stayed
Together at my father's – for I played,
As I remember, with the lady's shawl –
I might be six years old – but after all
She left him' . . . 'Why, her heart must have been tough:
How did it end?' 'And was not this enough?
They met – they parted' – 'Child, is there no more?
Something within that interval which bore
The stamp of *why* they parted, *how* they met?'   610
'Yet if thine aged eyes disdain to wet
Those wrinkled cheeks with youth's remembered tears,
Ask me no more, but let the silent years
Be closed and ceared over their memory
As yon mute marble where their corpses lie.'
I urged and questioned still, she told me how
All happened – but the cold world shall not know.

Composed 1818–19
First published 1824

THE TWO SPIRITS: AN ALLEGORY

First Spirit. O thou, who plumed with strong desire
          Would float above the Earth – beware!
        A shadow tracks thy flight of fire –
            Night is coming!
        Bright are the regions of the air,
        And when winds and beams [. . .]
        It were delight to wander there –
            Night is coming!

Second Spirit.   The deathless stars are bright above;
    If I should cross the shade of night   10
    Within my heart is the lamp of love,
        And that is day!
    And the moon will smile with gentle light
    On my golden plumes where'er they move;
    The meteors will linger around my flight,
        And make night day.
First Spirit.   But if the whirlwinds of darkness waken
    Hail and lightning and stormy rain –
    See, the bounds of the air are shaken,
        Night is coming!   20
    And swift the clouds of the hurricane
    Yon declining sun have overtaken,
    The clash of the hail sweeps o'er the plain,
        Night is coming!
Second Spirit.   I see the glare and I hear the sound –
    I'll sail on the flood of the tempest dark
    With the calm within and light around
        Which make night day;
    And thou, when the gloom is deep and stark,
    Look from thy dull earth slumberbound –   30
    My moonlike flight thou then mayst mark
        On high, far away.

—

Some say there is a precipice
Where one vast pine hangs frozen to ruin
O'er piles of snow and chasms of ice
    Mid Alpine mountains;
And that the languid storm pursuing
That wingèd shape forever flies
Round those hoar branches, aye renewing
    Its aëry fountains.   40

Some say when the nights are dry [and] clear
And the death-dews sleep on the morass,
Sweet whispers are heard by the traveller,
    Which make night day;

And a shape like his early love doth pass
Upborne by her wild and glittering hair,
And when he awakes on the fragrant grass
He finds night day.

Composed 1819?
First published 1824

from PROMETHEUS UNBOUND

A Lyrical Drama in Four Acts
Audisne haec, Amphiarae, sub terram abdite?

Preface

The Greek tragic writers, in selecting as their subject any portion of
their national history or mythology, employed in their treatment of
it a certain arbitrary discretion. They by no means conceived
themselves bound to adhere to the common interpretation or to
imitate in story as in title their rivals and predecessors. Such a system
would have amounted to a resignation of those claims to preference
over their competitors which incited the composition. The Aga-
memnonian story was exhibited on the Athenian theatre with as
many variations as dramas.

I have presumed to employ a similar licence. The *Prometheus* 10
Unbound of Aeschylus supposed the reconciliation of Jupiter with his
victim as the price of the disclosure of the danger threatened to his
empire by the consummation of his marriage with Thetis. Thetis,
according to this view of the subject, was given in marriage to Peleus,
and Prometheus, by the permission of Jupiter, delivered from his
captivity by Hercules. Had I framed my story on this model, I should
have done no more than have attempted to restore the lost drama of
Aeschylus; an ambition which, if my preference to this mode of
treating the subject had incited me to cherish, the recollection of the
high comparison such an attempt would challenge might well abate. 20
But, in truth, I was averse from a catastrophe so feeble as that of
reconciling the Champion with the Oppressor of mankind. The
moral interest of the fable, which is so powerfully sustained by the
sufferings and endurance of Prometheus, would be annihilated if we
could conceive of him as unsaying his high language and quailing

before his successful and perfidious adversary. The only imaginary being resembling in any degree Prometheus, is Satan; and Prometheus is, in my judgement, a more poetical character than Satan, because, in addition to courage, and majesty, and firm and patient opposition to omnipotent force, he is susceptible of being described as exempt from the taints of ambition, envy, revenge, and a desire for personal aggrandisement, which, in the Hero of *Paradise Lost*, interfere with the interest. The character of Satan engenders in the mind a pernicious casuistry which leads us to weigh his faults with his wrongs, and to excuse the former because the latter exceed all measure. In the minds of those who consider that magnificent fiction with a religious feeling, it engenders something worse. But Prometheus is, as it were, the type of the highest perfection of moral and intellectual nature, impelled by the purest and the truest motives to the best and noblest ends.

This Poem was chiefly written upon the mountainous ruins of the Baths of Caracalla, among the flowery glades, and thickets of odoriferous blossoming trees, which are extended in ever winding labyrinths upon its immense platforms and dizzy arches suspended in the air. The bright blue sky of Rome, and the effect of the vigorous awakening spring in that divinest climate, and the new life with which it drenches the spirits even to intoxication, were the inspiration of this drama.

The imagery which I have employed will be found, in many instances, to have been drawn from the operations of the human mind, or from those external actions by which they are expressed. This is unusual in modern poetry, although Dante and Shakespeare are full of instances of the same kind: Dante indeed more than any other poet, and with greater success. But the Greek poets, as writers to whom no resource of awakening the sympathy of their contemporaries was unknown, were in the habitual use of this power; and it is the study of their works (since a higher merit would probably be denied me) to which I am willing that my readers should impute this singularity.

One word is due in candour to the degree in which the study of contemporary writings may have tinged my composition, for such has been a topic of censure with regard to poems far more popular, and indeed more deservedly popular, than mine. It is impossible that any one who inhabits the same age with such writers as those who stand in the foremost ranks of our own, can conscientiously assure himself that his language and tone of thought may not have been modified by the study of the productions of those extraordinary intellects. It is true that, not the spirit of their genius, but the forms in which it has manifested itself, are due, less to the peculiarities of their own minds, than to the peculiarity of the moral and intellectual 70 condition of the minds among which they have been produced. Thus a number of writers possess the form, whilst they want the spirit of those whom, it is alleged, they imitate; because the former is the endowment of the age in which they live, and the latter must be the uncommunicated lightning of their own mind.

The peculiar style of intense and comprehensive imagery which distinguishes the modern literature of England has not been, as a general power, the product of the imitation of any particular writer. The mass of capabilities remains at every period materially the same; the circumstances which awaken it to action perpetually change. If 80 England were divided into forty republics, each equal in population and extent to Athens, there is no reason to suppose but that, under institutions not more perfect than those of Athens, each would produce philosophers and poets equal to those who (if we except Shakespeare) have never been surpassed. We owe the great writers of the golden age of our literature to that fervid awakening of the public mind which shook to dust the oldest and most oppressive form of the Christian religion. We owe Milton to the progress and development of the same spirit: the sacred Milton was, let it ever be remembered, a republican, and a bold inquirer into morals and 90 religion. The great writers of our own age are, we have reason to suppose, the companions and forerunners of some unimagined change in our social condition or the opinions which cement it. The cloud of mind is discharging its collected lightning, and the equilibrium between institutions and opinions is now restoring, or is about to be restored.

As to imitation, poetry is a mimetic art. It creates, but it creates by combination and representation. Poetical abstractions are beautiful and new, not because the portions of which they are composed had no previous existence in the mind of man or in nature, but 100 because the whole produced by their combination has some intelligible and beautiful analogy with those sources of emotion and thought, and with the contemporary condition of them: one great poet is a masterpiece of nature which another not only ought to study but must study. He might as wisely and as easily determine that his mind should no longer be the mirror of all that is lovely in the visible universe, as exclude from his contemplation the beautiful which exists in the writings of a great contemporary. The pretence of doing it would be a presumption in any but the greatest; the effect, even in him, would be strained, unnatural, and ineffectual. A poet is the   110 combined product of such internal powers as modify the nature of others; and of such external influences as excite and sustain these powers; he is not one, but both. Every man's mind is, in this respect, modified by all the objects of nature and art, by every word and every suggestion which he ever admitted to act upon his consciousness; it is the mirror upon which all forms are reflected, and in which they compose one form. Poets, not otherwise than philosophers, painters, sculptors, and musicians, are, in one sense, the creators, and, in another, the creations, of their age. From this subjection the loftiest do not escape. There is a similarity between Homer and Hesiod,   120 between Aeschylus and Euripides, between Virgil and Horace, between Dante and Petrarch, between Shakespeare and Fletcher, between Dryden and Pope; each has a generic resemblance under which their specific distinctions are arranged. If this similarity be the result of imitation, I am willing to confess that I have imitated.

Let this opportunity be conceded to me of acknowledging that I have, what a Scotch philosopher characteristically terms, 'a passion for reforming the world': what passion incited him to write and publish his book, he omits to explain. For my part I had rather be damned with Plato and Lord Bacon, than go to Heaven with Paley   130 and Malthus. But it is a mistake to suppose that I dedicate my poetical compositions solely to the direct enforcement of reform, or that I consider them in any degree as containing a reasoned system on the theory of human life. Didactic poetry is my abhorrence; nothing can be equally well expressed in prose that is not tedious and supererogatory in verse. My purpose has hitherto been simply to familiarize the highly refined imagination of the more select classes of poetical readers with beautiful idealisms of moral excellence; aware that, until the mind can love, and admire, and trust, and hope, and endure, reasoned principles of moral conduct are seeds cast upon the highway   140 of life which the unconscious passenger tramples into dust, although they would bear the harvest of his happiness. Should I live to accomplish what I purpose, that is, produce a systematical history of what appear to me to be the genuine elements of human society, let not the advocates of injustice and superstition flatter themselves that I should take Aeschylus rather than Plato as my model.

The having spoken of myself with unaffected freedom will need little apology with the candid; and let the uncandid consider that they injure me less than their own hearts and minds by misrepresentation. Whatever talents a person may possess to amuse and instruct others, be they ever so inconsiderable, he is yet bound to exert them: if his attempt be ineffectual, let the punishment of an unaccomplished purpose have been sufficient; let none trouble themselves to heap the dust of oblivion upon his efforts: the pile they raise will betray his grave which might otherwise have been unknown.   150

Act I

SCENE: *a ravine of icy rocks in the Indian Caucasus.*
PROMETHEUS *is discovered bound to the precipice.*
PANTHEA *and* IONE *are seated at his feet. Time, night. During the scene, morning slowly breaks.*

Prometheus. Monarch of Gods and Daemons, and all Spirits
       But One, who throng those bright and rolling worlds
       Which Thou and I alone of living things
       Behold with sleepless eyes! regard this Earth,
       Made multitudinous with thy slaves, whom thou
       Requitest for knee-worship, prayer and praise,
       And toil, and hecatombs of broken hearts,
       With fear and self-contempt and barren hope;
       Whilst me, who am thy foe, eyeless in hate,
       Hast thou made reign and triumph, to thy scorn,   10
       O'er mine own misery and thy vain revenge.
       Three thousand years of sleep-unsheltered hours,
       And moments aye divided by keen pangs
       Till they seemed years, torture and solitude,
       Scorn and despair, – these are mine empire:
       More glorious far than that which thou surveyest
       From thine unenvied throne, O Mighty God!
       Almighty, had I deigned to share the shame

57

Of thine ill tyranny, and hung not here
Nailed to this wall of eagle-baffling mountain,   20
Black, wintry, dead, unmeasured; without herb,
Insect, or beast, or shape or sound of life.
Ah me! alas, pain, pain ever, forever!

No change, no pause, no hope! Yet I endure.
I ask the Earth, have not the mountains felt?
I ask yon Heaven, the all-beholding Sun,
Has it not seen! the Sea, in storm or calm,
Heaven's ever-changing Shadow, spread below,
Have its deaf waves not heard my agony?
Ah me! alas, pain, pain ever, forever!   30

The crawling glaciers pierce me with the spears
Of their moon-freezing crystals; the bright chains
Eat with their burning cold into my bones.
Heaven's wingèd hound, polluting from thy lips
His beak in poison not his own, tears up
My heart; and shapeless sights come wandering by,
The ghastly people of the realm of dream,
Mocking me; and the Earthquake-fiends are charged
To wrench the rivets from my quivering wounds
When the rocks split and close again behind;   40
While from their loud abysses howling throng
The genii of the storm, urging the rage
Of whirlwind, and afflict me with keen hail.
And yet to me welcome is day and night,
Whether one breaks the hoar frost of the morn,
Or starry, dim, and slow, the other climbs
The leaden-coloured east; for then they lead
Their wingless, crawling Hours, one among whom
 – As some dark Priest hales the reluctant victim –
Shall drag thee, cruel King, to kiss the blood   50
From these pale feet, which then might trample thee
If they disdained not such a prostrate slave.
Disdain? Ah no! I pity thee. What ruin
Will hunt thee undefended through wide Heaven!
How will thy soul, cloven to its depth with terror,
Gape like a Hell within! I speak in grief,

Not exultation, for I hate no more,
As then ere misery made me wise. The curse
Once breathed on thee I would recall. Ye Mountains,
Whose many-voicèd Echoes, through the mist   60
Of cataracts, flung the thunder of that spell;
Ye icy Springs, stagnant with wrinkling frost,
Which vibrated to hear me, and then crept
Shuddering through India; thou serenest Air,
Through which the Sun walks burning without beams;
And ye swift Whirlwinds, who on poisèd wings
Hung mute and moveless o'er yon hushed abyss,
As thunder, louder than your own, made rock
The orbèd world; – if then my words had power,
Though I am changed so that aught evil wish   70
Is dead within, although no memory be
Of what is hate, let them not lose it now!
What was that curse? for ye all heard me speak.

First Voice (from the Mountains).
Thrice three hundred thousand years
   O'er the Earthquake's couch we stood:
Oft, as men convulsed with fears,
   We trembled in our multitude.

Second Voice (from the Springs).
Thunderbolts had parched our water,
   We had been stained with bitter blood,
And had run mute, mid shrieks of slaughter,   80
   Through a city and a solitude.

Third Voice (from the Air).
I had clothed, since Earth uprose,
   Its wastes in colours not their own;
And oft had my serene repose
   Been cloven by many a rending groan.

Fourth Voice (from the Whirlwinds).
We had soared beneath these mountains
   Unresting ages; nor had thunder,
Nor yon volcano's flaming fountains,
   Nor any power above or under
   Ever made us mute with wonder.   90

First Voice.   But never bowed our snowy crest

As at the voice of thine unrest.
Second Voice.　Never such a sound before
　　　To the Indian waves we bore.
　　　A pilot asleep on the howling sea
　　　Leaped up from the deck in agony
　　　And heard, and cried, 'Ah, woe is me!'
　　　And died as mad as the wild waves be.
Third Voice.　By such dread words from Earth to Heaven
　　　My still realm was never riven:　　　　　　　　100
　　　When its wound was closed, there stood
　　　Darkness o'er the day like blood.
Fourth Voice.　And we shrank back: for dreams of ruin
　　　To frozen caves our flight pursuing
　　　Made us keep silence – thus – and thus –
　　　Though silence is as hell to us.
The Earth.　The tongueless Caverns of the craggy hills
　　　Cried, 'Misery!' then the hollow Heaven replied,
　　　'Misery!' and the Ocean's purple waves,
　　　Climbing the land, howled to the lashing winds,　　110
　　　And the pale nations heard it, – 'Misery!'
Prometheus.　I hear a sound of voices – not the voice
　　　Which I gave forth. Mother, thy sons and thou
　　　Scorn him, without whose all-enduring will
　　　Beneath the fierce omnipotence of Jove,
　　　Both they and thou had vanished like thin mist
　　　Unrolled on the morning wind. Know ye not me,
　　　The Titan? he who made his agony
　　　The barrier to your else all-conquering foe?
　　　O rock-embosomed lawns, and snow-fed streams,　　120
　　　Now seen athwart frore vapours, deep below,
　　　Through whose o'ershadowing woods I wandered once
　　　With Asia, drinking life from her loved eyes,
　　　Why scorns the spirit which informs ye, now
　　　To commune with me? me alone, who checked –
　　　As one who checks a fiend-drawn charioteer –
　　　The falsehood and the force of Him who reigns
　　　Supreme, and with the groans of pining slaves
　　　Fills your dim glens and liquid wildernesses?
　　　Why answer ye not, still? Brethren!

The Earth.   They dare not.

Prometheus.   Who dares? for I would hear that curse again . . .
    Ha, what an awful whisper rises up!
    'Tis scarce like sound; it tingles through the frame
    As lightning tingles, hovering ere it strike.
    Speak, Spirit! from thine inorganic voice
    I only know that thou art moving near
    And love. How cursed I him?

The Earth.   How canst thou hear,
    Who knowest not the language of the dead?

Prometheus.   Thou art a living spirit; speak as they.

The Earth.   I dare not speak like life, lest Heaven's fell King   140
    Should hear, and link me to some wheel of pain
    More torturing than the one whereon I roll.
    Subtle thou art and good; and though the Gods
    Hear not this voice, yet thou art more than God,
    Being wise and kind: earnestly hearken now.

Prometheus.   Obscurely through my brain, like shadows dim,
    Sweep awful thoughts, rapid and thick. I feel
    Faint, like one mingled in entwining love;
    Yet 'tis not pleasure.

The Earth.   No, thou canst not hear:
    Thou art immortal, and this tongue is known   150
    Only to those who die . . .

Prometheus.   And what art thou,
    O melancholy Voice?

The Earth.   I am the Earth,
    Thy mother, she within whose stony veins,
    To the last fibre of the loftiest tree
    Whose thin leaves trembled in the frozen air,
    Joy ran, as blood within a living frame,
    When thou didst from her bosom, like a cloud
    Of glory, arise – a spirit of keen joy!
    And at thy voice her pining sons uplifted
    Their prostrate brows from the polluting dust,   160
    And our almighty Tyrant with fierce dread
    Grew pale, until his thunder chained thee here.
    Then – see those million worlds which burn and roll
    Around us: their inhabitants beheld

My spherèd light wane in wide Heaven; the sea
Was lifted by strange tempest, and new fire
From earthquake-rifted mountains of bright snow
Shook its portentous hair beneath Heaven's frown;
Lightning and Inundation vexed the plains;
Blue thistles bloomed in cities; foodless toads   170
Within voluptuous chambers panting crawled;
When Plague had fallen on man and beast and worm,
And Famine, and black Blight on herb and tree;
And in the corn, and vines, and meadow-grass
Teemed ineradicable poisonous weeds
Draining their growth, for my wan breast was dry
With grief; and the thin air, my breath, was stained
With the contagion of a mother's hate
Breathed on her child's destroyer – aye, I heard
Thy curse, the which, if thou rememberest not,   180
Yet my innumerable seas and streams,
Mountains, and caves, and winds, and yon wide air,
And the inarticulate people of the dead,
Preserve, a treasured spell. We meditate
In secret joy and hope those dreadful words,
But dare not speak them.
Prometheus.   Venerable Mother!
All else who live and suffer take from thee
Some comfort: flowers, and fruits, and happy sounds,
And love, though fleeting; these may not be mine.
But mine own words, I pray, deny me not.   190
The Earth.   They shall be told. Ere Babylon was dust,
The Magus Zoroaster, my dead child,
Met his own image walking in the garden.
That apparition, sole of men, he saw.
For know, there are two worlds of life and death:
One that which thou beholdest; but the other
Is underneath the grave, where do inhabit
The shadows of all forms that think and live
Till death unite them and they part no more;
Dreams and the light imaginings of men,   200
And all that faith creates or love desires,
Terrible, strange, sublime and beauteous shapes.

62

There thou art, and dost hang, a writhing shade
Mid whirlwind-peopled mountains; all the Gods
Are there, and all the Powers of nameless worlds,
Vast, sceptred Phantoms; heroes, men, and beasts;
And Demogorgon, a tremendous Gloom;
And he, the Supreme Tyrant, on his throne
Of burning gold. Son, one of these shall utter
The curse which all remember. Call at will   210
Thine own ghost, or the ghost of Jupiter,
Hades, or Typhon, or what mightier Gods
From all-prolific Evil since thy ruin
Have sprung, and trampled on my prostrate sons.
Ask, and they must reply: so the revenge
Of the Supreme may sweep through vacant shades,
As rainy wind through the abandoned gate
Of a fallen palace.
Prometheus.   Mother, let not aught
Of that which may be evil, pass again
My lips, or those of aught resembling me.   220
Phantasm of Jupiter, arise, appear!
Ione.   My wings are folded o'er mine ears;
        My wings are crossed over mine eyes;
    Yet through their silver shade appears,
        And through their lulling plumes arise,
    A Shape, a throng of sounds;
        May it be no ill to thee,
    O thou of many wounds!
    Near whom, for our sweet sister's sake,
    Ever thus we watch and wake.   230
Panthea.   The sound is of whirlwind underground,
        Earthquake, and fire, and mountains cloven;
    The Shape is awful like the sound,
        Clothed in dark purple, star-inwoven.
    A sceptre of pale gold
        To stay steps proud, o'er the slow cloud
    His veinèd hand doth hold.
    Cruel he looks but calm and strong,
    Like one who does, not suffers wrong.

Phantasm of Jupiter. Why have the secret powers of this strange world 240
    Driven me, a frail and empty phantom, hither
    On direst storms? What unaccustomed sounds
    Are hovering on my lips, unlike the voice
    With which our pallid race hold ghastly talk
    In darkness? And, proud Sufferer, who art thou?
Prometheus. Tremendous Image, as thou art must be
    He whom thou shadowest forth. I am his foe,
    The Titan. Speak the words which I would hear,
    Although no thought inform thine empty voice.
The Earth. Listen! And though your echoes must be mute,   250
    Grey mountains, and old woods, and haunted springs,
    Prophetic caves, and isle-surrounding streams,
    Rejoice to hear what yet ye cannot speak.
Phantasm. A spirit seizes me and speaks within:
    It tears me as fire tears a thunder-cloud.
Panthea. See, how he lifts his mighty looks! The Heaven
    Darkens above.
Ione.   He speaks! O shelter me!
Prometheus. I see the curse on gestures proud and cold,
    And looks of firm defiance, and calm hate,
    And such despair as mocks itself with smiles,   260
    Written as on a scroll . . . yet speak – O speak!
Phantasm. Fiend, I defy thee! with a calm, fixed mind,
      All that thou canst inflict I bid thee do;
    Foul Tyrant both of Gods and Humankind,
      One only being shalt thou not subdue.
    Rain then thy plagues upon me here,
    Ghastly disease, and frenzying fear;
    And let alternate frost and fire
    Eat into me, and be thine ire
    Lightning, and cutting hail, and legioned forms   270
    Of furies, driving by upon the wounding storms.

    Aye, do thy worst. Thou art omnipotent.
      O'er all things but thyself I gave thee power,
    And my own will. Be thy swift mischiefs sent
      To blast mankind, from yon etherial tower.
    Let thy malignant spirit move
    Its darkness over those I love:

    On me and mine I imprecate
    The utmost torture of thy hate,
    And thus devote to sleepless agony   280
    This undeclining head while thou must reign on high.

    But thou who art the God and Lord – O thou
        Who fillest with thy soul this world of woe,
    To whom all things of Earth and Heaven do bow
        In fear and worship – all-prevailing foe!
    I curse thee! let a sufferer's curse
    Clasp thee, his torturer, like remorse,
    Till thine Infinity shall be
    A robe of envenomed agony,
    And thine Omnipotence a crown of pain   290
    To cling like burning gold round thy dissolving brain.

    Heap on thy soul, by virtue of this Curse,
        Ill deeds; then be thou damned, beholding good –
    Both infinite as is the Universe,
        And thou, and thy self-torturing solitude.
    And awful image of calm power
    Though now thou sittest, let the hour
    Come, when thou must appear to be
    That which thou art internally;
    And after many a false and fruitless crime   300
    Scorn track thy lagging fall through boundless space and time.

Prometheus.   Were these my words, O Parent?
The Earth.   They were thine.
Prometheus.   It doth repent me: words are quick and vain;
    Grief for a while is blind, and so was mine.
    I wish no living thing to suffer pain.
The Earth.   Misery, O misery to me,
    That Jove at length should vanquish thee.
    Wail, howl aloud, Land and Sea;
    The Earth's rent heart shall answer ye.
    Howl, Spirits of the living and the dead;   310
    Your refuge, your defence lies fallen and vanquishèd.
First Echo.   Lies fallen and vanquishèd!
Second Echo.   Fallen and vanquishèd!
Ione.   Fear not: 'tis but some passing spasm;

65

    The Titan is unvanquished still.
But see, where through the azure chasm
    Of yon forked and snowy hill,
Trampling the slant winds on high
    With golden-sandalled feet, that glow
Under plumes of purple dye.   320
Like rose-ensanguined ivory,
    A Shape comes now,
Stretching on high from his right hand
A serpent-cinctured wand.
Panthea.   'Tis Jove's world-wandering herald, Mercury.
Ione.   And who are those with hydra tresses
    And iron wings that climb the wind,
Whom the frowning God represses
    Like vapours streaming up behind,
Clanging loud, an endless crowd?   330
Panthea.   These are Jove's tempest-walking hounds,
Whom he gluts with groans and blood,
When, charioted on sulphurous cloud,
    He bursts Heaven's bounds.
Ione.   Are they now led from the thin dead,
On new pangs to be fed?
Panthea.   The Titan looks as ever, firm, not proud.
First Fury.   Ha! I scent life!
Second Fury.   Let me but look into his eyes!
Third Fury.   The hope of torturing him smells like a heap
    Of corpses to a death-bird after battle   340
First Fury.   Darest thou delay, O Herald? – take cheer, Hounds
    Of Hell – what if the Son of Maia soon
    Should make us food and sport? Who can please long
    The Omnipotent?
Mercury.   Back to your towers of iron,
    And gnash beside the streams of fire and wail
    Your foodless teeth! . . . Geryon, arise! and Gorgon,
    Chimaera, and thou Sphinx, subtlest of fiends,
    Who ministered to Thebes Heaven's poisoned wine –
    Unnatural love, and more unnatural hate:
    These shall perform your task.
First Fury.   O mercy! mercy!   350

We die with our desire – drive us not back!
Mercury. Crouch then in silence.
                              Awful Sufferer,
To thee unwilling, most unwillingly
I come, by the great Father's will driven down,
To execute a doom of new revenge.
Alas! I pity thee, and hate myself
That I can do no more; aye from thy sight
Returning, for a season, Heaven seems Hell,
So thy worn form pursues me night and day,
Smiling reproach. Wise art thou, firm and good,   360
But vainly wouldst stand forth alone in strife
Against the Omnipotent; as yon clear lamps
That measure and divide the weary years
From which there is no refuge, long have taught
And long must teach. Even now thy Torturer arms
With the strange might of unimagined pains
The powers who scheme slow agonies in Hell,
And my commission is to lead them here,
Or what more subtle, foul, or savage fiends
People the abyss, and leave them to their task.   370
Be it not so! . . . There is a secret known
To thee and to none else of living things,
Which may transfer the sceptre of wide Heaven,
The fear of which perplexes the Supreme.
Clothe it in words, and bid it clasp his throne
In intercession; bend thy soul in prayer,
And, like a suppliant in some gorgeous fane,
Let the will kneel within thy haughty heart;
For benefits and meek submission tame
The fiercest and the mightiest.
Prometheus.   – Evil minds   380
Change good to their own nature. I gave all
He has; and in return he chains me here
Years, ages, night and day: whether the Sun
Split my parched skin, or in the moony night
The crystal-wingèd snow cling round my hair –
Whilst my belovèd race is trampled down
By his thought-executing ministers.

Such is the tyrant's recompense –'tis just:
He who is evil can receive no good;
And for a world bestowed, or a friend lost,   390
He can feel hate, fear, shame – not gratitude:
He but requites me for his own misdeed.
Kindness to such is keen reproach, which breaks
With bitter stings the light sleep of Revenge.
Submission, thou dost know, I cannot try:
For what submission but that fatal word,
The death-seal of mankind's captivity,
Like the Sicilian's hair-suspended sword
Which trembles o'er his crown, would he accept,
Or could I yield? – Which yet I will not yield.   400
Let others flatter Crime, where it sits throned
In brief Omnipotence; secure are they:
For Justice, when triumphant, will weep down
Pity, not punishment, on her own wrongs,
Too much avenged by those who err. I wait,
Enduring thus, the retributive hour
Which since we spake is even nearer now. –
But hark, the hell-hounds clamour: fear delay:
Behold! Heaven lowers under thy Father's frown.

Mercury.   O that we might be spared: I to inflict   410
  And thou to suffer! Once more answer me:
  Thou knowest not the period of Jove's power?
Prometheus.   I know but this, that it must come.
Mercury.   Alas!
  Thou canst not count thy years to come of pain?
Prometheus.   They last while Jove must reign: nor more, nor less
  Do I desire or fear.
Mercury.   Yet pause, and plunge
  Into Eternity, where recorded time,
  Even all that we imagine, age on age,
  Seems but a point, and the reluctant mind
  Flags wearily in its unending flight,   420
  Till it sink, dizzy, blind, lost, shelterless;
  Perchance it has not numbered the slow years
  Which thou must spend in torture, unreprieved.
Prometheus.   Perchance no thought can count them – yet they pass.

Mercury. If thou might'st dwell among the Gods the while,
  Lapped in voluptuous joy?
Prometheus.   I would not quit
  This bleak ravine, these unrepentant pains.
Mercury. Alas! I wonder at, yet pity thee.
Prometheus. Pity the self-despising slaves of Heaven,
  Not me, within whose mind sits peace serene,   430
  As light in the sun, throned . . . How vain is talk!
  Call up the fiends.
Ione.   O sister, look! White fire
  Has cloven to the roots yon huge snow-loaded cedar;
  How fearfully God's thunder howls behind!
Mercury. I must obey his words and thine – alas!
  Most heavily remorse hangs at my heart!
Panthea. See where the child of Heaven with wingèd feet
  Runs down the slanted sunlight of the dawn.
Ione. Dear sister, close thy plumes over thine eyes
  Lest thou behold and die – they come, they come   440
  Blackening the birth of day with countless wings,
  And hollow underneath, like death.
First Fury.   Prometheus!
Second Fury. Immortal Titan!
Third Fury.   Champion of Heaven's slaves!
Prometheus. He whom some dreadful voice invokes is here,
  Prometheus, the chained Titan. Horrible forms,
  What and who are ye? Never yet there came
  Phantasms so foul through monster-teeming Hell
  From the all-miscreative brain of Jove;
  Whilst I behold such execrable shapes,
  Methinks I grow like what I contemplate,   450
  And laugh and stare in loathsome sympathy.
First Fury. We are the ministers of pain and fear,
  And disappointment, and mistrust, and hate,
  And clinging crime; and, as lean dogs pursue
  Through wood and lake some struck and sobbing fawn,
  We track all things that weep, and bleed, and live,
  When the great King betrays them to our will.
Prometheus. O many fearful natures in one name,
  I know ye; and these lakes and echoes know

69

The darkness and the clangour of your wings.   460
But why more hideous than your loathèd selves
Gather ye up in legions from the deep?
Second Fury.   We knew not that: Sisters, rejoice, rejoice!
Prometheus.   Can aught exult in its deformity?
Second Fury.   The beauty of delight makes lovers glad,
Gazing on one another: so are we.
As from the rose which the pale priestess kneels
To gather for her festal crown of flowers
The aërial crimson falls, flushing her cheek,
So from our victim's destined agony   470
The shade which is our form invests us round,
Else are we shapeless as our mother Night.
Prometheus.   I laugh your power, and his who sent you here,
To lowest scorn. Pour forth the cup of pain.
First Fury.   Thou thinkest we will rend thee bone from bone,
And nerve from nerve, working like fire within?
Prometheus.   Pain is my element, as hate is thine;
Ye rend me now: I care not.
Second Fury.   Dost imagine
We will but laugh into thy lidless eyes?
Prometheus.   I weigh not what ye do, but what ye suffer,   480
Being evil. Cruel was the Power which called
You, or aught else so wretched, into light.
Third Fury.   Thou think'st we will live through thee, one by one,
Like animal life; and though we can obscure not
The soul which burns within, that we will dwell
Beside it, like a vain loud multitude
Vexing the self-content of wisest men;
That we will be dread thought beneath thy brain,
And foul desire round thine astonished heart,
And blood within thy labyrinthine veins   490
Crawling like agony?
Prometheus.   Why, ye are thus now;
Yet am I king over myself, and rule
The torturing and conflicting throngs within,
As Jove rules you when Hell grows mutinous.
Chorus of Furies.
From the ends of the Earth, from the ends of the Earth,

Where the night has its grave and the morning its birth,
     Come, come, come!
O ye who shake hills with the scream of your mirth
When cities sink howling in ruin; and ye
Who with wingless footsteps trample the Sea,   500
And close upon Shipwreck and Famine's track
Sit chattering with joy on the foodless wreck:
     Come, come, come!
   Leave the bed, low, cold, and red,
Strewed beneath a nation dead;
Leave the hatred – as in ashes
   Fire is left for future burning –
It will burst in bloodier flashes
   When ye stir it, soon returning;
Leave the self-contempt implanted   510
In young spirits, sense-enchanted,
   Misery's yet unkindled fuel;
Leave Hell's secrets, half-unchanted,
   To the maniac dreamer: cruel
More than ye can be with hate
   Is he with fear.
        Come, come, come!
We are steaming up from Hell's wide gate,
   And we burthen the blasts of the atmosphere,
   But vainly we toil till ye come here.   520

Ione.   Sister, I hear the thunder of new wings.

Panthea.   These solid mountains quiver with the sound
   Even as the tremulous air: their shadows make
   The space within my plumes more black than night.

First Fury.   Your call was as a wingèd car
   Driven on whirlwinds fast and far;
   It rapt us from red gulfs of war –

Second Fury.   From wide cities, famine-wasted –

Third Fury.   Groans half heard, and blood untasted –

Fourth Fury.   Kingly conclaves, stern and cold,   530
   Where blood with gold is bought and sold –

Fifth Fury.   From the furnace, white and hot,
   In which –

A Fury.   Speak not – whisper not!

71

I know all that ye would tell,
But to speak might break the spell
Which must bend the Invincible,
   The stern of thought;
He yet defies the deepest power of Hell.
Fury.   Tear the veil!
Another Fury.   It is torn!
Chorus.   The pale stars of the morn
Shine on a misery dire to be borne.   540
Dost thou faint, mighty Titan? We laugh thee to scorn.
Dost thou boast the clear knowledge thou waken'dst for man?
Then was kindled within him a thirst which outran
Those perishing waters: a thirst of fierce fever,
Hope, love, doubt, desire – which consume him for ever.
  One came forth of gentle worth
  Smiling on the sanguine earth;
  His words outlived him, like swift poison
    Withering up truth, peace, and pity.
  Look! where round the wide horizon   550
    Many a million-peopled city
  Vomits smoke in the bright air.
  Hark that outcry of despair!
  'Tis his mild and gentle ghost
    Wailing for the faith he kindled.
  Look again! The flames almost
    To a glow-worm's lamp have dwindled:
  The survivors round the embers
    Gather in dread.
      Joy, joy, joy!   560
Past ages crowd on thee, but each one remembers;
And the future is dark, and the present is spread
Like a pillow of thorns for thy slumberless head.
Semichorus I. Drops of bloody agony flow
  From his white and quivering brow.
  Grant a little respite now –
  See! A disenchanted nation
  Springs like day from desolation;
  To Truth its state is dedicate,
  And Freedom leads it forth, her mate;   570

A legioned band of linkèd brothers
Whom Love calls children –
Semichorus II. 'Tis another's –
See how kindred murder kin!
'Tis the vintage-time for Death and Sin:
Blood, like new wine, bubbles within,
Till Despair smothers
The struggling World – which slaves and tyrants win.

All the Furies vanish, except one.

Ione. Hark, sister! what a low yet dreadful groan
Quite unsuppressed is tearing up the heart
Of the good Titan, as storms tear the deep, 580
And beasts hear the sea moan in inland caves.
Darest thou observe how the fiends torture him?
Panthea. Alas! I looked forth twice, but will no more.
Ione. What didst thou see?
Panthea. A woeful sight: a youth
With patient looks nailed to a crucifix.
Ione. What next?
Panthea. The Heaven around, the Earth below
Was peopled with thick shapes of human death,
All horrible, and wrought by human hands,
Though some appeared the work of human hearts,
For men were slowly killed by frowns and smiles; 590
And other sights too foul to speak and live
Were wandering by. Let us not tempt worse fear
By looking forth: those groans are grief enough.
Fury. Behold an emblem: those who do endure
Deep wrongs for man, and scorn, and chains, but heap
Thousandfold torment on themselves and him.
Prometheus. Remit the anguish of that lighted stare;
Close those wan lips; let that thorn-wounded brow
Stream not with blood – it mingles with thy tears!
Fix, fix those tortured orbs in peace and death, 600
So thy sick throes shake not that crucifix,
So those pale fingers play not with thy gore.
O, horrible! Thy name I will not speak;
It hath become a curse. I see, I see

73

    The wise, the mild, the lofty, and the just,
    Whom thy slaves hate for being like to thee,
    Some hunted by foul lies from their heart's home,
    An early-chosen, late-lamented home,
    As hooded ounces cling to the driven hind;
    Some linked to corpses in unwholesome cells;   610
    Some – hear I not the multitude laugh loud? –
    Impaled in lingering fire: and mighty realms
    Float by my feet like sea-uprooted isles,
    Whose sons are kneaded down in common blood
    By the red light of their own burning homes.
Fury.   Blood thou canst see, and fire; and canst hear groans;
    Worse things, unheard, unseen, remain behind.
Prometheus. Worse?
Fury.   In each human heart terror survives
    The ravin it has gorged: the loftiest fear
    All that they would disdain to think were true: 620
    Hypocrisy and custom make their minds
    The fanes of many a worship, now outworn.
    They dare not devise good for man's estate,
    And yet they know not that they do not dare.
    The good want power, but to weep barren tears;
    The powerful goodness want: worse need for them.
    The wise want love; and those who love want wisdom;
    And all best things are thus confused to ill.
    Many are strong and rich, – and would be just –
    But live among their suffering fellow men   630
    As if none felt: they know not what they do.
Prometheus. Thy words are like a cloud of wingèd snakes;
    And yet I pity those they torture not.
Fury.   Thou pitiest them? I speak no more! (*Vanishes.*)
Prometheus.   Ah woe!
    Ah woe! Alas! pain, pain ever, for ever!
    I close my tearless eyes, but see more clear
    Thy works within my woe-illumèd mind,
    Thou subtle tyrant! . . . Peace is in the grave.
    The grave hides all things beautiful and good:
    I am a God and cannot find it there,   640
    Nor would I seek it: for, though dread revenge,

This is defeat, fierce King, not victory!
The sights with which thou torturest gird my soul
With new endurance, till the hour arrives
When they shall be no types of things which are.
Panthea. Alas! what sawest thou more?
Prometheus.   There are two woes:
  To speak, and to behold; thou spare me one.
  Names are there, Nature's sacred watchwords – they
  Were borne aloft in bright emblazonry;
  The nations thronged around, and cried aloud,   650
  As with one voice, 'Truth, Liberty, and Love!'
  Suddenly fierce confusion fell from Heaven
  Among them: there was strife, deceit, and fear;
  Tyrants rushed in, and did divide the spoil.
  This was the shadow of the truth I saw.
The Earth. I felt thy torture, Son, with such mixed joy
  As pain and virtue give. To cheer thy state
  I bid ascend those subtle and fair spirits
  Whose homes are the dim caves of human thought,
  And who inhabit, as birds wing the wind,   660
  Its world-surrounding ether; they behold
  Beyond that twilight realm, as in a glass,
  The future: may they speak comfort to thee!
Panthea. Look, sister, where a troop of spirits gather,
  Like flocks of clouds in spring's delightful weather,
  Thronging in the blue air!
Ione.   And see! more come,
  Like fountain-vapours when the winds are dumb,
  That climb up the ravine in scattered lines.
  And, hark! is it the music of the pines?
  Is it the lake? is it the waterfall?   670
Panthea. 'Tis something sadder, sweeter far than all.
Chorus of Spirits. From unremembered ages we
  Gentle guides and guardians be
  Of Heaven-oppressed mortality;
  And we breathe, and sicken not,
  The atmosphere of human thought:
  Be it dim, and dank, and grey,
  Like a storm-extinguished day,

Travelled o'er by dying gleams;
  Be it bright as all between   680
Cloudless skies and windless streams,
  Silent, liquid, and serene –
As the birds within the wind,
  As the fish within the wave,
As the thoughts of man's own mind
  Float through all above the grave;
We make there our liquid lair,
Voyaging cloudlike and unpent
Through the boundless element –
Thence we bear the prophecy   690
Which begins and ends in thee!

Ione. More yet come, one by one: the air around them
  Looks radiant as the air around a star.

First Spirit. On a battle-trumpet's blast
  I fled hither, fast, fast, fast,
  Mid the darkness upward cast,
  From the dust of creeds outworn,
  From the tyrant's banner torn,
  Gathering round me, onward borne,
  There was mingled many a cry –   700
  'Freedom! Hope! Death! Victory!'
  Till they faded through the sky;
  And one sound, above, around,
  One sound beneath, around, above,
  Was moving: 'twas the soul of love;
  'Twas the hope, the prophecy,
  Which begins and ends in thee.

Second Spirit. A rainbow's arch stood on the sea,
  Which rocked beneath, immoveably;
  And the triumphant Storm did flee   710
  Like a conqueror, swift and proud,
  Between, with many a captive cloud,
  A shapeless, dark and rapid crowd,
  Each by lightning riven in half;
  I heard the thunder hoarsely laugh –
  Mighty fleets were strewn like chaff
  And spread beneath, a hell of death

O'er the white waters. I alit
On a great ship lightning-split,
And speeded hither on the sigh   720
Of one who gave an enemy
His plank – then plunged aside to die.

Third Spirit.   I sate beside a Sage's bed,
And the lamp was burning red
Near the book where he had fed,
When a Dream with plumes of flame
To his pillow hovering came,
And I knew it was the same
Which had kindled long ago
Pity, eloquence, and woe;   730
And the world awhile below
Wore the shade its lustre made.
It has borne me here as fleet
As Desire's lightning feet:
I must ride it back ere morrow,
Or the sage will wake in sorrow.

Fourth Spirit.   On a Poet's lips I slept
Dreaming like a love-adept
In the sound his breathing kept;
Nor seeks nor finds he mortal blisses,   740
But feeds on the aërial kisses
Of shapes that haunt thought's wildernesses.
He will watch from dawn to gloom
The lake-reflected sun illume
The yellow bees i' the ivy-bloom,
Nor heed nor see, what things they be;
But from these create he can
Forms more real than living man,
Nurslings of immortality!
One of these awakened me,   750
And I sped to succour thee.

Ione.   Behold'st thou not two shapes from the east and west
Come, as two doves to one belovèd nest,
Twin nurslings of the all-sustaining air,
On swift still wings glide down the atmosphere?
And hark! their sweet, sad voices; 'tis despair

Mingled with love and then dissolved in sound.

Panthea. Canst thou speak, sister? all my words are drowned.

Ione. Their beauty gives me voice. See how they float
On their sustaining wings of skyey grain,   760
Orange and azure deepening into gold:
Their soft smiles light the air like a star's fire.

Chorus of Spirits. Hast thou beheld the form of Love?

Fifth Spirit.   As over wide dominions
I sped, like some swift cloud that wings the wide air's wildernesses,
That planet-crested Shape swept by on lightning-braided pinions,
Scattering the liquid joy of life from his ambrosial tresses:
His footsteps paved the world with light – but as I passed 'twas fading,
And hollow Ruin yawned behind: great sages bound in madness,
And headless patriots, and pale youths who perished,
    unupbraiding,
Gleamed in the night I wandered o'er – till thou, O King of sadness,770
Turned by thy smile the worst I saw to recollected gladness.

Sixth Spirit. Ah, sister! Desolation is a delicate thing:
It walks not on the earth, it floats not on the air,
But treads with lulling footstep, and fans with silent wing
The tender hopes which in their hearts the best and gentlest bear,
Who, soothed to false repose by the fanning plumes above,
And the music-stirring motion of its soft and busy feet,
Dream visions of aërial joy, and call the monster Love,
And wake, and find the shadow Pain – as he whom now we greet.

Chorus. Though Ruin now Love's shadow be,   780
Following him destroyingly
   On Death's white and wingèd steed,
Which the fleetest cannot flee –
   Trampling down both flower and weed,
Man and beast, and foul and fair,
Like a tempest through the air;
Thou shalt quell this Horseman grim,
Woundless though in heart or limb.

Prometheus. Spirits! how know ye this shall be?

Chorus. In the atmosphere we breathe –   790
As buds grow red when snow-storms flee
   From spring gathering up beneath,
Whose mild winds shake the elder brake,

And the wandering herdsmen know
That the white-thorn soon will blow –
Wisdom, Justice, Love, and Peace,
When they struggle to increase,
   Are to us as soft winds be
   To shepherd boys – the prophecy
   Which begins and ends in thee.   800

Ione.   Where are the Spirits fled?
Panthea.   Only a sense
Remains of them, like the omnipotence
Of music, when the inspired voice and lute
Languish, ere yet the responses are mute
Which through the deep and labyrinthine soul,
Like echoes through long caverns, wind and roll.

Prometheus.   How fair these air-born shapes! and yet I feel
Most vain all hope but love; and thou art far,
Asia! who, when my being overflowed,
Wert like a golden chalice to bright wine   810
Which else had sunk into the thirsty dust.
All things are still: alas! how heavily
This quiet morning weighs upon my heart;
Though I should dream, I could even sleep with grief
If slumber were denied not. I would fain
Be what it is my destiny to be,
The saviour and the strength of suffering man,
Or sink into the original gulf of things . . .
There is no agony, and no solace left;
Earth can console, Heaven can torment no more.   820

Panthea.   Hast thou forgotten one who watches thee
The cold dark night, and never sleeps but when
The shadow of thy spirit falls on her?

Prometheus.   I said all hope was vain but love: thou lovest.

Panthea.   Deeply in truth; but the eastern star looks white,
And Asia waits in that far Indian vale,
The scene of her sad exile – rugged once
And desolate and frozen, like this ravine;
But now invested with fair flowers and herbs,
And haunted by sweet airs and sounds, which flow   830
Among the woods and waters, from the ether

Of her transforming presence – which would fade
If it were mingled not with thine. Farewell!

ACT II, SCENE 4, ll. 19–128

The Cave of Demogorgon. ASIA *and* PANTHEA

Asia.   And who made terror, madness, crime, remorse,
      Which from the links of the great chain of things   20
      To every thought within the mind of man
      Sway and drag heavily, and each one reels
      Under the load towards the pit of death;
      Abandoned hope, and love that turns to hate;
      And self-contempt, bitterer to drink than blood;
      Pain, whose unheeded and familiar speech
      Is howling, and keen shrieks, day after day;
      And Hell, or the sharp fear of Hell?
Demogorgon.   He reigns.
Asia.   Utter his name: a world pining in pain
      Asks but his name: curses shall drag him down.   30
Demogorgon.   He reigns.
Asia.   I feel, I know it: who?
Demogorgon.   He reigns.
Asia.   Who reigns? There was the Heaven and Earth at first,
      And Light and Love; then Saturn, from whose throne
      Time fell, an envious shadow; such the state
      Of the earth's primal spirits beneath his sway,
      As the calm joy of flowers and living leaves
      Before the wind or sun has withered them
      And semivital worms; but he refused
      The birthrights of their being, knowledge, power,
      The skill which wields the elements, the thought   40
      Which pierces this dim universe like light,
      Self-empire, and the majesty of love;
      For thirst of which they fainted. Then Prometheus
      Gave wisdom, which is strength, to Jupiter,
      And with this law alone, 'Let man be free,'
      Clothed him with the dominion of wide Heaven.

To know nor faith, nor love, nor law, to be
Omnipotent but friendless is to reign;
And Jove now reigned; for on the race of man
First famine, and then toil, and then disease,   50
Strife, wounds, and ghastly death unseen before,
Fell; and the unseasonable seasons drove
With alternating shafts of frost and fire,
Their shelterless, pale tribes to mountain caves;
And in their desert hearts fierce wants he sent,
And mad disquietudes, and shadows idle
Of unreal good, which levied mutual war,
So ruining the lair wherein they raged.
Prometheus saw, and waked the legioned hopes
Which sleep within folded Elysian flowers,   60
Nepenthe, Moly, Amaranth, fadeless blooms,
That they might hide with thin and rainbow wings
The shape of Death; and Love he sent to bind
The disunited tendrils of that vine
Which bears the wine of life, the human heart;
And he tamed fire which, like some beast of chase,
Most terrible, but lovely, played beneath
The frown of man; and tortured to his will
Iron and gold, the slaves and signs of power,
And gems and poisons, and all subtlest forms   70
Hidden beneath the mountains and the waves.
He gave man speech, and speech created thought,
Which is the measure of the universe;
And Science struck the thrones of Earth and Heaven,
Which shook, but fell not; and the harmonious mind
Poured itself forth in all-prophetic song;
And music lifted up the listening spirit
Until it walked, exempt from mortal care,
Godlike, o'er the clear billows of sweet sound;
And human hands first mimicked and then mocked,   80
With moulded limbs more lovely than its own,
The human form, till marble grew divine;
And mothers, gazing, drank the love men see
Reflected in their race – behold, and perish.
He told the hidden power of herbs and springs,

81

And Disease drank and slept. Death grew like sleep.
He taught the implicated orbits woven
Of the wide-wandering stars; and how the Sun
Changes his lair, and by what secret spell
The pale Moon is transformed, when her broad eye   90
Gazes not on the interlunar sea.
He taught to rule, as life directs the limbs,
The tempest-wingèd chariots of the Ocean,
And the Celt knew the Indian. Cities then
Were built, and through their snow-like columns flowed
The warm winds, and the azure ether shone,
And the blue sea and shadowy hills were seen . . .
Such the alleviations of his state
Prometheus gave to man – for which he hangs
Withering in destined pain. But who rains down   100
Evil, the immedicable plague which, while
Man looks on his creation like a God
And sees that it is glorious, drives him on,
The wreck of his own will, the scorn of Earth,
The outcast, the abandoned, the alone?
Not Jove: while yet his frown shook heaven, ay, when
His adversary from adamantine chains
Cursed him, he trembled like a slave. Declare
Who is his master? Is he too a slave?

Demogorgon.   All spirits are enslaved which serve things evil: 110
Thou knowest if Jupiter be such or no.

Asia.   Whom calledst thou God?

Demogorgon.   I spoke but as ye speak,
For Jove is the supreme of living things.

Asia.   Who is the master of the slave?

Demogorgon.   If the abysm
Could vomit forth its secrets . . . but a voice
Is wanting, the deep truth is imageless;
For what would it avail to bid thee gaze
On the revolving world? what to bid speak
Fate, Time, Occasion, Chance and Change? To these
All things are subject but eternal Love.   120

Asia.   So much I asked before, and my heart gave
The response thou hast given; and of such truths

Each to itself must be the oracle. –
One more demand; and do thou answer me
As my own soul would answer, did it know
That which I ask. Prometheus shall arise
Henceforth the Sun of this rejoicing world:
When will the destined hour arrive?

Demogorgon.   Behold!

ACT III, SCENE 4, ll. 124–204

Spirit of the Hour.

   As I have said, I floated to the earth:
It was, as it is still, the pain of bliss
To move, to breathe, to be; I wandering went
Among the haunts and dwellings of mankind,
And first was disappointed not to see
Such mighty change as I had felt within
Expressed in outward things; but soon I looked,   130
And behold! thrones were kingless, and men walked
One with the other even as spirits do:
None fawned, none trampled; hate, disdain, or fear,
Self-love or self-contempt, on human brows
No more inscribed, as o'er the gate of Hell,
'All hope abandon, ye who enter here';
None frowned, none trembled, none with eager fear
Gazed on another's eye of cold command
Until the subject of a tyrant's will
Became, worse fate, the abject of his own,   140
Which spurred him, like an outspent horse, to death;
None wrought his lips in truth-entangling lines
Which smiled the lie his tongue disdained to speak;
None, with firm sneer, trod out in his own heart
The sparks of love and hope till there remained
Those bitter ashes, a soul self-consumed,
And the wretch crept a vampire among men,
Infecting all with his own hideous ill;
None talked that common, false, cold, hollow talk
Which makes the heart deny the *yes* it breathes,   150
Yet question that unmeant hypocrisy

With such a self-mistrust as has no name.
And women, too, frank, beautiful, and kind
As the free heaven which rains fresh light and dew
On the wide earth, passed – gentle, radiant forms,
From custom's evil taint exempt and pure,
Speaking the wisdom once they could not think,
Looking emotions once they feared to feel,
And changed to all which once they dared not be,
Yet being now, made earth like Heaven; nor pride,   160
Nor jealousy, nor envy, nor ill shame,
The bitterest of those drops of treasured gall,
Spoilt the sweet taste of the nepenthe, love.

Thrones, altars, judgement-seats, and prisons – wherein
And beside which, by wretched men were borne
Sceptres, tiaras, swords, and chains, and tomes
Of reasoned wrong, glozed on by ignorance –
Were like those monstrous and barbaric shapes,
The ghosts of a no-more-remembered fame,
Which, from their unworn obelisks, look forth   170
In triumph o'er the palaces and tombs
Of those who were their conquerors, mouldering round.
These imaged to the pride of kings and priests
A dark yet mighty faith, a power as wide
As is the world it wasted, and are now
But an astonishment; even so the tools
And emblems of its last captivity,
Amid the dwellings of the peopled earth,
Stand, not o'erthrown, but unregarded now.
And those foul shapes, abhorred by God and man –   180
Which, under many a name and many a form,
Strange, savage, ghastly, dark and execrable,
Were Jupiter, the tyrant of the world;
And which the nations, panic-stricken, served
With blood, and hearts broken by long hope, and love
Dragged to his altars soiled and garlandless,
And slain amid men's unreclaiming tears,
Flattering the thing they feared, which fear was hate –
Frown, mouldering fast, o'er their abandoned shrines;
The painted veil, by those who were, called life,   190

Which mimicked, as with colours idly spread,
All men believed or hoped, is torn aside;
The loathsome mask has fallen, the man remains
Sceptreless, free, uncircumscribed – but man:
Equal, unclassed, tribeless and nationless;
Exempt from awe, worship, degree; the king
Over himself; just, gentle, wise – but man:
Passionless? no – yet free from guilt or pain
Which were, for his will made, or suffered them;
Nor yet exempt, though ruling them like slaves,   200
From chance, and death, and mutability,
The clogs of that which else might oversoar
The loftiest star of unascended Heaven,
Pinnacled dim in the intense inane.

ACT IV, ll. 93–193 and ll. 356–578

Chorus of Spirits.   We come from the mind
                Of humankind,
Which was late so dusk, and obscene, and blind;
                Now 'tis an ocean
                Of clear emotion,
A heaven of serene and mighty motion;

            From that deep abyss
            Of wonder and bliss,   100
Whose caverns are crystal palaces;
            From those skyey towers
            Where Thought's crowned Powers
Sit watching your dance, ye happy Hours;

            From the dim recesses
            Of woven caresses,
Where lovers catch ye by your loose tresses;
            From the azure isles,
            Where sweet Wisdom smiles,
Delaying your ships with her siren wiles;   110

            From the temples high
            Of man's ear and eye,

Roofed over Sculpture and Poesy;
    From the murmurings
    Of the unsealed springs
Where Science bedews her daedal wings.

    Year after years,
    Through blood and tears,
And a thick hell of hatreds and hopes and fears,
    We waded and flew,   120
    And the islets were few
Where the bud-blighted flowers of happiness grew.

    Our feet now, every palm,
    Are sandalled with calm,
And the dew of our wings is a rain of balm;
    And, beyond our eyes,
    The human love lies,
Which makes all it gazes on Paradise.
Chorus of Spirits and Hours.
Then weave the web of the mystic measure;
    From the depths of the sky and the ends of the earth,   130
Come, swift Spirits of might and of pleasure,
    Fill the dance and the music of mirth,
As the waves of a thousand streams rush by
To an ocean of splendour and harmony!
Chorus of Spirits.   Our spoil is won,
    Our task is done,
We are free to dive, or soar, or run;
    Beyond and around,
    Or within the bound
Which clips the world with darkness round.   140

    We'll pass the eyes
    Of the starry skies
Into the hoar deep to colonize;
    Death, Chaos, and Night,
    From the sound of our flight
Shall flee, like mist from a tempest's might;

    And Earth, Air, and Light,
    And the Spirit of Might

Which drives round the stars in their fiery flight;
    And Love, Thought, and Breath,   150
    The powers that quell Death,
Wherever we soar shall assemble beneath;

    And our singing shall build
    In the void's loose field
A world for the Spirit of Wisdom to wield;
    We will take our plan
    From the new world of man,
And our work shall be called the Promethean.

Chorus of Hours.
    Break the dance, and scatter the song;
    Let some depart, and some remain.   160
Semichorus I.   We, beyond heaven, are driven along –
Semichorus II.   Us the enchantments of earth retain –
Semichorus I.   Ceaseless, and rapid, and fierce, and free,
    With the Spirits which build a new earth and sea,
    And a Heaven where yet Heaven could never be –
Semichorus II.   Solemn, and slow, and serene, and bright,
    Leading the Day, and outspeeding the Night,
    With the Powers of a world of perfect light –
Semichorus I.   We whirl, singing loud, round the gathering sphere,
    Till the trees, and the beasts, and the clouds appear   170
    From its chaos made calm by love, not fear –
Semichorus II.   We encircle the oceans and mountains of earth,
    And the happy forms of its death and birth
    Change to the music of our sweet mirth.

Chorus of Hours and Spirits.
    Break the dance, and scatter the song;
    Let some depart, and some remain.
    Wherever we fly we lead along
    In leashes, like starbeams, soft yet strong,
    The clouds that are heavy with Love's sweet rain.

Panthea.   Ha! they are gone!
Ione.   Yet feel you no delight   180
From the past sweetness?
Panthea.   As the bare green hill,
    When some soft cloud vanishes into rain,
    Laughs with a thousand drops of sunny water
    To the unpavilioned sky!

Ione.   Even whilst we speak
        New notes arise . . . What is that awful sound?
Panthea.   'Tis the deep music of the rolling world,
        Kindling within the strings of the waved air
        Aeolian modulations.
Ione.   Listen too,
        How every pause is filled with under-notes,
        Clear, silver, icy, keen, awakening tones   190
        Which pierce the sense, and live within the soul,
        As the sharp stars pierce winter's crystal air
        And gaze upon themselves within the sea.

                           *   *   *

The Moon.   The snow upon my lifeless mountains
        Is loosened into living fountains,
        My solid oceans flow, and sing, and shine;
            A spirit from my heart bursts forth,
            It clothes with unexpected birth   360
        My cold bare bosom: Oh, it must be thine
            On mine, on mine!

        Gazing on thee I feel, I know
        Green stalks burst forth, and bright flowers grow,
        And living shapes upon my bosom move;
            Music is in the sea and air,
            Wingèd clouds soar here and there,
        Dark with the rain new buds are dreaming of:
            'Tis Love, all Love!
The Earth.   It interpenetrates my granite mass,   370
        Through tangled roots and trodden clay doth pass
        Into the utmost leaves and delicatest flowers;
            Upon the winds, among the clouds 'tis spread;
            It wakes a life in the forgotten dead,
        They breathe a spirit up from their obscurest bowers;

        And like a storm, bursting its cloudy prison
        With thunder, and with whirlwind, has arisen
        Out of the lampless caves of unimagined being,
            With earthquake shock and swiftness making shiver

Thought's stagnant chaos, unremoved for ever,   380
Till Hate, and Fear, and Pain, light-vanquished shadows, fleeing,

 Leave Man – who was a many-sided mirror,
 Which could distort to many a shape of error
This true fair world of things – a sea reflecting Love;
 Which over all his kind, as the sun's heaven
 Gliding o'er ocean, smooth, serene, and even,
Darting from starry depths radiance and life, doth move:

 Leave Man – even as a leprous child is left,
 Who follows a sick beast to some warm cleft
Of rocks, through which the might of healing springs is poured; 390
 Then when it wanders home with rosy smile,
 Unconscious, and its mother fears awhile
It is a Spirit, then weeps on her child restored –

 Man, oh, not men! a chain of linkèd thought,
 Of love and might to be divided not,
Compelling the elements with adamantine stress,
 As the sun rules, even with a tyrant's gaze,
 The unquiet republic of the maze
Of planets, struggling fierce towards heaven's free wilderness;

 Man, one harmonious soul of many a soul,   400
 Whose nature is its own divine control,
Where all things flow to all, as rivers to the sea;
 Familiar acts are beautiful through love;
 Labour, and Pain, and Grief, in life's green grove
Sport like tame beasts – none knew how gentle they could be!

 His will, with all mean passions, bad delights,
 And selfish cares, its trembling satellites,
A spirit ill to guide, but mighty to obey,
 Is a tempest-wingèd ship, whose helm
 Love rules, through waves which dare not overwhelm,   410
Forcing life's wildest shores to own its sovereign sway.

 All things confess his strength. Through the cold mass
 Of marble and of colour his dreams pass –
Bright threads whence mothers weave the robes their children wear;
 Language is a perpetual Orphic song,

89

Which rules with daedal harmony a throng
Of thoughts and forms, which else senseless and shapeless were.

The lightning is his slave; heaven's utmost deep
Gives up her stars, and like a flock of sheep
They pass before his eye, are numbered, and roll on.   420
 The Tempest is his steed – he strides the air;
 And the abyss shouts from her depth laid bare,
'Heaven, hast thou secrets? Man unveils me; I have none.'

The Moon. The shadow of white Death has passed
 From my path in heaven at last,
A clinging shroud of solid frost and sleep;
 And through my newly woven bowers
 Wander happy paramours,
Less mighty, but as mild as those who keep
 Thy vales more deep.   430

The Earth. As the dissolving warmth of dawn may fold
 A half-unfrozen dew-globe, green and gold
And crystalline, till it becomes a wingèd mist
 And wanders up the vault of the blue day,
 Outlives the noon, and on the sun's last ray
Hangs o'er the sea, a fleece of fire and amethyst –

The Moon. Thou art folded, thou art lying
 In the light which is undying
Of thine own joy, and heaven's smile divine;
 All suns and constellations shower   440
 On thee a light, a life, a power
Which doth array thy sphere; thou pourest thine
 On mine, on mine!

The Earth. I spin beneath my pyramid of night,
 Which points into the heavens, dreaming delight,
Murmuring victorious joy in my enchanted sleep;
 As a youth lulled in love-dreams, faintly sighing,
 Under the shadow of his beauty lying,
Which round his rest a watch of light and warmth doth keep.

The Moon. As in the soft and sweet eclipse,   450
 When soul meets soul on lovers' lips,
High hearts are calm, and brightest eyes are dull;
 So, when thy shadow falls on me,
 Then am I mute and still, by thee

Covered; of thy love, Orb most beautiful,
    Full, oh, too full!

Thou art speeding round the sun,
Brightest world of many a one,
Green and azure sphere, which shinest
With a light which is divinest 460
Among all the lamps of heaven
To whom life and light is given;
I, thy crystal paramour,
Borne beside thee by a power
Like the polar paradise,
Magnet-like, of lovers' eyes;
I, a most enamoured maiden,
Whose weak brain is overladen
With the pleasure of her love,
Maniac-like around thee move, 470
Gazing, an insatiate bride,
On thy form from every side,
Like a Maenad round the cup
Which Agave lifted up
In the weird Cadmaean forest.
Brother, wheresoe'er thou soarest
I must hurry, whirl and follow
Through the heavens wide and hollow,
Sheltered, by the warm embrace
Of thy soul, from hungry space; 480
Drinking from thy sense and sight
Beauty, majesty, and might,
As a lover or chameleon
Grows like what it looks upon,
As a violet's gentle eye
Gazes on the azure sky
Until its hue grows like what it beholds,
As a grey and watery mist
Grows like solid amethyst
Athwart the western mountain it enfolds, 490
    When the sunset sleeps
      Upon its snow –
The Earth. And the weak day weeps
    That it should be so.

    Oh gentle Moon, the voice of thy delight
    Falls on me like thy clear and tender light
    Soothing the seaman, borne the summer night
       Through isles forever calm;
    O gentle Moon, thy crystal accents pierce
    The caverns of my pride's deep universe,   500
    Charming the tiger Joy, whose tramplings fierce
       Made wounds which need thy balm.
Panthea.   I rise as from a bath of sparkling water,
    A bath of azure light, among dark rocks,
    Out of the stream of sound.
Ione.   Ah me! sweet sister,
    The stream of sound has ebbed away from us,
    And you pretend to rise out of its wave,
    Because your words fall like the clear soft dew
    Shaken from a bathing wood-nymph's limbs and hair.
Panthea.   Peace! peace! a mighty Power, which is as darkness,   510
    Is rising out of earth, and from the sky
    Is showered like night, and from within the air
    Bursts, like eclipse which had been gathered up
    Into the pores of sunlight: the bright Visions,
    Wherein the singing spirits rode and shone,
    Gleam like pale meteors through a watery night.
Ione.   There is a sense of words upon mine ear –
Panthea.   A universal sound like words . . . Oh, list!
Demogorgon.   Thou Earth, calm empire of a happy soul,
      Sphere of divinest shapes and harmonies,   520
    Beautiful Orb! gathering as thou dost roll
      The love which paves thy path along the skies:
The Earth.   I hear: I am as a drop of dew that dies!
Demogorgon.   Thou Moon, which gazest on the nightly Earth
      With wonder, as it gazes upon thee,
    Whilst each to men, and beasts, and the swift birth
      Of birds, is beauty, love, calm, harmony:
The Moon.   I hear: I am a leaf shaken by thee!
Demogorgon.   Ye Kings of suns and stars, Daemons and Gods,
      Aetherial Dominations, who possess   530
    Elysian, windless, fortunate abodes
      Beyond heaven's constelled wilderness:

A Voice from Above.
      Our great Republic hears: we are blest, and bless.
Demogorgon. Ye happy dead, whom beams of brightest verse
      Are clouds to hide, not colours to portray,
    Whether your nature is that universe
    Which once ye saw and suffered –
A Voice from Beneath.   Or as they
      Whom we have left, we change and pass away.
Demogorgon. Ye elemental Genii, who have homes
      From man's high mind even to the central stone   540
    Of sullen lead, from heaven's star-fretted domes
    To the dull weed some sea worm battens on:

Confused Voice. We hear: thy words waken Oblivion.
Demogorgon. Spirits whose homes are flesh; ye beasts and birds;
      Ye worms and fish; ye living leaves and buds;
    Lightning and wind; and ye untameable herds,
    Meteors and mists, which feed air's solitudes:
A Voice. Thy voice to us is wind among still woods.
Demogorgon. Man, who wert once a despot and a slave;
      A dupe and a deceiver; a decay;   550
    A traveller from the cradle to the grave
    Through the dim night of this immortal day:
All. Speak: thy strong words may never pass away.
Demogorgon. This is the day, which down the void abysm
      At the Earth-born's spell yawns for Heaven's despotism,
      And Conquest is dragged captive through the deep;
    Love, from its awful throne of patient power
    In the wise heart, from the last giddy hour
      Of dread endurance, from the slippery steep,
    And narrow verge of crag-like agony, springs   560
    And folds over the world its healing wings.

    Gentleness, Virtue, Wisdom, and Endurance –
    These are the seals of that most firm assurance
      Which bars the pit over Destruction's strength;
    And if, with infirm hand, Eternity,
    Mother of many acts and hours, should free
      The serpent that would clasp her with his length,

These are the spells by which to re-assume
An empire o'er the disentangled Doom:

To suffer woes which Hope thinks infinite;   570
To forgive wrongs darker than death or night;
    To defy Power, which seems omnipotent;
To love, and bear; to hope, till Hope creates
From its own wreck the thing it contemplates;
    Neither to change, nor falter, nor repent: –
This, like thy glory, Titan, is to be
Good, great and joyous, beautiful and free;
This is alone Life, Joy, Empire, and Victory.

Composed 1818–19
First published 1820

SONNET: LIFT NOT THE PAINTED VEIL

Lift not the painted veil which those who live
Call Life; though unreal shapes be pictured there
And it but mimic all we would believe
With colours idly spread, – behind, lurk Fear
And Hope, twin Destinies, who ever weave
Their shadows o'er the chasm, sightless and drear.
I knew one who had lifted it . . . he sought,
For his lost heart was tender, things to love
But found them not, alas! nor was there aught
The world contains, the which he could approve.   10
Through the unheeding many he did move,
A splendour among shadows, a bright blot
Upon this gloomy scene, a Spirit that strove
For truth, and like the Preacher found it not.

Composed 1819?
First published 1824

SONNET: TO THE REPUBLIC OF BENEVENTO

Nor happiness, nor majesty, nor fame,
Nor peace, nor strength, nor skill in arms or arts,

Shepherd those herds whom Tyranny makes tame:
Verse echoes not one beating of their hearts;
History is but the shadow of their shame;
Art veils her glass, or from the pageant starts
As to oblivion their blind millions fleet,
Staining that Heaven with obscene imagery
Of their own likeness. – What are numbers, knit
By force or custom? Man, who man would be,   10
Must rule the empire of himself; in it
Must be supreme, establishing his throne
On vanquished will, quelling the anarchy
Of hopes and fears, being himself alone.

Composed 1820?
First published 1824

SONNET: ENGLAND IN 1819

An old, mad, blind, despised and dying King;
Princes, the dregs of their dull race, who flow
Through public scorn, – mud from a muddy spring;
Rulers who neither see nor feel nor know,
But leechlike to their fainting Country cling
Till they drop, blind in blood, without a blow;
A people starved and stabbed in the untilled field;
An army whom liberticide and prey
Makes as a two-edged sword to all who wield;
Golden and sanguine laws which tempt and slay;   10
Religion Christless, Godless, a book sealed;
A senate, Time's worst statute, unrepealed, –
Are graves, from which a glorious Phantom may
Burst, to illumine our tempestuous day.

Composed 1819
First published 1839

SONG: MEN OF ENGLAND

I

Men of England, wherefore plough
For the lords who lay ye low?
Wherefore weave with toil and care
The rich robes your tyrants wear?

II

Wherefore feed, and clothe, and save,
From the cradle to the grave,
Those ungrateful drones who would
Drain your sweat – nay, drink your blood?

III

Wherefore, Bees of England, forge
Many a weapon, chain and scourge, 10
That these stingless drones may spoil
The forced produce of your toil?

IV

Have ye leisure, comfort, calm,
Shelter, food, love's gentle balm?
Or what is it ye buy so dear
With your pain and with your fear?

V

The seed ye sow, another reaps;
The wealth ye find, another keeps;
The robes ye weave, another wears;
The arms ye forge, another bears. 20

VI

Sow seed – but let no tyrant reap;
Find wealth – let no impostor heap;
Weave robes – let not the idle wear;
Forge arms – in your defence to bear.

VII

Shrink to your cellars, holes, and cells;
In halls ye deck another dwells.
Why shake the chains ye wrought? Why see
The steel ye tempered glance on ye?

VIII

With plough and spade, and hoe and loom,
Trace your grave, and build your tomb,   30
And weave your winding-sheet – till fair
England be your sepulchre.

Composed 1819
First published 1839

THE MASK OF ANARCHY

Written on the Occasion of the Massacre at
Manchester

As I lay asleep in Italy
There came a voice from over the Sea,
And with great power it forth led me
To walk in the Visions of Poesy.

I met Murder on the way –
He had a mask like Castlereagh,
Very smooth he looked, yet grim;
Seven bloodhounds followed him;

All were fat; and well they might
Be in admirable plight,   10
For one by one, and two by two,
He tossed them human hearts to chew
Which from his wide cloak he drew.

Next came Fraud, and he had on,
Like Eldon, an ermined gown;
His big tears, for he wept well,
Turned to mill-stones as they fell,

And the little children who
Round his feet played to and fro,
Thinking every tear a gem,   20
Had their brains knocked out by them.

Clothed with the Bible, as with light,
And the shadows of the night,
Like Sidmouth, next, Hypocrisy
On a crocodile rode by.

And many more Destructions played
In this ghastly masquerade,
All disguised, even to the eyes,
Like Bishops, lawyers, peers and spies.

Last came Anarchy: he rode   30
On a white horse, splashed with blood;
He was pale even to the lips,
Like Death in the Apocalypse.

And he wore a kingly crown;
And in his grasp a sceptre shone;
On his brow this mark I saw –
'I AM GOD AND KING AND LAW.'

With a pace stately and fast,
Over English land he passed,
Trampling to a mire of blood   40
The adoring multitude.

And a mighty troop around,
With their trampling shook the ground,
Waving each a bloody sword,
For the service of their Lord.

And with glorious triumph, they
Rode through England proud and gay,
Drunk as with intoxication
Of the wine of desolation.

O'er fields and towns, from sea to sea,   50
Passed that Pageant swift and free,
Tearing up and trampling down,

Till they came to London town.

And each dweller, panic-stricken,
Felt his heart with terror sicken
Hearing the tempestuous cry
Of the triumph of Anarchy.

For with pomp to meet him came
Clothed in arms like blood and flame
The hired Murderers, who did sing,   60
'Thou art God and Law and King.

'We have waited weak and lone
For thy coming, Mighty One!
Our purses are empty, our swords are cold
Give us glory and blood and gold.'

Lawyers and priests, a motley crowd,
To the earth their pale brows bowed,
Like a bad prayer not overloud,
Whispering – 'Thou art Law and God.'

Then all cried with one accord,   70
'Thou art King and God and Lord;
Anarchy, to Thee we bow,
Be Thy name made holy now!'

And Anarchy, the Skeleton,
Bowed and grinned to every one,
As well as if his education
Had cost ten millions to the Nation.

For he knew the Palaces
Of our Kings were rightly his;
His the sceptre, crown, and globe,   80
And the gold-inwoven robe.

So he sent his slaves before
To seize upon the Bank and Tower,
And was proceeding with intent
To meet his pensioned Parliament,

When One fled past, a maniac maid,
And her name was Hope, she said;

But she looked more like Despair,
And she cried out in the air:

'My father Time is weak and grey   90
With waiting for a better day –
See how idiot-like he stands
Fumbling with his palsied hands!

He has had child after child
And the dust of death is piled
Over every one but me –
Misery, oh, Misery!'

Then she lay down in the street
Right before the horses' feet,
Expecting with a patient eye   100
Murder, Fraud and Anarchy,

When between her and her foes
A mist, a light, an image rose,
Small at first, and weak and frail
Like the vapour of a vale,

Till as clouds grow on the blast,
Like tower-crowned giants striding fast,
And glare with lightnings as they fly
And speak in thunder to the sky,

It grew – a Shape arrayed in mail   110
Brighter than the viper's scale,
And upborne on wings whose grain
Was as the light of sunny rain.

On its helm, seen far away,
A planet, like the Morning's lay;
And those plumes its light rained through
Like a shower of crimson dew.

With step as soft as wind it passed
O'er the heads of men – so fast
That they knew the presence there   120
And looked – but all was empty air.

As flowers beneath May's footstep waken,
As stars from Night's loose hair are shaken,
As waves arise when loud winds call,
Thoughts sprung where'er that step did fall.

And the prostrate multitude
Looked – and ankle-deep in blood,
Hope, that maiden most serene,
Was walking with a quiet mien;

And Anarchy, the ghastly birth,   130
Lay dead earth upon the earth –
The Horse of Death tameless as wind
Fled, and with his hoofs did grind
To dust the murderers thronged behind.

A rushing light of clouds and splendour,
A sense awakening and yet tender
Was heard and felt – and at its close
These words of joy and fear arose

As if their own indignant Earth
Which gave the Sons of England birth   140
Had felt their blood upon her brow,
And shuddering with a mother's throe

Had turned every drop of blood
By which her face had been bedewed
To an accent unwithstood –
As if her heart cried out aloud:

'Men of England, Heirs of Glory,
Heroes of unwritten story,
Nurslings of one mighty Mother,
Hopes of her and one another,   150

'Rise like Lions after slumber
In unvanquishable number,
Shake your chains to Earth like dew
Which in sleep had fallen on you –
Ye are many – they are few.

'What is Freedom? – ye can tell
That which slavery is, too well –

For its very name has grown
To an echo of your own.

' 'Tis to work and have such pay   160
As just keeps life from day to day
In your limbs, as in a cell
For the tyrants' use to dwell,

'So that ye for them are made
Loom and plough and sword and spade,
With or without your own will bent
To their defence and nourishment;

' 'Tis to see your children weak
With their mothers pine and peak
When the winter winds are bleak –   170
They are dying whilst I speak;

' 'Tis to hunger for such diet
As the rich man in his riot
Casts to the fat dogs that lie
Surfeiting beneath his eye;

' 'Tis to let the Ghost of Gold
Take from Toil a thousandfold
More than e'er its substance could
In the tyrannies of old –

'Paper coin, that forgery   180
Of the title deeds, which ye
Hold to something of the worth
Of the inheritance of Earth;

' 'Tis to be a slave in soul
And to hold no strong control
Over your own will, but be
All that others make of ye;

'And at length when ye complain
With a murmur weak and vain,
'Tis to see the tyrants' crew   190
Ride over your wives and you –
Blood is on the grass like dew.

'Then it is to feel revenge
Fiercely thirsting to exchange
Blood for blood, and wrong for wrong –
Do not thus when ye are strong

'Birds find rest, in narrow nest
When weary of their wingèd quest
Beasts find fare, in woody lair
When storm and snow are in the air;   200

'Horses, oxen, have a home
When from daily toil they come;
Household dogs, when the wind roars
Find a home within warm doors;

'Asses, swine, have litter spread
And with fitting food are fed;
All things have a home but one –
Thou, O Englishman, hast none!

'This is slavery – savage men
Or wild beasts within a den   210
Would endure not as ye do –
But such ills they never knew.

'What art thou, Freedom? O, could slaves
Answer from their living graves
This demand, tyrants would flee
Like a dream's dim imagery.

'Thou art not as imposters say
A shadow soon to pass away,
A superstition, and a name
Echoing from the cave of Fame: 220

'For the labourer thou art bread
And a comely table spread,
From his daily labour come,
In a neat and happy home;

'Thou art clothes and fire and food
For the trampled multitude –
No – in countries that are free
Such starvation cannot be
As in England now we see.

103

'To the rich thou art a check –   230
When his foot is on the neck
Of his victim, thou dost make
That he treads upon a snake.

'Thou art Justice – ne'er for gold
May thy righteous laws be sold
As laws are in England – thou
Shieldst alike both high and low.

'Thou art Wisdom – Freemen never
Dream that God will damn forever
All who think those things untrue   240
Of which Priests make such ado.

'Thou art Peace – never by thee
Would blood and treasure wasted be
As tyrants wasted them, when all
Leagued to quench thy flame in Gaul.

'What if English toil and blood
Was poured forth, even as a flood?
It availed, O Liberty,
To dim, but not extinguish thee.

'Thou art Love – the rich have kissed   250
Thy feet and, like him following Christ,
Give their substance to the free
And through the rough world follow thee,

'Or turn their wealth to arms, and make
War for thy belovèd sake
On wealth and war and fraud – whence they
Drew the power which is their prey.

'Science, Poetry and Thought
Are thy lamps; they make the lot
Of the dwellers in a cot   260
Such, they curse their Maker not.

'Spirit, Patience, Gentleness,
All that can adorn and bless
Art thou . . . let deeds, not words, express
Thine exceeding loveliness –

'Let a great Assembly be
Of the fearless and the free
On some spot of English ground
Where the plains stretch wide around.

'Let the blue sky overhead,   270
The green earth on which ye tread,
All that must eternal be
Witness the Solemnity.

'From the corners uttermost
Of the bounds of English coast,
From every hut, village and town
Where those who live and suffer, moan
For others' misery or their own –

'From the workhouse and the prison
Where pale as corpses newly risen   280
Women, children, young and old
Groan for pain and weep for cold –

'From the haunts of daily life
Where is waged the daily strife
With common wants and common cares
Which sows the human heart with tares –

'Lastly from the palaces
Where the murmur of distress
Echoes, like the distant sound
Of a wind alive around   290

'Those prison-halls of wealth and fashion
Where some few feel such compassion
For those who groan and toil and wail
As must make their brethren pale,

'Ye who suffer woes untold,
Or to feel or to behold
Your lost country bought and sold
With a price of blood and gold –

'Let a vast Assembly be,

And with great solemnity   300
Declare with measured words that ye
Are, as God has made ye, free –

'Be your strong and simple words
Keen to wound as sharpened swords,
And wide as targes let them be
With their shade to cover ye.

'Let the tyrants pour around
With a quick and startling sound
Like the loosening of a sea
Troops of armed emblazonry.   310

'Let the charged artillery drive
Till the dead air seems alive
With the clash of clanging wheels
And the tramp of horses' heels.

'Let the fixèd bayonet
Gleam with sharp desire to wet
Its bright point in English blood
Looking keen, as one for food.

'Let the horsemen's scimitars
Wheel and flash like sphereless stars   320
Thirsting to eclipse their burning
In a sea of death and mourning.

'Stand ye calm and resolute,
Like a forest close and mute,
With folded arms and looks which are
Weapons of unvanquished war,

'And let Panic who outspeeds
The career of armèd steeds
Pass, a disregarded shade,
Through your phalanx undismayed.   330

'Let the Laws of your own land,
Good or ill, between ye stand,
Hand to hand and foot to foot,
Arbiters of the dispute,

'The old laws of England – they
Whose reverend heads with age are grey,
Children of a wiser day,
And whose solemn voice must be
Thine own echo – Liberty!

'On those who first should violate   340
Such sacred heralds in their state
Rest the blood that must ensue . . .
And it will not rest on you.

'And if then the tyrants dare,
Let them ride among you there,
Slash and stab and maim and hew –
What they like, that let them do.

'With folded arms, and steady eyes,
And little fear, and less surprise,
Look upon them as they slay   350
Till their rage has died away.

'Then they will return with shame
To the place from which they came,
And the blood thus shed will speak
In hot blushes on their cheek.

'Every woman in the land
Will point at them as they stand –
They will hardly dare to greet
Their acquaintance in the street.

'And the bold, true warriors   360
Who have hugged Danger in wars
Will turn to those who would be free,
Ashamed of such base company.

'And that slaughter, to the Nation
Shall steam up like inspiration,
Eloquent, oracular –
A volcano heard afar.

'And these words shall then become
Like oppression's thundered doom

Ringing through each heart and brain   370
Heard again, again, again –

'Rise like lions after slumber
In unvanquishable number,
Shake your chains to earth like dew
Which in sleep had fallen on you –
Ye are many – they are few –'

Composed 1819
First published 1832

from PETER BELL THE THIRD

Hell is a city much like London –
    A populous and a smoky city;
There are all sorts of people undone,
And there is little or no fun done;   150
    Small justice shown, and still less pity.

                    *   *   *

There is a great talk of Revolution –
    And a great chance of despotism –
German soldiers – camps – confusion –
Tumults – lotteries – rage – delusion –
    Gin – suicide – and methodism;

Taxes too, on wine and bread,
    And meat, and beer, and tea, and cheese,
From which those patriots pure are fed
Who gorge before they reel to bed   180
    The tenfold essence of all these.

There are mincing women, mewing
    (Like cats, who *amant misere*)
Of their own virtue, and pursuing
Their gentler sisters to that ruin,
    Without which – what were chastity?

Lawyers – judges – old hobnobbers
    Are there – Bailiffs – Chancellors –
Bishops – great and little robbers –

Rhymesters – pamphleteers – stock-jobbers –   190
   Men of glory in the wars, –

Things whose trade is, over ladies
   To lean, and flirt, and stare, and simper,
Till all that is divine in woman
Grows cruel, courteous, smooth, inhuman,
   Crucified 'twixt a smile and whimper.

Thrusting, toiling, wailing, moiling,
   Frowning, preaching – such a riot!
Each with never ceasing labour
Whilst he thinks he cheats his neighbour   200
   Cheating his own heart of quiet.

*   *   *

All things that Peter saw and felt
   Had a peculiar aspect to him;
And when they came within the belt
Of his own nature, seemed to melt
   Like cloud to cloud, into him.

And so the outward world uniting
   To that within him, he became
Considerably uninviting   280
To those who, meditation slighting,
   Were moulded in a different frame.

And he scorned them, and they scorned him;
   And he scorned all they did; and they
Did all that men of their own trim
Are wont to do to please their whim,
   Drinking, lying, swearing, play.

Such were his fellow servants; thus
   His virtue, like our own, was built
Too much on that indignant fuss   290
Hypocrite Pride stirs up in us
   To bully one another's guilt.

He had a mind which was somehow
   At once circumference and centre
Of all he might or feel or know;

Nothing went ever out, although
   Something did ever enter.

He had as much imagination
   As a pint-pot: – he never could
Fancy another situation,   300
From which to dart his contemplation,
   Than that wherein he stood.

Yet his was individual mind,
   And new created all he saw
In a new manner, and refined
Those new creations, and combined
   Them, by a master-spirit's law;

Thus – though unimaginative,
   An apprehension clear, intense,
Of his mind's work, had made alive   310
The things it wrought on; I believe
   Wakening a sort of thought in sense.

But from the first 'twas Peter's drift
   To be a kind of moral eunuch;
He touched the hem of Nature's shift,
Felt faint – and never dared uplift
   The closest, all-concealing tunic.

*   *   *

He was a mighty poet – and
   A subtle-souled Psychologist;
All things he seemed to understand   380
Of old or new – of sea or land –
   But his own mind – which was a mist.

This was a man who might have turned
   Hell into Heaven – and so in gladness
A Heaven unto himself have earned;
But he in shadows undiscerned
   Trusted, – and damned himself to madness.

He spoke of poetry, and how
   'Divine it was – a light – a love –
A spirit which like wind doth blow   390

As it listeth, to and fro;
    A dew rained down from God above;

'A power which comes and goes like dream,
    And which none can ever trace –
Heaven's light on Earth – Truth's brightest beam.'
And when he ceased there lay the gleam
    Of those words upon his face.

Now Peter, when he heard such talk,
    Would, heedless of a broken pate,
Stand like a man asleep, or baulk   400
Some wishing guest of knife or fork,
    Or drop and break his master's plate.

At night he oft would start and wake
    Like a lover, and began
In a wild measure songs to make
On moor, and glen, and rocky lake,
    And on the heart of man,

And on the universal sky –
    And the wide earth's bosom green, –
And the sweet, strange mystery   410
Of what beyond these things may lie
    And yet remain unseen.

For in his thought he visited
    The spots in which, ere dead and damned,
He his wayward life had led;
Yet knew not whence the thoughts were fed
    Which thus his fancy crammed.

And these obscure remembrances
    Stirred such harmony in Peter,
That, whensoever he should please,   420
He could speak of rocks and trees
    In poetic metre.

For though it was without a sense
    Of memory, yet he remembered well
Many a ditch and quickset fence;
Of lakes he had intelligence,
    He knew something of heath and fell.

He had also dim recollections
   Of pedlars tramping on their rounds;
Milk pans and pails; and odd collections   430
Of saws, and proverbs; and reflections
   Old parsons make in burying-grounds.

But Peter's verse was clear, and came
   Announcing from the frozen hearth
Of a cold age, that none might tame
The soul of that diviner flame
   It augured to the Earth;

Like gentle rains, on the dry plains,
   Making that green which late was grey,
Or like the sudden moon, that stains   440
   With a broad light like day.

Composed 1819
First published 1839

ODE TO THE WEST WIND

I

O wild West Wind, thou breath of Autumn's being,
Thou, from whose unseen presence the leaves dead
Are driven, like ghosts from an enchanter fleeing,

Yellow, and black, and pale, and hectic red,
Pestilence-stricken multitudes: O thou,
Who chariotest to their dark wintry bed

The wingèd seeds, where they lie cold and low,
Each like a corpse within its grave, until
Thine azure sister of the Spring shall blow

Her clarion o'er the dreaming earth, and fill   10
(Driving sweet buds like flocks to feed in air)
With living hues and odours plain and hill:

Wild Spirit, which art moving everywhere;
Destroyer and Preserver; hear, O hear!

II

Thou on whose stream, 'mid the steep sky's commotion,
Loose clouds like Earth's decaying leaves are shed,
Shook from the tangled boughs of Heaven and Ocean,

Angels of rain and lightning: there are spread
On the blue surface of thine airy surge,
Like the bright hair uplifted from the head   20

Of some fierce Maenad, even from the dim verge
Of the horizon to the zenith's height,
The locks of the approaching storm. Thou dirge

Of the dying year, to which this closing night
Will be the dome of a vast sepulchre,
Vaulted with all thy congregated might

Of vapours, from whose solid atmosphere
Black rain, and fire, and hail will burst: O hear!

III

Thou who didst waken from his summer dreams
The blue Mediterranean, where he lay,   30
Lulled by the coil of his crystalline streams,

Beside a pumice isle in Baiae's bay,
And saw in sleep old palaces and towers
Quivering within the wave's intenser day,

All overgrown with azure moss and flowers
So sweet, the sense faints picturing them! Thou
For whose path the Atlantic's level powers

Cleave themselves into chasms, while far below
The sea-blooms and the oozy woods which wear
The sapless foliage of the ocean, know   40

Thy voice, and suddenly grow grey with fear,
And tremble and despoil themselves: O hear!

IV

If I were a dead leaf thou mightest bear;
If I were a swift cloud to fly with thee;
A wave to pant beneath thy power, and share

113

The impulse of thy strength, only less free
Than thou, O Uncontrollable! If even
I were as in my boyhood, and could be

The comrade of thy wanderings over Heaven,
As then, when to outstrip thy skiey speed   50
Scarce seemed a vision; I would ne'er have striven

As thus with thee in prayer in my sore need.
Oh! lift me as a wave, a leaf, a cloud!
I fall upon the thorns of life! I bleed!

A heavy weight of hours has chained and bowed
One too like thee: tameless, and swift, and proud.

V

Make me thy lyre, even as the forest is:
What if my leaves are falling like its own!
The tumult of thy mighty harmonies

Will take from both a deep, autumnal tone,   60
Sweet though in sadness. Be thou, Spirit fierce,
My spirit! Be thou me, impetuous one!

Drive my dead thoughts over the universe
Like withered leaves to quicken a new birth!
And, by the incantation of this verse,

Scatter, as from an unextinguished hearth
Ashes and sparks, my words among mankind!
Be through my lips to unawakened Earth

The trumpet of a prophecy! O, Wind,
If Winter comes, can Spring be far behind?   70

Composed 1819
First published 1820

THE CLOUD

I bring fresh showers for the thirsting flowers
    From the seas and the streams;

I bear light shade for the leaves when laid
    In their noon-day dreams.
From my wings are shaken the dews that waken
    The sweet buds every one,
When rocked to rest on their mother's breast,
    As she dances about the sun.
I wield the flail of the lashing hail,
    And whiten the green plains under,   10
And then again I dissolve it in rain,
    And laugh as I pass in thunder.

I sift the snow on the mountains below,
    And their great pines groan aghast;
And all the night 'tis my pillow white,
    While I sleep in the arms of the blast.
Sublime on the towers of my skyey bowers,
    Lightning my pilot sits;
In a cavern under is fettered the thunder,
    It struggles and howls at fits;   20
Over earth and ocean, with gentle motion,
    This pilot is guiding me,
Lured by the love of the genii that move
    In the depths of the purple sea;
Over the rills, and the crags, and the hills,
    Over the lakes and the plains,
Wherever he dream, under mountain or stream,
    The Spirit he loves remains;
And I all the while bask in Heaven's blue smile,
    Whilst he is dissolving in rains.   30

The sanguine sunrise, with his meteor eyes,
    And his burning plumes outspread,
Leaps on the back of my sailing rack,
    When the morning star shines dead;
As on the jag of a mountain crag,
    Which an earthquake rocks and swings,
An eagle alit one moment may sit
    In the light of its golden wings;
And when sunset may breathe, from the lit sea beneath,
    Its ardours of rest and of love,   40

And the crimson pall of eve may fall
    From the depth of Heaven above,
With wings folded I rest, on mine airy nest,
    As still as a brooding dove.

That orbèd maiden with white fire laden,
    Whom mortals call the moon,
Glides glimmering o'er my fleece-like floor,
    By the midnight breezes strewn;
And wherever the beat of her unseen feet,
    Which only the angels hear,   50
May have broken the woof of my tent's thin roof,
    The stars peep behind her, and peer;
And I laugh to see them whirl and flee
    Like a swarm of golden bees,
When I widen the rent in my wind-built tent,
    Till the calm rivers, lakes, and seas,
Like strips of the sky fallen through me on high,
    Are each paved with the moon and these.

I bind the sun's throne with a burning zone,
    And the moon's with a girdle of pearl;   60
The volcanoes are dim, and the stars reel and swim,
    When the whirlwinds my banner unfurl.
From cape to cape, with a bridge-like shape,
    Over a torrent sea,
Sunbeam-proof, I hang like a roof –
    The mountains its columns be.
The triumphal arch through which I march
    With hurricane, fire, and snow,
When the powers of the air are chained to my chair,
    Is the million-coloured bow;   70
The sphere-fire above its soft colours wove,
    While the moist earth was laughing below.

I am the daughter of Earth and Water,
    And the nursling of the Sky;
I pass through the pores of the oceans and shores;
    I change, but I cannot die –
For after the rain, when with never a stain
    The pavilion of Heaven is bare,

And the winds and sunbeams, with their convex gleams,
    Build up the blue dome of air, 80
I silently laugh at my own cenotaph,
    And out of the caverns of rain,
Like a child from the womb, like a ghost from the tomb,
    I arise and unbuild it again.

Composed 1820
First published 1820

TO A SKYLARK

Hail to thee, blithe Spirit!
    Bird thou never wert,
That from Heaven, or near it,
    Pourest thy full heart
In profuse strains of unpremeditated art.

    Higher still and higher
    From the earth thou springest
Like a cloud of fire;
    The blue deep thou wingest,
And singing still dost soar, and soaring ever singest. 10

    In the golden lightning
    Of the sunken Sun,
O'er which clouds are bright'ning,
    Thou dost float and run;
Like an unbodied joy whose race is just begun.

    The pale purple even
    Melts around thy flight;
Like a star of Heaven
    In the broad day-light
Thou art unseen, – but yet I hear thy shrill delight, 20

    Keen as are the arrows
    Of that silver sphere
Whose intense lamp narrows
    In the white dawn clear,
Until we hardly see – we feel that it is there.

117

All the earth and air
　　With thy voice is loud,
As, when night is bare,
　　From one lonely cloud
The moon rains out her beams, and Heaven is overflowed.　　30

　　What thou art we know not;
　　　　What is most like thee?
　　From rainbow clouds there flow not
　　　　Drops so bright to see,
As from thy presence showers a rain of melody.

　　Like a Poet hidden
　　　　In the light of thought,
　　Singing hymns unbidden
　　　　Till the world is wrought
To sympathy with hopes and fears it heeded not;　　40

　　Like a high-born maiden
　　　　In a palace-tower,
　　Soothing her love-laden
　　　　Soul in secret hour
With music sweet as love, which overflows her bower;

　　Like a glow-worm golden
　　　　In a dell of dew,
　　Scattering unbeholden
　　　　Its aërial hue
Among the flowers and grass which screen it from the view;　　50

　　Like a rose embowered
　　　　In its own green leaves,
　　By warm winds deflowered,
　　　　Till the scent it gives
Makes faint with too much sweet those heavy-wingèd thieves:

　　Sound of vernal showers
　　　　On the twinkling grass,
　　Rain-awakened flowers,
　　　　All that ever was
Joyous and clear and fresh, thy music doth surpass.　　60

　　Teach us, Sprite or Bird,
　　　　What sweet thoughts are thine;

I have never heard
    Praise of love or wine
That panted forth a flood of rapture so divine:

    Chorus Hymeneal
      Or triumphal chaunt
    Matched with thine, would be all
      But an empty vaunt,
A thing wherein we feel there is some hidden want.   70

    What objects are the fountains
      Of thy happy strain?
    What fields or waves or mountains?
      What shapes of sky or plain?
What love of thine own kind? what ignorance of pain?

    With thy clear keen joyance
      Languor cannot be –
    Shadow of annoyance
      Never came near thee:
Thou lovest – but ne'er knew love's sad satiety.   80

    Waking or asleep,
      Thou of death must deem
    Things more true and deep
      Than we mortals dream,
Or how could thy notes flow in such a crystal stream?

    We look before and after
      And pine for what is not:
    Our sincerest laughter
      With some pain is fraught;
Our sweetest songs are those that tell of saddest thought.   90

    Yet if we could scorn
      Hate and pride and fear,
    If we were things born
      Not to shed a tear,
I know not how thy joy we ever should come near.

    Better than all measures
      Of delightful sound –

Better than all treasures
        That in books are found –
Thy skill to poet were, thou scorner of the ground!   100

        Teach me half the gladness
        That thy brain must know,
    Such harmonious madness
        From my lips would flow,
The world should listen then – as I am listening now.

Composed 1820
First published 1820

LETTER TO MARIA GISBORNE

The spider spreads her webs, whether she be
In poet's tower, cellar or barn or tree;
The silk-worm in the dark green mulberry leaves
His winding sheet and cradle ever weaves;
So I, a thing whom moralists call worm,
Sit spinning still round this decaying form
From the fine threads of rare and subtle thought –
No net of words in garish colours wrought
To catch the idle buzzers of the day –
But a soft cell where, when that fades away,   10
Memory may clothe in wings my living name
And feed it with the asphodels of fame,
Which in those hearts that most remember me
Grow, making love an immortality.

Whoever should behold me now, I wist,
Would think I were a mighty mechanist,
Bent with sublime Archimedean art
To breathe a soul into the iron heart
Of some machine portentous, or strange gin,
Which, by the force of figured spells, might win   20
Its way over the sea, and sport therein;
For round the walls are hung dread engines, such
As Vulcan never wrought for Jove to clutch
Ixion or the Titan; – or the quick
Wit of that man of God, St Dominic,

120

To convince Atheist, Turk or heretic;
Or those in philanthropic council met,
Who thought to pay some interest for the debt
They owed to Jesus Christ for their salvation,
By giving a faint foretaste of damnation   30
To Shakespeare, Sidney, Spenser, and the rest
Who made our land an island of the blest,
When lamplike Spain, who now relumes her fire
On Freedom's hearth, grew dim with Empire –
With thumbscrews, wheels, with tooth and spike and jag,
Which fishers found under the utmost crag
Of Cornwall, and the storm-encompassed isles,
Where to the sky the rude sea rarely smiles
Unless in treacherous wrath, as on the morn
When the exulting elements, in scorn,   40
Satiated with destroyed destruction, lay
Sleeping in beauty on their mangled prey,
As panthers sleep; – and other strange and dread
Magical forms the brick floor overspread –
Proteus transformed to metal did not make
More figures or more strange; nor did he take
Such shapes of unintelligible brass,
Or heap himself in such a horrid mass
Of tin and iron not to be understood,
And forms of unimaginable wood,   50
To puzzle Tubal Cain and all his brood:
Great screws, and cones, and wheels, and groovèd blocks,
The elements of what will stand the shocks
Of wave and wind and time. – Upon the table
More knacks and quips there be than I am able
To catalogize in this verse of mine: –
A pretty bowl of wood, not full of wine
But quicksilver, that dew which the gnomes drink
When at their subterranean toil they swink,
Pledging the demons of the earthquake, who   60
Reply to them in lava, cry halloo!
And call out to the cities o'er their head –
Roofs, towers, and shrines, the dying and the dead,
Crash through the chinks of earth – and then all quaff

Another rouse, and hold their ribs and laugh.
This quicksilver no gnome has drunk – within
The walnut bowl it lies, veinèd and thin,
In colour like the wake of light that stains
The Tuscan deep, when from the moist moon rains
The inmost shower of its white fire – the breeze   70
Is still – blue heaven smiles over the pale seas.
And in this bowl of quicksilver – for I
Yield to the impulse of an infancy
Outlasting manhood – I have made to float
A rude idealism of a paper boat: –
A hollow screw with cogs – Henry will know
The thing I mean, and laugh at me, if so
He fears not I should do more mischief. – Next
Lie bills and calculations much perplexed,
With steam boats, frigates and machinery quaint   80
Traced over them in blue and yellow paint.
Then comes a range of mathematical
Instruments, for plans nautical and statical;
A heap of rosin, a queer broken glass
With ink in it; a china cup that was
What it will never be again, I think,
A thing from which sweet lips were wont to drink
The liquor doctors rail at – and which I
Will quaff in spite of them – and when we die
We'll toss up who died first of drinking tea,   90
And cry out, 'Heads or tails?' where'er we be.
Near that a dusty paint box, some odd hooks,
A half-burnt match, an ivory block, three books
Where conic sections, spherics, logarithms,
To great Laplace from Saunderson and Sims,
Lie heaped in their harmonious disarray
Of figures – disentangle them who may.
Baron de Tott's memoirs beside them lie,
And some odd volumes of old chemistry.
Near those a most inexplicable tin thing   100
With lead in the middle – I'm conjecturing
How to make Henry understand – but no,
I'll leave, as Spenser says, with many mo,

This secret in the pregnant womb of time,
Too vast a matter for so weak a rhyme.

And here like some weird Archimage sit I,
Plotting dark spells and devilish enginery, –
The self-impelling steam-wheels of the mind
Which pump up oaths from clergymen, and grind
The gentle spirit of our meek reviews   110
Into a powdery foam of salt abuse,
Ruffling the ocean of their self-content –
I sit, and smile or sigh, as is my bent,
But not for them – Libeccio rushes round
With an inconstant and an idle sound,
I heed him more than them – the thundersmoke
Is gathering on the mountains, like a cloak
Folded athwart their shoulders broad and bare;
The ripe corn under the undulating air
Undulates like an ocean; – and the vines   120
Are trembling wide in all their trellised lines –
The murmur of the awakening sea doth fill
The empty pauses of the blast – the hill
Looks hoary through the white electric rain –
And from the glens beyond, in sullen strain,
The interrupted thunder howls; above
One chasm of Heaven smiles, like the eye of Love,
O'er the unquiet world; – while such things are,
How could one worth your friendship heed this war
Of worms? the shriek of the world's carrion jays,   130
Their censure, or their wonder, or their praise?

You are not here! . . . the quaint witch Memory sees
In vacant chairs your absent images,
And points where once you sat, and now should be
But are not. – I demand if ever we
Shall meet as then we met, – and she replies
Veiling in awe her second-sighted eyes,
'I know the past alone – but summon home
My sister Hope, she speaks of all to come.'
But I, an old diviner, who know well   140
Every false verse of that sweet oracle

Turned to the sad enchantress once again,
And sought a respite from my gentle pain
In citing every passage o'er and o'er
Of our communion – how on the sea shore
We watched the ocean and the sky together
Under the roof of blue Italian weather;
How I ran home through last year's thunderstorm,
And felt the transverse lightning linger warm
Upon my cheek – and how we often made   150
Feasts for each other, where good will outweighed
The frugal luxury of our country cheer,
As well it might, were it less firm and clear
Than ours must ever be; – and how we spun
A shroud of talk to hide us from the sun
Of this familiar life, which seems to be
But is not, – or is but quaint mockery
Of all we would believe; and sadly blame
The jarring and inexplicable frame
Of this wrong world – and then anatomize   160
The purposes and thoughts of men whose eyes
Were closed in distant years – or widely guess
The issue of the earth's great business,
When we shall be as we no longer are,
Like babbling gossips safe, who hear the war
Of winds, and sigh, but tremble not; – or how
You listened to some interrupted flow
Of visionary rhyme, in joy and pain
Struck from the inmost fountains of my brain
With little skill perhaps; – or how we sought   170
Those deepest wells of passion and of thought
Wrought by wise poets in the waste of years,
Staining their sacred waters with our tears,
Quenching a thirst ever to be renewed!
Or how I, wisest lady! then indued
The language of a land which now is free
And, winged with thoughts of truth and majesty,
Flits round the tyrant's sceptre like a cloud,
And bursts the peopled prisons, cries aloud,
'My name is Legion!' – that majestic tongue   180

124

Which Calderon over the desert flung
Of ages and of nations; and which found
An echo in our hearts, and with the sound
Startled oblivion; – thou wert then to me
As is a nurse, when inarticulately
A child would talk as its grown parents do.
If living winds the rapid clouds pursue,
If hawks chase doves through the aetherial way,
Huntsmen the innocent deer, and beasts their prey,
Why should not we rouse with the spirit's blast   190
Out of the forest of the pathless past
These recollected pleasures?

             You are now
In London, that great sea, whose ebb and flow
At once is deaf and loud, and on the shore
Vomits its wrecks, and still howls on for more.
Yet in its depth what treasures! – You will see
That which was Godwin, – greater none than he
Though fallen – and fallen on evil times – to stand
Among the spirits of our age and land,
Before the dread tribunal of *to come*   200
The foremost – while Rebuke cowers, pale and dumb.
You will see Coleridge – he who sits obscure
In the exceeding lustre and the pure
Intense irradiation of a mind,
Which, with its own internal lightning blind,
Flags wearily through darkness and despair –
A cloud-encircled meteor of the air,
A hooded eagle among blinking owls. –
You will see Hunt – one of those happy souls
Who are the salt of the earth, and without whom   210
This world would smell like what it is – a tomb; –
Who is, what others seem; his room no doubt
Is still adorned with many a cast from Shout,
With graceful flowers, tastefully placed about;
And coronals of bay from ribbons hung,
And brighter wreaths in neat disorder flung,
The gifts of the most learn'd among some dozens
Of female friends, sisters-in-law and cousins.

And there is he with his eternal puns,
Which beat the dullest brain for smiles, like duns   220
Thundering for money at a poet's door;
Alas, it is no use to say 'I'm poor!'
Or oft in graver mood, when he will look
Things wiser than were ever read in book,
Except in Shakespeare's wisest tenderness. –
You will see Hogg – and I cannot express
His virtues, though I know that they are great,
Because he locks, then barricades, the gate
Within which they inhabit; – of his wit
And wisdom, you'll cry out when you are bit.   230
He is a pearl within an oyster shell,
One of the richest of the deep. And there
Is English Peacock with his mountain Fair,
Turned into a Flamingo, – that shy bird
That gleams i' the Indian air. Have you not heard
When a man marries, dies, or turns Hindu,
His best friends hear no more of him? – but you
Will see him and will like him too, I hope,
With the milk-white Snowdonian Antelope
Matched with this Cameleopard. – His fine wit   240
Makes such a wound, the knife is lost in it;
A strain too learnèd for a shallow age,
Too wise for selfish bigots; let his page
Which charms the chosen spirits of the time
Fold itself up for the serener clime
Of years to come and find its recompense
In that just expectation. – Wit and sense,
Virtue and human knowledge, all that might
Make this dull world a business of delight,
Are all combined in Horace Smith. – And these,   250
With some exceptions which I need not tease
Your patience by descanting on, are all
You and I know in London.

                    I recall
My thoughts, and bid you look upon the night.
As water does a sponge, so the moonlight
Fills the void, hollow, universal air –

What see you? – unpavilioned heaven is fair,
Whether the moon, into her chamber gone,
Leaves midnight to the golden stars, or wan
Climbs with diminished beams the azure steep;   260
Or whether clouds sail o'er the inverse deep,
Piloted by the many-wandering blast,
And the rare stars rush through them dim and fast: –
All this is beautiful in every land. –
But what see you beside? – a shabby stand
Of hackney coaches – a brick house or wall
Fencing some lordly court, white with the scrawl
Of our unhappy politics; or worse –
A wretched woman reeling by, whose curse
Mixed with the watchman's, partner of her trade,   270
You must accept in place of serenade –
Or yellow-haired Pollonia murmuring
To Henry some unutterable thing. –
I see a chaos of green leaves and fruit
Built round dark caverns, even to the root
Of the living stems which feed them – in whose bowers
There sleep in their dark dew the folded flowers;
Beyond, the surface of the unsickled corn
Trembles not in the slumbering air, and borne
In circles quaint, and ever-changing dance,   280
Like wingèd stars the fire-flies flash and glance,
Pale in the open moonshine, but each one
Under the dark trees seems a little sun,
A meteor tamed, a fixed star gone astray
From the silver regions of the Milky Way; –
Afar the Contadino's song is heard,
Rude, but made sweet by distance – and a bird
Which cannot be the nightingale, and yet
I know none else that sings so sweet as it
At this late hour; – and then all is still –   290
Now, Italy or London – which you will!

        Next winter you must pass with me; I'll have
My house by that time turned into a grave
Of dead despondence and low-thoughted care,
And all the dreams which our tormentors are.

Oh, that Hunt, Hogg, Peacock and Smith were there,
With every thing belonging to them fair!
We will have books, Spanish, Italian, Greek;
And ask one week to make another week
As like his father as I'm unlike mine,   300
Which is not his fault, as you may divine.
Though we eat little flesh and drink no wine,
Yet let's be merry: we'll have tea and toast,
Custards for supper, and an endless host
Of syllabubs and jellies and mince-pies,
And other such lady-like luxuries –
Feasting on which, we will philosophize!
And we'll have fires out of the Grand Duke's wood
To thaw the six weeks' winter in our blood.
And then we'll talk; – what shall we talk about?   310
Oh! there are themes enough for many a bout
Of thought-entangled descant; – as to nerves,
With cones and parallelograms and curves
I've sworn to strangle them if once they dare
To bother me – when you are with me there,
And they shall never more sip laudanum
From Helicon or Himeros; – well, come,
And in despite of God and of the devil,
We'll make our friendly philosophic revel
Outlast the leafless time; – till buds and flowers   320
Warn the obscure inevitable hours
Sweet meeting by sad parting to renew –
'Tomorrow to fresh woods and pastures new.'

Composed 1820
First published 1824

from THE WITCH OF ATLAS

The deep recesses of her odorous dwelling
    Were stored with magic treasures – sounds of air,
Which had the power all spirits of compelling,
    Folded in cells of crystal silence there;
Such as we hear in youth, and think the feeling

128

Will never die – yet ere we are aware,
The feeling and the sound are fled and gone,
And the regret they leave remains alone.   160

And there lay Visions swift and sweet and quaint,
    Each in its thin sheath like a chrysalis,
Some eager to burst forth, some weak and faint
    With the soft burthen of intensest bliss;
It was its work to bear to many a saint
    Whose heart adores the shrine which holiest is,
Even Love's – and others white, green, grey and black,
And of all shapes – and each was at her beck.

And odours in a kind of aviary
    Of ever blooming Eden-trees she kept,   170
Clipt in a floating net a love-sick Fairy
    Had woven from dew beams while the moon yet slept –
As bats at the wired window of a dairy
    They beat their vans; and each was an adept,
When loosed and missioned, making wings of winds,
To stir sweet thoughts or sad, in destined minds.

And liquors clear and sweet, whose healthful might
    Could medicine the sick soul to happy sleep,
And change eternal death into a night
    Of glorious dreams – or if eyes needs must weep,   180
Could make their tears all wonder and delight,
    She in her crystal vials did closely keep –
If men could drink of those clear vials, 'tis said
The living were not envied of the dead.

Her cave was stored with scrolls of strange device,
    The works of some Saturnian Archimage,
Which taught the expiations at whose price
    Men from the Gods might win that happy age
Too lightly lost, redeeming native vice;
    And which might quench the earth-consuming rage   190
Of gold and blood – till men should live and move
Harmonious as the sacred stars above.

And how all things that seem untameable,
    Not to be checked and not to be confined,

Obey the spells of wisdom's wizard skill;
   Time, earth and fire – the ocean and the wind
And all their shapes – and man's imperial will –
   And other scrolls whose writings did unbind
The inmost lore of Love – let the profane
Tremble to ask what secrets they contain.   200

         *   *   *

A pleasure sweet doubtless it was to see
   Mortals subdued in all the shapes of sleep: 530
Here lay two sister-twins in infancy;
   There, a lone youth who in his dreams did weep;
Within, two lovers linkèd innocently
   In their loose locks which over both did creep
Like ivy from one stem; and there lay calm
Old age with snow bright hair and folded palm.

But other troubled forms of sleep she saw,
   Not to be mirrored in a holy song –
Distortions foul of supernatural awe,
   And pale imaginings of visioned wrong   540
And all the code of custom's lawless law
   Written upon the brows of old and young:
'This', said the wizard maiden, 'is the strife
Which stirs the liquid surface of man's life.'

And little did the sight disturb her soul.
   We, the weak mariners of that wide lake
Where'er its shores extend or billows roll,
   Our course unpiloted and starless make
O'er its wild surface to an unknown goal –
   But she in the calm depths her way could take,   550
Where in bright bowers immortal forms abide
Beneath the weltering of the restless tide.

And she saw princes couched under the flow
   Of sunlike gems; and round each temple-court
In dormitories ranged, row after row,
   She saw the priests asleep – all of one sort
For all were educated to be so –
   The peasants in their huts, and in the port

The sailors she saw cradled on the waves,
And the dead lulled within their dreamless graves.   560

And all the forms in which those spirits lay
   Were to her sight like the diaphanous
Veils, in which those sweet ladies oft array
   Their delicate limbs, who would conceal from us
Only their scorn of all concealment; they
   Move in the light of their own beauty thus.
But these and all now lay with sleep upon them
And little thought a Witch was looking on them.

She, all those human figures breathing there
   Beheld as living spirits – to her eyes   570
The naked beauty of the soul lay bare,
   And often through a rude and worn disguise
She saw the inner form most bright and fair –
   And then she had a charm of strange device,
Which, murmured on mute lips with tender tone,
Could make the spirit mingle with her own.

Composed 1820
First published 1824

from EPIPSYCHIDION

I never was attached to that great sect
Whose doctrine is, that each one should select   150
Out of the crowd a mistress or a friend,
And all the rest, though fair and wise, commend
To cold oblivion, though it is in the code
Of modern morals, and the beaten road
Which those poor slaves with weary footsteps tread,
Who travel to their home among the dead
By the broad highway of the world, and so
With one chained friend, perhaps a jealous foe,
The dreariest and the longest journey go.

   True Love in this differs from gold and clay,   160
That to divide is not to take away.
Love is like understanding, that grows bright,

131

Gazing on many truths; 'tis like thy light,
Imagination! which from earth and sky,
And from the depths of human phantasy,
As from a thousand prisms and mirrors, fills
The Universe with glorious beams, and kills
Error, the worm, with many a sun-like arrow
Of its reverberated lightning. Narrow
The heart that loves, the brain that contemplates,   170
The life that wears, the spirit that creates
One object, and one form, and builds thereby
A sepulchre for its eternity.

    Mind from its object differs most in this:
Evil from good; misery from happiness;
The baser from the nobler; the impure
And frail, from what is clear and must endure.
If you divide suffering and dross, you may
Diminish till it is consumed away;
If you divide pleasure and love and thought,   180
Each part exceeds the whole; and we know not
How much, while any yet remains unshared,
Of pleasure may be gained, of sorrow spared:
This truth is that deep well, whence sages draw
The unenvied light of hope; the eternal law
By which those live, to whom this world of life
Is as a garden ravaged, and whose strife
Tills for the promise of a later birth
The wilderness of this Elysian earth.

Composed 1820–1
First published 1821

SONG ('Rarely, rarely, comest thou')

Rarely, rarely, comest thou,
  Spirit of Delight!
Wherefore hast thou left me now
  Many a day and night?
Many a weary night and day
'Tis since thou art fled away.

132

How shall ever one like me
   Win thee back again?
With the joyous and the free
   Thou wilt scoff at pain.
Spirit false! that hast forgot
All but those who need thee not.

As a lizard with the shade
   Of a trembling leaf,
Thou with sorrow art dismayed;
   Even the sighs of grief
Reproach thee, that thou art not near,
And reproach thou wilt not hear.

Let me set my mournful ditty
   To a merry measure;
Thou wilt never come for pity,
   Thou wilt come for pleasure;
Pity then will cut away
Those cruel wings, and thou wilt stay.

I love all that thou lovest,
   Spirit of Delight!
The fresh Earth in new leaves dressed,
   And the starry night;
Autumn evening, and the morn
When the golden mists are born.

I love snow, and all the forms
   Of the radiant frost;
I love waves and winds and storms –
   Every thing almost
Which is Nature's, and may be
Untainted by man's misery.

I love tranquil solitude,
   And such society
As is quiet, wise and good;
   Between thee and me
What difference? – but thou dost possess
The things I seek, not love them less.

I love Love – though he has wings,
  And like light can flee –
But above all other things,
  Spirit, I love thee –
Thou art Love and Life! O come,
Make once more my heart thy home.

Composed 1820
First published 1824

ADONAIS

An Elegy on the Death of John Keats,
Author of *Endymion*, *Hyperion*, etc.

Thou wert the morning star among the living,
      Ere thy fair light had fled –
Now, having died, thou art as Hesperus, giving
      New splendour to the dead.

I

I weep for Adonais – he is dead!
O, weep for Adonais! though our tears
Thaw not the frost which binds so dear a head!
And thou, sad Hour, selected from all years
To mourn our loss, rouse thy obscure compeers,
And teach them thine own sorrow, say: with me
Died Adonais; till the Future dares
Forget the Past, his fate and fame shall be
An echo and a light unto eternity!

II

Where wert thou, mighty Mother, when he lay,   10
When thy Son lay, pierced by the shaft which flies
In darkness? where was lorn Urania
When Adonais died? With veilèd eyes,
Mid listening Echoes, in her Paradise

She sate, while one, with soft enamoured breath,
Rekindled all the fading melodies
With which, like flowers that mock the corse beneath,
He had adorned and hid the coming bulk of death.

III

O, weep for Adonais – he is dead!
Wake, melancholy Mother, wake and weep!   20
Yet wherefore? Quench within their burning bed
Thy fiery tears, and let thy loud heart keep
Like his, a mute and uncomplaining sleep;
For he is gone, where all things wise and fair
Descend; – oh, dream not that the amorous Deep
Will yet restore him to the vital air;
Death feeds on his mute voice, and laughs at our despair.

IV

Most musical of mourners, weep again!
Lament anew, Urania! – He died,
Who was the Sire of an immortal strain,   30
Blind, old, and lonely, when his country's pride,
The priest, the slave, and the liberticide
Trampled and mocked with many a loathèd rite
Of lust and blood; he went, unterrified,
Into the gulf of death; but his clear Sprite
Yet reigns o'er earth; the third among the sons of light.

V

Most musical of mourners, weep anew!
Not all to that bright station dared to climb;
And happier they their happiness who knew,
Whose tapers yet burn through that night of time   40
In which suns perished; others more sublime,
Struck by the envious wrath of man or God,
Have sunk, extinct in their refulgent prime;
And some yet live, treading the thorny road
Which leads through toil and hate, to Fame's serene abode.

VI

But now, thy youngest, dearest one, has perished –
The nursling of thy widowhood, who grew,
Like a pale flower by some sad maiden cherished,
And fed with true love tears, instead of dew;
Most musical of mourners, weep anew!   50
Thy extreme hope, the loveliest and the last,
The bloom, whose petals nipped before they blew,
Died on the promise of the fruit, is waste;
The broken lily lies – the storm is overpast.

VII

To that high Capital, where kingly Death
Keeps his pale court in beauty and decay,
He came; and bought, with price of purest breath,
A grave among the eternal. – Come away!
Haste, while the vault of blue Italian day
Is yet his fitting charnel-roof! while still   60
He lies, as if in dewy sleep he lay;
Awake him not! surely he takes his fill
Of deep and liquid rest, forgetful of all ill.

VIII

He will awake no more, oh, never more! –
Within the twilight chamber spreads apace
The shadow of white Death, and at the door
Invisible Corruption waits to trace
His extreme way to her dim dwelling-place;
The eternal Hunger sits, but pity and awe
Soothe her pale rage, nor dares she to deface   70
So fair a prey, till darkness, and the law
Of change, shall o'er his sleep the mortal curtain draw.

IX

O, weep for Adonais! – The quick Dreams,
The passion-wingèd Ministers of thought,
Who were his flocks, whom near the living streams

Of his young spirit he fed, and whom he taught
The love which was its music, wander not, –
Wander no more, from kindling brain to brain,
But droop there, whence they sprung; and mourn their lot
Round the cold heart, where, after their sweet pain,   80
They ne'er will gather strength, or find a home again.

X

And one with trembling hands clasps his cold head,
And fans him with her moonlight wings, and cries,
'Our love, our hope, our sorrow, is not dead;
See, on the silken fringe of his faint eyes,
Like dew upon a sleeping flower, there lies
A tear some Dream has loosened from his brain.'
Lost Angel of a ruined Paradise!
She knew not 'twas her own; as with no stain
She faded, like a cloud which had outwept its rain.   90

XI

One from a lucid urn of starry dew
Washed his light limbs as if embalming them;
Another clipped her profuse locks, and threw
The wreath upon him, like an anadem,
Which frozen tears instead of pearls begem;
Another in her wilful grief would break
Her bow and wingèd reeds, as if to stem
A greater loss with one which was more weak;
And dull the barbèd fire against his frozen cheek.

XII

Another Splendour on his mouth alit,   100
That mouth, whence it was wont to draw the breath
Which gave it strength to pierce the guarded wit,
And pass into the panting heart beneath
With lightning and with music: the damp death
Quenched its caress upon his icy lips;
And, as a dying meteor stains a wreath

Of moonlight vapour, which the cold night clips,
It flushed through his pale limbs, and passed to its eclipse.

XIII

And others came . . . Desires and Adorations,
Wingèd Persuasions and veiled Destinies,   110
Splendours, and Glooms, and glimmering Incarnations
Of hopes and fears, and twilight Phantasies;
And Sorrow, with her family of Sighs,
And Pleasure, blind with tears, led by the gleam
Of her own dying smile instead of eyes,
Came in slow pomp; – the moving pomp might seem
Like pageantry of mist on an autumnal stream.

XIV

All he had loved, and moulded into thought,
From shape, and hue, and odour, and sweet sound,
Lamented Adonais. Morning sought   120
Her eastern watch-tower, and her hair unbound,
Wet with the tears which should adorn the ground,
Dimmed the aërial eyes that kindle day;
Afar the melancholy thunder moaned,
Pale Ocean in unquiet slumber lay,
And the wild winds flew round, sobbing in their dismay.

XV

Lost Echo sits amid the voiceless mountains,
And feeds her grief with his remembered lay,
And will no more reply to winds or fountains,
Or amorous birds perched on the young green spray,   130
Or herdsman's horn, or bell at closing day,
Since she can mimic not his lips, more dear
Than those for whose disdain she pined away
Into a shadow of all sounds: – a drear
Murmur, between their songs, is all the woodmen hear.

XVI

Grief made the young Spring wild, and she threw down

Her kindling buds, as if she Autumn were,
Or they dead leaves; since her delight is flown,
For whom should she have waked the sullen year?
To Phoebus was not Hyacinth so dear   140
Nor to himself Narcissus, as to both
Thou, Adonais: wan they stand and sere
Amid the faint companions of their youth,
With dew all turned to tears; odour, to sighing ruth.

XVII

Thy spirit's sister, the lorn nightingale
Mourns not her mate with such melodious pain;
Not so the eagle, who like thee could scale
Heaven, and could nourish in the sun's domain
Her mighty youth with morning, doth complain,
Soaring and screaming round her empty nest,   150
As Albion wails for thee: the curse of Cain
Light on his head who pierced thy innocent breast,
And scared the angel soul that was its earthly guest!

XVIII

Ah, woe is me! Winter is come and gone,
But grief returns with the revolving year;
The airs and streams renew their joyous tone;
The ants, the bees, the swallows reappear;
Fresh leaves and flowers deck the dead Season's bier;
The amorous birds now pair in every brake,
And build their mossy homes in field and brere;   160
And the green lizard, and the golden snake,
Like unimprisoned flames, out of their trance awake.

XIX

Through wood and stream and field and hill and Ocean
A quickening life from the Earth's heart has burst
As it has ever done, with change and motion,
From the great morning of the world when first
God dawned on Chaos; in its stream immersed,
The lamps of Heaven flash with a softer light;

All baser things pant with life's sacred thirst;
Diffuse themselves; and spend in love's delight   170
The beauty and the joy of their renewèd might.

XX

The leprous corpse touched by this spirit tender
Exhales itself in flowers of gentle breath;
Like incarnations of the stars, when splendour
Is changed to fragrance, they illumine death
And mock the merry worm that wakes beneath;
Nought we know, dies. Shall that alone which knows
Be as a sword consumed before the sheath
By sightless lightning? – the intense atom glows
A moment, then is quenched in a most cold repose.   180

XXI

Alas! that all we loved of him should be,
But for our grief, as if it had not been,
And grief itself be mortal! Woe is me!
Whence are we, and why are we? of what scene
The actors or spectators? Great and mean
Meet massed in death, who lends what life must borrow.
As long as skies are blue, and fields are green,
Evening must usher night, night urge the morrow,
Month follow month with woe, and year wake year to sorrow.

XXII

He will awake no more, oh, never more!   190
'Wake thou,' cried Misery, 'childless Mother, rise
Out of thy sleep, and slake, in thy heart's core,
A wound more fierce than his with tears and sighs.'
And all the Dreams that watched Urania's eyes,
And all the Echoes whom their sister's song
Had held in holy silence, cried: 'Arise!'
Swift as a Thought by the snake Memory stung,
From her ambrosial rest the fading Splendour sprung.

XXIII

She rose like an autumnal Night, that springs
Out of the East, and follows wild and drear   200
The golden Day, which, on eternal wings,
Even as a ghost abandoning a bier,
Has left the Earth a corpse. Sorrow and fear
So struck, so roused, so rapt Urania;
So saddened round her like an atmosphere
Of stormy mist; so swept her on her way
Even to the mournful place where Adonais lay.

XXIV

Out of her secret Paradise she sped,
Through camps and cities rough with stone, and steel,
And human hearts, which to her airy tread   210
Yielding not, wounded the invisible
Palms of her tender feet where'er they fell:
And barbèd tongues, and thoughts more sharp than they,
Rend the soft Form they never could repel,
Whose sacred blood, like the young tears of May,
Paved with eternal flowers that undeserving way.

XXV

In the death-chamber for a moment Death,
Shamed by the presence of that living Might,
Blushed to annihilation, and the breath
Revisited those lips, and life's pale light   220
Flashed through those limbs, so late her dear delight.
'Leave me not wild and drear and comfortless,
As silent lightning leaves the starless night!
Leave me not!' cried Urania: her distress
Roused Death: Death rose and smiled, and met her vain caress.

XXVI

'Stay yet awhile! speak to me once again;
Kiss me, so long but as a kiss may live;
And in my heartless breast and burning brain

141

That word, that kiss, shall all thoughts else survive,
With food of saddest memory kept alive,   230
Now thou art dead, as if it were a part
Of thee, my Adonais! I would give
All that I am to be as thou now art!
But I am chained to Time, and cannot thence depart!

XXVII

'Oh gentle child, beautiful as thou wert,
Why didst thou leave the trodden paths of men
Too soon, and with weak hands though mighty heart
Dare the unpastured dragon in his den?
Defenceless as thou wert, oh where was then
Wisdom the mirrored shield, or scorn the spear?   240
Or hadst thou waited the full cycle, when
Thy spirit should have filled its crescent sphere,
The monsters of life's waste had fled from thee like deer.

XXVIII

'The herded wolves, bold only to pursue;
The obscene ravens, clamorous o'er the dead;
The vultures to the conqueror's banner true
Who feed where Desolation first has fed,
And whose wings rain contagion; – how they fled,
When like Apollo, from his golden bow,
The Pythian of the age one arrow sped   250
And smiled! – The spoilers tempt no second blow,
They fawn on the proud feet that spurn them lying low.

XXIX

'The sun comes forth, and many reptiles spawn;
He sets, and each ephemeral insect then
Is gathered into death without a dawn,
And the immortal stars awake again;
So is it in the world of living men:
A godlike mind soars forth, in its delight
Making earth bare and veiling heaven, and when
It sinks, the swarms that dimmed or shared its light   260

Leave to its kindred lamps the spirit's awful night.'

XXX

Thus ceased she: and the mountain shepherds came,
Their garlands sere, their magic mantles rent;
The Pilgrim of Eternity, whose fame
Over his living head like Heaven is bent,
An early but enduring monument,
Came, veiling all the lightnings of his song
In sorrow; from her wilds Ierne sent
The sweetest lyrist of her saddest wrong,
And love taught grief to fall like music from his tongue.   270

XXXI

Midst others of less note, came one frail Form,
A phantom among men; companionless
As the last cloud of an expiring storm
Whose thunder is its knell; he, as I guess,
Had gazed on Nature's naked loveliness,
Actaeon-like, and now he fled astray
With feeble steps o'er the world's wilderness,
And his own thoughts, along that rugged way,
Pursued, like raging hounds, their father and their prey.

XXXII

A pardlike Spirit beautiful and swift –   280
A Love in desolation masked; – a Power
Girt round with weakness; – it can scarce uplift
The weight of the superincumbent hour;
It is a dying lamp, a falling shower,
A breaking billow; – even whilst we speak
Is it not broken? On the withering flower
The killing sun smiles brightly: on a cheek
The life can burn in blood, even while the heart may break.

XXXIII

His head was bound with pansies overblown,
And faded violets, white, and pied, and blue;   290

143

And a light spear topped with a cypress cone,
Round whose rude shaft dark ivy tresses grew
Yet dripping with the forest's noonday dew,
Vibrated, as the ever-beating heart
Shook the weak hand that grasped it; of that crew
He came the last, neglected and apart;
A herd-abandoned deer struck by the hunter's dart.

XXXIV

All stood aloof, and at his partial moan
Smiled through their tears; well knew that gentle band
Who in another's fate now wept his own –   300
As in the accents of an unknown land
He sung new sorrow; sad Urania scanned
The Stranger's mien, and murmured: 'Who art thou?'
He answered not, but with a sudden hand
Made bare his branded and ensanguined brow,
Which was like Cain's or Christ's – Oh! that it should be so!

XXXV

What softer voice is hushed over the dead?
Athwart what brow is that dark mantle thrown?
What form leans sadly o'er the white death-bed,
In mockery of monumental stone,   310
The heavy heart heaving without a moan?
If it be He, who, gentlest of the wise,
Taught, soothed, loved, honoured the departed one,
Let me not vex, with inharmonious sighs,
The silence of that heart's accepted sacrifice.

XXXVI

Our Adonais has drunk poison – oh!
What deaf and viperous murderer could crown
Life's early cup with such a draught of woe?
The nameless worm would now itself disown:
It felt, yet could escape, the magic tone   320
Whose prelude held all envy, hate, and wrong,

But what was howling in one breast alone,
Silent with expectation of the song,
Whose master's hand is cold, whose silver lyre unstrung.

XXXVII

Live thou, whose infamy is not thy fame!
Live! fear no heavier chastisement from me,
Thou noteless blot on a remembered name!
But be thyself, and know thyself to be!
And ever at thy season be thou free
To spill the venom when thy fangs o'erflow: 330
Remorse and Self-contempt shall cling to thee;
Hot Shame shall burn upon thy secret brow,
And like a beaten hound tremble thou shalt – as now.

XXXVIII

Nor let us weep that our delight is fled
Far from these carrion kites that scream below;
He wakes or sleeps with the enduring dead;
Thou canst not soar where he is sitting now. –
Dust to the dust! but the pure spirit shall flow
Back to the burning fountain whence it came,
A portion of the Eternal, which must glow   340
Through time and change, unquenchably the same,
Whilst thy cold embers choke the sordid hearth of shame.

XXXIX

Peace, peace! he is not dead, he doth not sleep –
He hath awakened from the dream of life –
'Tis we, who lost in stormy visions, keep
With phantoms an unprofitable strife,
And in mad trance, strike with our spirit's knife
Invulnerable nothings. – *We* decay
Like corpses in a charnel; fear and grief
Convulse us and consume us day by day,   350
And cold hopes swarm like worms within our living clay.

XL

He has outsoared the shadow of our night;
Envy and calumny and hate and pain,
And that unrest which men miscall delight,
Can touch him not and torture not again;
From the contagion of the world's slow stain
He is secure, and now can never mourn
A heart grown cold, a head grown grey in vain;
Nor, when the spirit's self has ceased to burn,
With sparkless ashes load an unlamented urn.   360

XLI

He lives, he wakes – 'tis Death is dead, not he;
Mourn not for Adonais. – Thou, young Dawn,
Turn all thy dew to splendour, for from thee
The spirit thou lamentest is not gone;
Ye caverns and ye forests, cease to moan!
Cease, ye faint flowers and fountains, and thou Air
Which like a mourning veil thy scarf hadst thrown
O'er the abandoned Earth, now leave it bare
Even to the joyous stars which smile on its despair!

XLII

He is made one with Nature: there is heard   370
His voice in all her music, from the moan
Of thunder, to the song of night's sweet bird;
He is a presence to be felt and known
In darkness and in light, from herb and stone,
Spreading itself where'er that Power may move
Which has withdrawn his being to its own;
Which wields the world with never wearied love,
Sustains it from beneath, and kindles it above.

XLIII

He is a portion of the loveliness
Which once he made more lovely: he doth bear   380
His part, while the one Spirit's plastic stress

Sweeps through the dull dense world, compelling there
All new successions to the forms they wear;
Torturing th'unwilling dross that checks its flight
To its own likeness, as each mass may bear;
And bursting in its beauty and its might
From trees and beasts and men into the Heaven's light.

XLIV

The splendours of the firmament of time
May be eclipsed, but are extinguished not;
Like stars to their appointed height they climb,   390
And death is a low mist which cannot blot
The brightness it may veil. When lofty thought
Lifts a young heart above its mortal lair,
And love and life contend in it, for what
Shall be its earthly doom, the dead live there
And move like winds of light on dark and stormy air.

XLV

The inheritors of unfulfilled renown
Rose from their thrones, built beyond mortal thought,
Far in the Unapparent. Chatterton
Rose pale, his solemn agony had not   400
Yet faded from him; Sidney, as he fought
And as he fell and as he lived and loved
Sublimely mild, a Spirit without spot,
Arose; and Lucan, by his death approved;
Oblivion as they rose shrank like a thing reproved.

XLVI

And many more, whose names on Earth are dark,
But whose transmitted effluence cannot die
So long as fire outlives the parent spark,
Rose, robed in dazzling immortality.
'Thou art become as one of us,' they cry,   410
'It was for thee yon kingless sphere has long
Swung blind in unascended majesty,
Silent alone amid an Heaven of song.
Assume thy wingèd throne, thou Vesper of our throng!'

XLVII

Who mourns for Adonais? oh, come forth,
Fond wretch! and know thyself and him aright.
Clasp with thy panting soul the pendulous Earth;
As from a centre, dart thy spirit's light
Beyond all worlds, until its spacious might
Satiate the void circumference: then shrink
Even to a point within our day and night;
And keep thy heart light lest it make thee sink
When hope has kindled hope, and lured thee to the brink.

420

XLVIII

Or go to Rome, which is the sepulchre,
O, not of him, but of our joy: 'tis nought
That ages, empires, and religions there
Lie buried in the ravage they have wrought;
For such as he can lend, – they borrow not
Glory from those who made the world their prey;
And he is gathered to the kings of thought
Who waged contention with their time's decay,
And of the past are all that cannot pass away.

430

XLIX

Go thou to Rome, – at once the Paradise,
The grave, the city, and the wilderness;
And where its wrecks like shattered mountains rise,
And flowering weeds, and fragrant copses dress
The bones of Desolation's nakedness,
Pass, till the Spirit of the spot shall lead
Thy footsteps to a slope of green access
Where, like an infant's smile, over the dead,
A light of laughing flowers along the grass is spread.

440

L

And grey walls moulder round, on which dull Time
Feeds, like slow fire upon a hoary brand;
And one keen pyramid with wedge sublime,

Pavilioning the dust of him who planned
This refuge for his memory, doth stand
Like flame transformed to marble; and beneath,
A field is spread, on which a newer band
Have pitched in Heaven's smile their camp of death,
Welcoming him we lose with scarce extinguished breath.　450

LI

Here pause: these graves are all too young as yet
To have outgrown the sorrow which consigned
Its charge to each; and if the seal is set,
Here, on one fountain of a mourning mind,
Break it not thou! too surely shalt thou find
Thine own well full, if thou returnest home,
Of tears and gall. From the world's bitter wind
Seek shelter in the shadow of the tomb.
What Adonais is, why fear we to become?

LII

The One remains, the many change and pass;　460
Heaven's light forever shines, Earth's shadows fly;
Life, like a dome of many-coloured glass,
Stains the white radiance of Eternity,
Until Death tramples it to fragments. – Die,
If thou wouldst be with that which thou dost seek!
Follow where all is fled! – Rome's azure sky,
Flowers, ruins, statues, music, words, are weak
The glory they transfuse with fitting truth to speak.

LIII

Why linger, why turn back, why shrink, my Heart?
Thy hopes are gone before: from all things here　470
They have departed; thou shouldst now depart!
A light is passed from the revolving year,
And man, and woman; and what still is dear
Attracts to crush, repels to make thee wither.
The soft sky smiles, – the low wind whispers near:
'Tis Adonais calls! oh, hasten thither,
No more let Life divide what Death can join together.

LIV

That Light whose smile kindles the Universe,
That Beauty in which all things work and move,
That Benediction which the eclipsing Curse 480
Of birth can quench not, that sustaining Love
Which through the web of being blindly wove
By man and beast and earth and air and sea,
Burns bright or dim, as each are mirrors of
The fire for which all thirst, now beams on me,
Consuming the last clouds of cold mortality.

LV

The breath whose might I have invoked in song
Descends on me; my spirit's bark is driven
Far from the shore, far from the trembling throng
Whose sails were never to the tempest given; 490
The massy earth and spherèd skies are riven!
I am borne darkly, fearfully, afar;
Whilst, burning through the inmost veil of Heaven,
The soul of Adonais, like a star,
Beacons from the abode where the Eternal are.

Composed 1821
First published 1821

CHORUS from HELLAS

The world's great age begins anew,
    The golden years return,
The earth doth like a snake renew
    Her winter weeds outworn;
Heaven smiles, and faiths and empires gleam
Like wrecks of a dissolving dream.

A brighter Hellas rears its mountains
    From waves serener far,
A new Peneus rolls his fountains
    Against the morning-star; 10
Where fairer Tempes bloom, there sleep

Young Cyclads on a sunnier deep.

 A loftier Argo cleaves the main
  Fraught with a later prize;
 Another Orpheus sings again,
  And loves, and weeps, and dies;
A new Ulysses leaves once more
Calypso for his native shore.

 O, write no more the tale of Troy,
  If earth Death's scroll must be!   20
 Nor mix with Laian rage the joy
  Which dawns upon the free;
Although a subtler Sphinx renew
Riddles of death Thebes never knew.

 Another Athens shall arise,
  And to remoter time
 Bequeath, like sunset to the skies,
  The splendour of its prime;
And leave, if nought so bright may live,
All earth can take or Heaven can give.   30

 Saturn and Love their long repose
  Shall burst, more bright and good
 Than all who fell, than One who rose,
  Than many unsubdued;
Not gold, not blood, their altar dowers,
But votive tears and symbol flowers.

 O cease! must hate and death return?
  Cease! must men kill and die?
 Cease! drain not to its dregs the urn
  Of bitter prophecy.   40
The world is weary of the past,
O might it die or rest at last!

Composed 1821
First published 1822

'Do you not hear the aziola cry?
Methinks she must be nigh –'
  Said Mary, as we sate
In dusk, ere stars were lit or candles brought –
  And I, who thought
This Aziola was some tedious woman,
Asked, 'Who is Aziola?' – How elate
I felt to know that it was nothing human,
No mockery of myself to fear or hate!
  And Mary saw my soul,   10
And laughed and said –'Disquiet yourself not,
  'Tis nothing but a little downy owl.'

Sad aziola, many an eventide
  Thy music I had heard
By wood and stream, meadow and mountain-side,
  And fields and marshes wide,
Such as nor voice, nor lute, nor wind, nor bird
  The soul ever stirred –
Unlike and far sweeter than them all.
Sad aziola, from that moment I   20
Loved thee and thy sad cry.

Composed 1821
First published 1829

MUTABILITY ('The flower that smiles today')

The flower that smiles today
  Tomorrow dies;
All that we wish to stay
  Tempts and then flies;
What is this world's delight?
Lightning that mocks the night,
  Brief even as bright. –

Virtue, how frail it is! –
  Friendship, how rare! –
Love, how it sells poor bliss   10

    For proud despair!
But these, though soon they fall,
Survive their joy, and all
    Which ours we call. –

Whilst skies are blue and bright,
    Whilst flowers are gay,
Whilst eyes that change ere night
    Make glad the day;
Whilst yet the calm hours creep,
Dream thou – and from thy sleep   20
    Then wake to weep.

Composed 1821
First published 1824

       T O — ('Music, when soft voices die')

Music, when soft voices die,
Vibrates in the memory. –
Odours, when sweet violets sicken,
Live within the sense they quicken. –

Rose leaves, when the rose is dead,
Are heaped for the beloved's bed –
And so thy thoughts, when thou art gone,
Love itself shall slumber on . . .

Composed 1821
First published 1824

      TO JANE: THE INVITATION

Best and brightest, come away –
Fairer far than this fair day
Which, like thee to those in sorrow,
Comes to bid a sweet good-morrow
To the rough year just awake
In its cradle on the brake. –
The brightest hour of unborn spring

Through the winter wandering
Found, it seems, this halcyon morn
To hoar February born; 10
Bending from Heaven in azure mirth
It kissed the forehead of the earth
And smiled upon the silent sea,
And bade the frozen streams be free
And waked to music all their fountains,
And breathed upon the frozen mountains,
And like a prophetess of May
Strewed flowers upon the barren way,
Making the wintry world appear
Like one on whom thou smilest, dear. 20

Away, away from men and towns
To the wild wood and the downs,
To the silent wilderness
Where the soul need not repress
Its music lest it should not find
An echo in another's mind,
While the touch of Nature's art
Harmonizes heart to heart. –
I leave this notice on my door
For each accustomed visitor – 30
'I am gone into the fields
To take what this sweet hour yields.
Reflection, you may come tomorrow,
Sit by the fireside with Sorrow –
You, with the unpaid bill, Despair,
You, tiresome verse-reciter Care,
I will pay you in the grave,
Death will listen to your stave –
Expectation too, be off!
Today is for itself enough – 40
Hope, in pity mock not woe
With smiles, nor follow where I go;
Long having lived on thy sweet food,
At length I find one moment's good
After long pain – with all your love
This you never told me of.'

Radiant Sister of the day,
Awake, arise and come away
To the wild woods and the plains
And the pools where winter rains   50
Image all their roof of leaves,
Where the pine its garland weaves
Of sapless green and ivy dun
Round stems that never kiss the Sun –
Where the lawns and pastures be
And the sandhills of the sea –
Where the melting hoar-frost wets
The daisy-star that never sets,
And wind-flowers, and violets,
Which yet join not scent to hue,   60
Crown the pale year weak and new,
When the night is left behind
In the deep east dun and blind
And the blue noon is over us,
And the multitudinous
Billows murmur at our feet
Where the earth and ocean meet,
And all things seem only one
In the universal Sun. –

Composed 1822
First published 1824

TO JANE: THE RECOLLECTION

Now the last day of many days,
All beautiful and bright as thou,
The loveliest and the last, is dead.
Rise, Memory, and write its praise!
Up to thy wonted work! come, trace
The epitaph of glory fled;
For now the Earth has changed its face,
A frown is on the Heaven's brow.

I

We wandered to the pine forest
  That skirts the ocean foam;
The lightest wind was in its nest,   10
  The tempest in its home;
The whispering waves were half asleep,
  The clouds were gone to play,
And on the bosom of the deep
  The smile of Heaven lay;
It seemed as if the hour were one
  Sent from beyond the skies,
Which scattered from above the sun
  A light of Paradise.   20

II

We paused amid the pines that stood
  The giants of the waste,
Tortured by storms to shapes as rude
  As serpents interlaced,
And soothed by every azure breath
  That under Heaven is blown
To harmonies and hues beneath,
  As tender as its own;
Now all the tree-tops lay asleep
  Like green waves on the sea,   30
As still as in the silent deep
  The ocean woods may be.

III

How calm it was! the silence there
  By such a chain was bound
That even the busy woodpecker
  Made stiller with her sound
The inviolable quietness;
  The breath of peace we drew
With its soft motion made not less
  The calm that round us grew. –   40
There seemed from the remotest seat

156

Of the white mountain-waste,
To the soft flower beneath our feet
    A magic circle traced,
A spirit interfused around
    A thrilling silent life,
To momentary peace it bound
    Our mortal nature's strife; –
And still I felt the centre of
    The magic circle there   50
Was one fair form that filled with love
    The lifeless atmosphere.

                    IV

We paused beside the pools that lie
    Under the forest bough –
Each seemed as 'twere a little sky
    Gulfed in a world below;
A firmament of purple light
    Which in the dark earth lay
More boundless than the depth of night
    And purer than the day,   60
In which the lovely forests grew
    As in the upper air,
More perfect, both in shape and hue,
    Than any spreading there;
There lay the glade, the neighbouring lawn,
    And through the dark green wood
The white sun twinkling like the dawn
    Out of a speckled cloud.

                    V

Sweet views, which in our world above
    Can never well be seen,   70
Were imaged in the water's love
    Of that fair forest green;
And all was interfused beneath
    With an Elysian glow,
An atmosphere without a breath,

157

A softer day below –
Like one beloved, the scene had lent
  To the dark water's breast,
Its every leaf and lineament
  With more than truth exprest;   80
Until an envious wind crept by,
  Like an unwelcome thought
Which from the mind's too faithful eye
  Blots one dear image out. –
Though thou art ever fair and kind
  And forests ever green,
Less oft is peace in S[helley]'s mind
  Than calm in water seen.

Composed 1822
First published 1824

TO—('One word is too often profaned')

One word is too often profaned
  For me to profane it,
One feeling too falsely disdained
  For thee to disdain it;
One hope is too like despair
  For prudence to smother,
And pity from thee more dear
  Than that from another.

I can give not what men call love;
  But wilt thou accept not   10
The worship the heart lifts above
  And the Heavens reject not, –
The desire of the moth for the star,
  Of the night for the morrow,
The devotion to something afar
  From the sphere of our sorrow?

Composed 1821?
First published 1824

TO EDWARD WILLIAMS

I

The serpent is shut out from Paradise –
  The wounded deer must seek the herb no more
    In which its heart's cure lies –
  The widowed dove must cease to haunt a bower
Like that from which its mate with feignèd sighs
    Fled in the April hour. –
  I, too, must seldom seek again
Near happy friends a mitigated pain.

II

Of hatred I am proud, – with scorn content;
  Indifference, which once hurt me, now is grown
    Itself indifferent.
  But, not to speak of love, Pity alone
Can break a spirit already more than bent.
    The miserable one
  Turns the mind's poison into food:
Its medicine is tears, its evil, good.

III

Therefore, if now I see you seldomer,
  Dear friends, dear *friend*, know that I only fly
    Your looks, because they stir
  Griefs that should sleep, and hopes that cannot die.
The very comfort which they minister
    I scarce can bear; yet I,
  So deeply is the arrow gone,
Should quickly perish if it were withdrawn.

IV

When I return to my cold home, you ask
  Why I am not as I have lately been?
    You spoil me for the task
  Of acting a forced part in life's dull scene, –
Of wearing on my brow the idle mask
    Of author, great or mean,

10

20

30

In the world's carnival. I sought
Peace thus, and but in you I found it not.

V

Full half an hour, today, I tried my lot
    With various flowers, and every one still said,
        'She loves me, loves me not.'
    And if this meant a Vision long since fled –
If it meant Fortune, Fame, or Peace of thought,
        If it meant – (but I dread
    To speak what you may know too well)
Still there was truth in the sad oracle.   40

VI

The crane o'er seas and forests seeks her home;
    No bird so wild, but has its quiet nest,
        When it no more would roam;
    The sleepless billows on the Ocean's breast
Break like a bursting heart, and die in foam
        And thus, at length, find rest;
    Doubtless there is a place of peace
Where my weak heart and all its throbs will cease.

VII

I asked her yesterday if she believed
    That I had resolution. One who *had*   50
        Would ne'er have thus relieved
    His heart with words, but what his judgement bade
Would do, and leave the scorner unrelieved. –
        These verses were too sad
    To send to you, but that I know,
Happy yourself, you feel another's woe.

Composed 1822
First published 1834

WITH A GUITAR, TO JANE

Ariel to Miranda: – Take
This slave of music for the sake
Of him who is the slave of thee;
And teach it all the harmony,
In which thou canst, and only thou,
Make the delighted spirit glow,
Till joy denies itself again
And, too intense, is turned to pain;
For by permission and command
Of thine own prince Ferdinand,   10
Poor Ariel sends this silent token
Of more than ever can be spoken;
Your guardian spirit, Ariel, who
From life to life must still pursue
Your happiness, for thus alone
Can Ariel ever find his own;
From Prospero's enchanted cell,
As the mighty verses tell,
To the throne of Naples, he
Lit you o'er the trackless sea,   20
Flitting on, your prow before,
Like a living meteor.
When you die, the silent Moon
In her interlunar swoon
Is not sadder in her cell
Than deserted Ariel;
When you live again on Earth,
Like an unseen Star of birth
Ariel guides you o'er the sea
Of life from your nativity;   30
Many changes have been run
Since Ferdinand and you begun
Your course of love, and Ariel still
Has tracked your steps and served your will;
Now, in humbler, happier lot
This is all remembered not;
And now, alas! the poor sprite is
Imprisoned for some fault of his

In a body like a grave: –
From you, he only dares to crave
For his service and his sorrow
A smile today, a song tomorrow.

The artist who this idol wrought
To echo all harmonious thought
Felled a tree, while on the steep
The woods were in their winter sleep
Rocked in that repose divine
On the wind-swept Apennine;
And dreaming, some of autumn past,
And some of spring approaching fast,
And some of April buds and showers,
And some of songs in July bowers,
And all of love, – and so this tree –
O that such our death may be –
Died in sleep, and felt no pain,
To live in happier form again,
From which, beneath Heaven's fairest star,
The artist wrought this loved guitar,
And taught it justly to reply
To all who question skilfully
In language gentle as thine own;
Whispering in enamoured tone
Sweet oracles of woods and dells
And summer winds in sylvan cells,
For it had learnt all harmonies
Of the plains and of the skies,
Of the forest and the mountains,
And the many-voicèd fountains,
The clearest echoes of the hills,
The softest notes of falling rills,
The melodies of birds and bees,
The murmuring of summer seas,
And pattering rain and breathing dew
And airs of evening; – and it knew
That seldom-heard mysterious sound,
Which, driven on its diurnal round
As it floats through boundless day,

40

50

60

70

Our world enkindles on its way –
All this it knows, but will not tell
To those who cannot question well 80
The spirit that inhabits it:
It talks according to the wit
Of its companions, and no more
Is heard than has been felt before
By those who tempt it to betray
These secrets of an elder day. –
But, sweetly as its answers will
Flatter hands of perfect skill,
It keeps its highest holiest tone
For our beloved Jane alone. – 90

Composed 1822
First published 1832

TO JANE ('The keen stars were twinkling')

The keen stars were twinkling
And the fair moon was rising among them,
    Dear Jane.
The guitar was tinkling
But the notes were not sweet till you sung them
    Again. –

As the moon's soft splendour
O'er the faint cold starlight of Heaven
    Is thrown –
So your voice most tender 10
To the strings without soul had then given
    Its own.

The stars will awaken,
Though the moon sleep a full hour later,
    Tonight;
No leaf will be shaken
While the dews of your melody scatter
    Delight.

Though the sound overpowers,
Sing again, with your dear voice revealing 20

A tone
Of some world far from ours,
Where music and moonlight and feeling
　　Are one.

Composed 1822
First published 1832

LINES WRITTEN IN THE BAY OF LERICI

Bright wanderer, fair coquette of Heaven,
To whom alone it has been given
To change and be adored for ever,
Envy not this dim world, for never
But once within its shadow grew
One fair as [thou], but far more true. –
She left me at the silent time
When the moon had ceased to climb
The azure dome of Heaven's steep,
And, like an albatross asleep,　　　　　　　　　　　10
Balanced on her wings of light,
Hovered in the purple night,
Ere she sought her Ocean nest
In the chambers of the west. –
She left me, and I stayed alone
Thinking over every tone,
Which though now silent to the ear
The enchanted heart could hear
Like notes which die when born, but still
Haunt the echoes of the hill:　　　　　　　　　　　20
And feeling over – O too much –
The soft vibrations of her touch,
As if her gentle hand even now
Lightly trembled on my brow;
And thus although she absent were
Memory gave me all of her
That even fancy dares to claim. –
Her presence had made weak and tame
All passions, and I lived alone,
In the time which is our own;　　　　　　　　　　　30

164

The past and future were forgot
As they had been, and would be, not. –
But soon, the guardian angel gone,
The demon reassumed his throne
In my faint heart . . . I dare not speak
My thoughts; but thus disturbed and weak
I sate and watched the vessels glide
Along the Ocean bright and wide,
Like spirit-wingèd chariots sent
O'er some serenest element   40
For ministrations strange and far;
As if to some Elysian star
They sailed for drink to medicine
Such sweet and bitter pain as mine. –
And the wind that winged their flight
From the land came fresh and light,
And the scent of sleeping flowers
And the coolness of the hours
Of dew, and the sweet warmth of day
Was scattered o'er the twinkling bay;   50
And the fisher with his lamp
And spear, about the low rocks damp
Crept, and struck the fish who came
To worship the delusive flame:
Too happy they, whose pleasure sought
Extinguishes all sense and thought
Of the regret that pleasure[. . .],
Destroying life alone, not peace.

Composed 1822
First published 1862

THE TRIUMPH OF LIFE

Swift as a spirit hastening to his task
　Of glory and of good, the Sun sprang forth
Rejoicing in his splendour, and the mask

　Of darkness fell from the awakened Earth.
The smokeless altars of the mountain snows
　Flamed above crimson clouds, and at the birth

Of light, the Ocean's orison arose
    To which the birds tempered their matin lay.
All flowers in field or forest which unclose

    Their trembling eyelids to the kiss of day,   10
Swinging their censers in the element,
    With orient incense lit by the new ray,

Burned slow and inconsumably, and sent
    Their odorous sighs up to the smiling air,
And in succession due, did Continent,

    Isle, Ocean, and all things that in them wear
The form and character of mortal mould
    Rise as the Sun their father rose, to bear

Their portion of the toil which he of old
    Took as his own and then imposed on them;   20
But I, whom thoughts which must remain untold

    Had kept as wakeful as the stars that gem
The cone of night, now they were laid asleep,
    Stretched my faint limbs beneath the hoary stem

Which an old chestnut flung athwart the steep
    Of a green Apennine: before me fled
The night; behind me rose the day; the Deep

    Was at my feet, and Heaven above my head;
When a strange trance over my fancy grew
    Which was not slumber, for the shade it spread   30

Was so transparent that the scene came through
    As clear as when a veil of light is drawn
O'er evening hills, they glimmer; and I knew

    That I had felt the freshness of that dawn,
Bathed in the same cold dew my brow and hair,
    And sate as thus upon that slope of lawn

Under the selfsame bough, and heard as there
    The birds, the fountains and the Ocean hold
Sweet talk in music through the enamoured air.

And then a Vision on my brain was rolled . . .   40

———

As in that trance of wondrous thought I lay
  This was the tenour of my waking dream:
Methought I sate beside a public way

  Thick strewn with summer dust, and a great stream
Of people there was hurrying to and fro
  Numerous as gnats upon the evening gleam,

All hastening onward, yet none seemed to know
  Whither he went, or whence he came, or why
He made one of the multitude, yet so

  Was borne amid the crowd as through the sky   50
One of the million leaves of summer's bier. –
  Old age and youth, manhood and infancy,

Mixed in one mighty torrent did appear,
  Some flying from the thing they feared and some
Seeking the object of another's fear,

  And others as with steps towards the tomb
Pored on the trodden worms that crawled beneath,
  And others mournfully within the gloom

Of their own shadow walked, and called it death . . .
  And some fled from it as it were a ghost,   60
Half fainting in the affliction of vain breath.

  But more, with motions which each other crossed,
Pursued or shunned the shadows the clouds threw
  Or birds within the noonday ether lost,

Upon that path where flowers never grew;
  And weary with vain toil and faint for thirst
Heard not the fountains whose melodious dew

  Out of their mossy cells forever burst,
Nor felt the breeze which from the forest told
  Of grassy paths, and wood lawns interspersed   70

With overarching elms and caverns cold,
    And violet banks where sweet dreams brood, but they
Pursued their serious folly as of old . . .

    And as I gazed, methought that in the way
The throng grew wilder, as the woods of June
    When the south wind shakes the extinguished day –

And a cold glare, intenser than the noon
    But icy cold, obscured with [blinding] light
The Sun as he the stars. Like the young moon

    When on the sunlit limits of the night   80
Her white shell trembles amid crimson air,
    And whilst the sleeping tempest gathers might

Doth, as a herald of its coming, bear
    The ghost of her dead mother, whose dim form
Bends in dark ether from her infant's chair, –

    So came a chariot on the silent storm
Of its own rushing splendour, and a Shape
    So sate within as one whom years deform

Beneath a dusky hood and double cape
    Crouching within the shadow of a tomb,   90
And o'er what seemed the head, a cloud like crape

    Was bent, a dun and faint etherial gloom
Tempering the light; upon the chariot's beam
    A Janus-visaged Shadow did assume

The guidance of that wonder-wingèd team.
    The shapes which drew it in thick lightnings
Were lost: I heard alone on the air's soft stream

    The music of their ever-moving wings.
All the four faces of that charioteer
    Had their eyes banded . . . little profit brings   100

Speed in the van and blindness in the rear,
    Nor then avail the beams that quenched the Sun,
Or that these banded eyes could pierce the sphere

    Of all that is, has been, or will be done. –
So ill was the car guided, but it passed

168

With solemn speed majestically on . . .

The crowd gave way, and I arose aghast,
  Or seemed to rise, so mighty was the trance,
And saw like clouds upon the thunder-blast

  The million with fierce song and maniac dance   110
Raging around; such seemed the jubilee
  As when to greet some conqueror's advance

Imperial Rome poured forth her living sea
  From senate-house and prison and theatre,
When Freedom left those who upon the free

  Had bound a yoke which soon they stooped to bear.
Nor wanted here the true similitude
  Of a triumphal pageant, for where'er

The chariot rolled a captive multitude
  Was driven; all those who had grown old in power   120
Or misery, – all who have their age subdued,

  By action or by suffering, and whose hour
Was drained to its last sand in weal or woe,
  So that the trunk survived both fruit and flower;

All those whose fame or infamy must grow
  Till the great winter lay the form and name
Of their green earth with them forever low; –

  All but the sacred few who could not tame
Their spirits to the Conqueror, but as soon
  As they had touched the world with living flame   130

Fled back like eagles to their native noon,
  Or those who put aside the diadem
Of earthly thrones or gems, till the last one

  Were there; – for they of Athens and Jerusalem
Were neither mid the mighty captives seen,
  Nor mid the ribald crowd that followed them

Or fled before . . . Now swift, fierce and obscene
  The wild dance maddens in the van, and those
Who lead it, fleet as shadows on the green,

Outspeed the chariot and without repose 140
Mixed with each other in tempestuous measure
　　To savage music . . . Wilder as it grows,

They, tortured by the agonizing pleasure,
　　Convulsed, and on the rapid whirlwinds spun
Of that fierce spirit, whose unholy leisure

　Was soothed by mischief since the world begun,
Throw back their heads and loose their streaming hair,
　　And in their dance round her who dims the Sun

Maidens and youths fling their wild arms in air
　　As their feet twinkle; they recede, and now 150
Bending within each other's atmosphere

　Kindle invisibly; and as they glow,
Like moths by light attracted and repelled,
　　Oft to their bright destruction come and go,

Till – like two clouds into one vale impelled
　　That shake the mountains when their lightnings mingle
And die in rain, – the fiery band which held

　Their natures, snaps . . . ere the shock cease to tingle,
One falls and then another in the path
　　Senseless, nor is the desolation single, – 160

Yet ere I can say *where*, the chariot hath
　　Passed over them; nor other trace I find
But as of foam after the Ocean's wrath

　Is spent upon the desert shore. – Behind,
Old men, and women foully disarrayed,
　　Shake their grey hair in the insulting wind,

Limp in the dance and strain with limbs decayed
　　To reach the car of light which leaves them still
Farther behind and deeper in the shade.

　But not the less with impotence of will 170
They wheel, though ghastly shadows interpose
　　Round them and round each other, and fulfil

Their work and to the dust whence they arose
  Sink, and corruption veils them as they lie,
And frost in these performs what fire in those.

  Struck· to the heart by this sad pageantry,
Half to myself I said, 'And what is this?
  Whose shape is that within the car? and why' –

I would have added – 'is all here amiss?'
  But a voice answered: 'Life' . . . I turned and knew   180
(O Heaven have mercy on such wretchedness!)

  That what I thought was an old root which grew
To strange distortion out of the hill side
  Was indeed one of that deluded crew,

And that the grass which methought hung so wide
  And white, was but his thin discoloured hair,
And that the holes it vainly sought to hide

  Were or had been eyes. –'If thou canst forbear
To join the dance, which I had well forborne,'
  Said the grim Feature, of my thought aware,   190

'I will unfold that which to this deep scorn
  Led me and my companions, and relate
The progress of the pageant since the morn;

  'If thirst of knowledge doth not thus abate,
Follow it even to the night, but I
  Am weary' . . . Then like one who with the weight

Of his own words is staggered, wearily
  He paused, and ere he could resume, I cried,
'First, who art thou?' . . . 'Before thy memory

  'I feared, loved, hated, suffered, did, and died,   200
And if the spark with which Heaven lit my spirit
  Earth had with purer nutriment supplied,

'Corruption would not now thus much inherit
  Of what was once Rousseau – nor this disguise
Stained that within which still disdains to wear it. –

  'If I have been extinguished, yet there rise
A thousand beacons from the spark I bore.'

'And who are those chained to the car?' 'The wise,

'The great, the unforgotten: they who wore
  Mitres and helms and crowns, or wreaths of light,   210
Signs of thought's empire over thought; their lore

  'Taught them not this – to know themselves; their might
Could not repress the mutiny within,
  And for the morn of truth they feigned, deep night

'Caught them ere evening.' 'Who is he with chin
  Upon his breast, and hands crossed on his chain?'
'The child of a fierce hour; he sought to win

  'The world, and lost all it did contain
Of greatness, in its hope destroyed; and more
  Of fame and peace than Virtue's self can gain   220

'Without the opportunity which bore
  Him on its eagle's pinion to the peak
From which a thousand climbers have before

  'Fall'n as Napoleon fell.' – I felt my cheek
Alter, to see the great form pass away
  Whose grasp had left the giant worlds so weak

That every pygmy kicked it as it lay –
  And much I grieved to think how power and will
In opposition rule our mortal day –

  And why God made irreconcilable   230
Good and the means of good; and for despair
  I half disdained mine eye's desire to fill

With the spent vision of the times that were
  And scarce have ceased to be . . . 'Dost thou behold,'
Said then my guide, 'those spoilers spoiled, Voltaire,

  'Frederick, and Kant, Catherine, and Leopold,
Chained hoary anarchs, demagogue and sage
  Whose name the fresh world thinks already old,

'For in the battle Life and they did wage
  She remained conqueror – I was overcome   240
By my own heart alone, which neither age

'Nor tears nor infamy nor now the tomb
Could temper to its object.' – 'Let them pass,'
  I cried, 'the world and its mysterious doom

'Is not so much more glorious than it was
  That I desire to worship those who drew
New figures on its false and fragile glass

  'As the old faded.' – 'Figures ever new
Rise on the bubble, paint them how you may;
  We have but thrown, as those before us threw,   250

'Our shadows on it as it passed away.
  But mark, how chained to the triumphal chair
The mighty phantoms of an elder day –

  'All that is mortal of great Plato there
Expiates the joy and woe his master knew not –
  That star that ruled his doom was far too fair,

'And Life, where long that flower of Heaven grew not,
  Conquered the heart by love which gold or pain
Or age or sloth or slavery could subdue not;

  'And near him walk the [. . .] twain,   260
The tutor and his pupil, whom Dominion
  Followed as tame as vulture in a chain. –

'The world has darkened beneath either pinion
  Of him whom from the flock of conquerors
Fame singled as her thunderbearing minion;

  'The other long outlived both woes and wars,
Throned in the thoughts of men, and still had kept
  The jealous keys of truth's eternal doors

'If Bacon's spirit [. . .] had not leapt
  Like lightning out of darkness; he compelled   270
The Proteus shape of Nature's as it slept.

  'To wake and to unbar the caves that held
The treasure of the secrets of its reign. –
  See the great bards of old, who inly quelled

'The passions which they sung, as by their strain
    May well be known: their living melody
Tempers its own contagion to the vein

    'Of those who are infected with it – I
Have suffered what I wrote, or viler pain! –

    'And so my words were seeds of misery,   280
Even as the deeds of others.' – 'Not as theirs,'
    I said – he pointed to a company

In which I recognized amid the heirs
    Of Caesar's crime, from him to Constantine,
The Anarchs old whose force and murderous snares

    Had founded many a sceptre-bearing line
And spread the plague of blood and gold abroad,
    And Gregory and John and men divine

Who rose like shadows between Man and God
    Till that eclipse, still hanging under Heaven,   290
Was worshipped by the world o'er which they strode

    For the true Sun it quenched. – 'Their power was given
But to destroy,' replied the leader; 'I
    Am one of those who have created, even

'If it be but a world of agony.' –
    'Whence camest thou and whither goest thou?
How did thy course begin,' I said, 'and why?

    'Mine eyes are sick of this perpetual flow
Of people, and my heart of one sad thought. –
    Speak.' – 'Whence I came, partly I seem to know,   300

'And how and by what paths I have been brought
    To this dread pass, methinks even thou mayst guess;
Why this should be, my mind can compass not.

    'Whither the conqueror hurries me, still less.
But follow thou, and from spectator turn
    Actor or victim in this wretchedness,

'And what thou wouldst be taught I then may learn
    From thee. – Now listen . . . In the April prime
When all the forest tips began to burn

'With kindling green, touched by the azure clime 310
Of the young year, I found myself asleep
  Under a mountain, which from unknown time

'Had yawned into a cavern high and deep,
  And from it came a gentle rivulet
Whose water like clear air in its calm sweep

  'Bent the soft grass and kept for ever wet
The stems of the sweet flowers, and filled the grove
  With sound which all who hear must needs forget

'All pleasure and all pain, all hate and love,
  Which they had known before that hour of rest: 320
A sleeping mother then would dream not of

  'The only child who died upon her breast
At eventide, a king would mourn no more
  The crown of which his brow was dispossessed

'When the sun lingered o'er the Ocean floor
  To gild his rival's new prosperity;
Thou wouldst forget thus vainly to deplore

  'Ills, which if ills, can find no cure from thee,
The thought of which no other sleep will quell,
  Nor other music blot from memory – 330

'So sweet and deep is the oblivious spell.
  Whether my life had been before that sleep
The Heaven which I imagine, or a Hell

  'Like this harsh world in which I wake to weep,
I know not. I arose and for a space
  The scene of woods and waters seemed to keep,

'Though it was now broad day, a gentle trace
  Of light diviner than the common Sun
Sheds on the common Earth, but all the place

  'Was filled with many sounds woven into one 340
Oblivious melody, confusing sense
  Amid the gliding waves and shadows dun;

'And as I looked, the bright omnipresence
  Of morning through the orient cavern flowed,
And the Sun's image radiantly intense

'Burned on the waters of the well that glowed
Like gold, and threaded all the forest maze
  With winding paths of emerald fire; – there stood

'Amid the Sun, as he amid the blaze
  Of his own glory, on the vibrating   350
Floor of the fountain, paved with flashing rays,

'A Shape all light, which with one hand did fling
Dew on the earth, as if she were the Dawn,
  Whose invisible rain forever seemed to sing

'A silver music on the mossy lawn,
  And still before her on the dusky grass
Iris her many-coloured scarf had drawn. –

'In her right hand she bore a crystal glass
Mantling with bright Nepenthe; – the fierce splendour
  Fell from her as she moved under the mass   360

'Of the deep cavern, and with palms so tender
  Their tread broke not the mirror of its billow,
Glided along the river, and did bend her

'Head under the dark boughs, till like a willow
Her fair hair swept the bosom of the stream
  That whispered with delight to be their pillow. –

'As one enamoured is upborne in dream
  O'er lily-paven lakes mid silver mist
To wondrous music, so this Shape might seem

'Partly to tread the waves with feet which kissed   370
The dancing foam, partly to glide along
  The airs that roughened the moist amethyst,

'Or the slant morning beams that fell among
  The trees, or the soft shadows of the trees;
And her feet ever to the ceaseless song

'Of leaves and winds and waves and birds and bees
And falling drops moved in a measure new
  Yet sweet, as on the summer evening breeze

176

'Up from the lake a shape of golden dew
  Between two rocks, athwart the rising moon,   380
Dances i' the wind, where eagle never flew. –

  'And still her feet, no less than the sweet tune
To which they moved, seemed as they moved, to blot
  The thoughts of him who gazed on them; and soon

'All that was, seemed as if it had been not,
  As if the gazer's mind was strewn beneath
Her feet like embers, and she, thought by thought,

  'Trampled its fires into the dust of death,
As day upon the threshold of the east
  Treads out the lamps of night, until the breath   390

'Of darkness reillumines even the least
  Of Heaven's living eyes – like Day she came,
Making the night a dream; and ere she ceased

  'To move, as one between desire and shame
Suspended, I said: "If, as it doth seem,
  Thou comest from the realm without a name

'"Into this valley of perpetual dream,
  Show whence I came, and where I am, and why –
Pass not away upon the passing stream."

  '"Arise and quench thy thirst," was her reply.   400
And as a shut lily, stricken by the wand
  Of dewy morning's vital alchemy,

'I rose; and bending at her sweet command,
  Touched with faint lips the cup she raised,
And suddenly my brain became as sand

  'Where the first wave had more than half erased
The track of deer on desert Labrador,
  Whilst the empty wolf from which they fled amazed

'Leaves his stamp visibly upon the shore
  Until the second bursts – so on my sight   410
Burst a new Vision never seen before;

177

'And the fair Shape waned in the coming light,
As veil by veil the silent splendour drops
 From Lucifer, amid the chrysolite

'Of sunrise, ere it strike the mountain tops –
 And as the presence of that fairest planet,
Although unseen, is felt by one who hopes

'That his day's path may end as he began it
In that star's smile, whose light is like the scent
 Of a jonquil when evening breezes fan it, 420

'Or the soft notes in which his dear lament
 The Brescian shepherd breathes, or the caress
That turned his weary slumber to content. –

'So knew I in that light's severe excess
The presence of that Shape which on the stream
 Moved, as I moved along the wilderness,

'More dimly than a day-appearing dream,
 The ghost of a forgotten form of sleep,
A light from Heaven whose half-extinguished beam

'Through the sick day in which we wake to weep 430
Glimmers, forever sought, forever lost. –
 So did that Shape its obscure tenor keep

'Beside my path, as silent as a ghost;
 But the new Vision, and its cold bright car,
With savage music, stunning music, crossed

'The forest, and as if from some dread war
Triumphantly returning, the loud million
 Fiercely extolled the fortune of her star.

'A moving arch of victory the vermilion
 And green and azure plumes of Iris had 440
Built high over her wind-winged pavilion,

'And underneath, etherial glory clad
The wilderness, and far before her flew
 The tempest of the splendour which forbade

178

'Shadow to fall from leaf or stone; – the crew
  Seemed in that light like atomies that dance
Within a sunbeam. – Some upon the new

'Embroidery of flowers that did enhance
The grassy vesture of the desert, played,
  Forgetful of the chariot's swift advance;   450

'Others stood gazing till within the shade
  Of the great mountain its light left them dim. –
Others outspeeded it, and others made

'Circles around it like the clouds that swim
Round the high moon in a bright sea of air;
  And more did follow, with exulting hymn,

'The chariot and the captives fettered there;
  But all like bubbles on an eddying flood
Fell into the same track at last and were

'Borne onward. – I among the multitude   460
Was swept; me sweetest flowers delayed not long,
  Me not the shadow nor the solitude,

'Me not the falling stream's Lethean song,
  Me, not the phantom of that early form
Which moved upon its motion, – but among

'The thickest billows of the living storm
I plunged, and bared my bosom to the clime
  Of that cold light, whose airs too soon deform. –

'Before the chariot had begun to climb
  The opposing steep of that mysterious dell,   470
Behold a wonder worthy of the rhyme

'Of him whom from the lowest depths of Hell
Through every Paradise and through all glory
  Love led serene, and who returned to tell

'In words of hate and awe the wondrous story
  How all things are transfigured, except Love;
For deaf as is a sea which wrath makes hoary

'The world can hear not the sweet notes that move
The sphere whose light is melody to lovers –

A wonder worthy of his rhyme: the grove 480

'Grew dense with shadows to its inmost covers,
    The earth was grey with phantoms, and the air
Was peopled with dim forms, as when there hovers

'A flock of vampire-bats before the glare
Of the tropic sun, bringing ere evening
    Strange night upon some Indian isle, – thus were

'Phantoms diffused around, and some did fling
    Shadows of shadows, yet unlike themselves,
Behind them; some like eaglets on the wing

'Were lost in the white blaze; others like elves 490
Danced in a thousand unimagined shapes
    Upon the sunny streams and grassy shelves;

'And others sate chattering like restless apes
    On vulgar paws and voluble like fire;
Some made a cradle of the ermined capes

'Of kingly mantles; some upon the tiar
Of pontiffs sate like vultures; others played
    Within the crown which girt with empire

'A baby's or an idiot's brow, and made
    Their nests in it; the old anatomies 500
Sate hatching their bare brood under the shade

'Of demons' wings, and laughed from their dead eyes
To reassume the delegated power
    Arrayed in which these worms did monarchize

'Who make this earth their charnel. – Others more
    Humble, like falcons sate upon the fist
Of common men, and round their heads did soar,

'Or like small gnats and flies, as thick as mist
On evening marshes, thronged about the brow
    Of lawyer, statesman, priest and theorist; 510

'And others like discoloured flakes of snow
    On fairest bosoms and the sunniest hair
Fell, and were melted by the youthful glow

'Which they extinguished; for like tears, they were
A veil to those from whose faint lids they rained
  In drops of sorrow. – I became aware

'Of whence those forms proceeded which thus stained
  The track in which we moved; after brief space
From every form the beauty slowly waned,

  'From every firmest limb and fairest face   520
The strength and freshness fell like dust, and left
  The action and the shape without the grace

'Of life; the marble brow of youth was cleft
  With care, and in the eyes where once hope shone
Desire like a lioness bereft

  'Of its last cub, glared ere it died; each one
Of that great crowd sent forth incessantly
  These shadows, numerous as the dead leaves blown

'In Autumn evening from a poplar tree –
  Each, like himself and like each other were,   530
At first, but soon distorted, seemed to be

  'Obscure clouds moulded by the casual air;
And of this stuff the car's creative ray
  Wrought all the busy phantoms that were there

'As the Sun shapes the clouds – thus, on the way,
  Mask after mask fell from the countenance
And form of all, and long before the day

  'Was old, the joy which waked like Heaven's glance
The sleepers in the oblivious valley, died,
  And some grew weary of the ghastly dance   540

'And fell, as I have fallen, by the wayside;
  Those soonest from whose forms most shadows passed
And least of strength and beauty did abide.' –

  'Then, what is Life?' I said . . . The cripple cast
His eye upon the car which now had rolled
  Onward, as if that look must be the last

And answered: 'Happy those for whom the fold
  Of

Composed 1822
First published 1824

AN ADDRESS TO THE PEOPLE ON THE DEATH OF THE
PRINCESS CHARLOTTE

I. The Princess Charlotte is dead. She no longer moves, nor thinks, nor feels. She is as inanimate as the clay with which she is about to mingle. It is a dreadful thing to know that she is a putrid corpse who but a few days since was full of life and hope; a woman young, innocent, and beautiful, snatched from the bosom of domestic peace, and leaving that single vacancy which none can die and leave not.

II. Thus much the death of the Princess Charlotte has in common with the death of thousands. How many women die in childbed and leave their families of motherless children and their husbands to live 10 on, blighted by the remembrance of that heavy loss? How many women of active and energetic virtues, mild, affectionate, and wise, whose life is as a chain of happiness and union which, once being broken, leaves those whom it bound to perish, have died, and have been deplored with bitterness, which is too deep for words? Some have perished in penury or shame, and their orphan baby has survived, a prey to the scorn and neglect of strangers. Men have watched by the bedside of their expiring wives and have gone mad when the hideous death-rattle was heard within the throat, regardless of the rosy child sleeping in the lap of the unobservant nurse. The coun- 20 tenance of the physician had been read by the stare of this distracted husband, until the legible despair sunk into his heart. All this has been and is. You walk with a merry heart through the streets of this great city and think not that such are the scenes acting all around you. You do not number in your thought the mothers who die in childbed. It is the most horrible of ruins: in sickness, in old age, in battle, death comes as to his own home; but in the season of joy and hope, when life should succeed to life, and the assembled family expects one more, the youngest and the best beloved – that the wife, the mother – she for whom each member of the family was so dear to one another, 30 should die! Yet thousands of the poorest poor whose misery is aggravated by what cannot be spoken now suffer this. And have they no affections? Do not their hearts beat in their bosoms and the tears gush from their eyes? Are they not human flesh and blood? Yet none weep for them – none mourn for them – none when their coffins are carried to the grave (if indeed the parish furnishes a coffin for all) turn aside and moralize upon the sadness they have left behind.

182

III. The Athenians did well to celebrate with public mourning the death of those who had guided the republic with their valour and their understanding, or illustrated it with their genius. Men do well 40 to mourn for the dead: it proves that we love something besides ourselves; and he must have a hard heart who can see his friend depart to rottenness and dust and speed him without emotion on his voyage to 'that bourne whence no traveller returns'. To lament for those who have benefited the state is a habit of piety yet more favourable to the cultivation of our best affections. When Milton died it had been well that the universal English nation had been clothed in solemn black, and that the muffled bells had tolled from town to town. The French nation should have enjoined a public mourning at the deaths of Rousseau and Voltaire. We cannot truly grieve for every one who 50 dies beyond the circle of those especially dear to us; yet in the extinction of the objects of public love and admiration and gratitude, there is something, if we enjoy a liberal mind, which has departed from within that circle. It were well done also, that men should mourn for any public calamity which has befallen their country or the world, though it be not death. This helps to maintain that connection between one man and another, and all men considered as a whole, which is the bond of social life. There should be public mourning when those events take place which make all good men mourn in their hearts – the rule of foreign or domestic tyrants, the 60 abuse of public faith, the wresting of old and venerable laws to the murder of the innocent, the established insecurity of all those, the flower of the nation, who cherish an unconquerable enthusiasm for public good. Thus, if Horne Tooke and Hardy had been convicted of high treason, it had been good that there had been not only the sorrow and the indignation which would have filled all hearts but the external symbols of grief. When the French Republic was extinguished, the world ought to have mourned.

IV. But this appeal to the feelings of men should not be made lightly, or in any manner that tends to waste on inadequate objects 70 those fertilizing streams of sympathy which a public mourning should be the occasion of pouring forth. This solemnity should be used only to express a wide and intelligible calamity, and one which is felt to be such by those who feel for their country and for mankind; its character ought to be universal, not particular.

V. The news of the death of the Princess Charlotte, and of the execution of [Jeremiah] Brandreth, [Isaac] Ludlam, and [William] Turner, arrived nearly at the same time. If beauty, youth, innocence, amiable manners, and the exercise of the domestic virtues could alone justify public sorrow when they are extinguished forever, this interesting Lady would well deserve that exhibition. She was the last and the best of her race. But there were thousands of others equally distinguished as she for private excellencies who have been cut off in youth and hope. The accident of her birth neither made her life more virtuous nor her death more worthy of grief. For the public she had done nothing either good or evil; her education had rendered her incapable of either in a large and comprehensive sense. She was born a princess; and those who are destined to rule mankind are dispensed with acquiring that wisdom and that experience which is necessary even to rule themselves. She was not like Lady Jane Grey, or Queen Elizabeth, a woman of profound and various learning. She had accomplished nothing, and aspired to nothing, and could understand nothing respecting those great political questions which involve the happiness of those over whom she was destined to rule. Yet this should not be said in blame, but in compassion; let us speak no evil of the dead. Such is the misery, such the impotence of royalty. Princes are prevented from the cradle from becoming anything which may deserve that greatest of all rewards next to a good conscience, public admiration and regret.

VI. The execution of Brandreth, Ludlam, and Turner is an event of quite a different character from the death of the Princess Charlotte. These men were shut up in a horrible dungeon for many months, with the fear of a hideous death and of everlasting hell thrust before their eyes; and at last were brought to the scaffold and hung. They too had domestic affections and were remarkable for the exercise of private virtues. Perhaps their low station permitted the growth of those affections in a degree not consistent with a more exalted rank. They had sons, and brothers, and sisters, and fathers, who loved them, it should seem, more than the Princess Charlotte could be loved by those whom the regulations of her rank had held in perpetual estrangement from her. Her husband was to her as father, mother, and brethren. Ludlam and Turner were men of mature years, and the affections were ripened and strengthened within them. What these sufferers felt shall not be said. But what must have been the long and various agony of their kindred may be inferred from Edward Turner, who, when he saw his brother dragged along upon the hurdle, shrieked horribly and fell in a fit, and was carried away like a corpse by two men. How fearful must have been their agony, sitting in solitude on that day when the tempestuous voice of horror from the crowd told them that the head so dear to them was severed from the body! Yes – they listened to the maddening shriek which burst from the multitude; they heard the rush of ten thousand terror-stricken feet, the groans and the hootings which told them that the mangled and distorted head was then lifted into the air. The sufferers were dead. What is death? Who dares to say that which will come after the grave? Brandreth was calm, and evidently believed that the consequences of our errors were limited by that tremendous barrier. Ludlam and Turner were full of fears, lest God should plunge them in everlasting fire. Mr Pickering, the clergyman, was evidently anxious that Brandreth should not by a false confidence lose the single opportunity of reconciling himself with the Ruler of the future world. None knew what death was, or could know. Yet these men were presumptuously thrust into that unfathomable gulf by other men who knew as little and who reckoned not the present or the future sufferings of their victims. Nothing is more horrible than that man should for any cause shed the life of man. For all other calamities there is a remedy or a consolation. When that Power through which we live ceases to maintain the life which it had conferred, then is grief and agony, and the burthen which must be borne; such sorrow improves the heart. But when man sheds the blood of man, revenge, and hatred, and a long train of executions, and assassinations, and proscriptions is perpetuated to remotest time.

VII. Such are the particular, and some of the general considerations depending on the death of these men. But however deplorable, if it were a mere private or customary grief, the public, as the public, should not mourn. But it is more than this. The events which led to the death of those unfortunate men are a public calamity. I will not impute blame to the jury who pronounced them guilty of high treason; perhaps the law requires that such should be the denomination of their offence. Some restraint ought indeed to be imposed on those thoughtless men who imagine they can find in violence a remedy for violence, even if their oppressors had tempted them to this occasion of their ruin. They are instruments of evil, not so guilty as the hands that wielded them, but fit to inspire caution. But their death by hanging and beheading, and the circumstances of which it is the characteristic and the consequence, constitute a calamity such as the English nation ought to mourn with an unassuageable grief.

VIII. Kings and their ministers have in every age been distinguished from other men by a thirst for expenditure and bloodshed. There existed in this country, until the American war, a check, sufficiently feeble and pliant indeed, to this desolating propensity. Until America proclaimed itself a republic, England was perhaps the freest and most glorious nation subsisting on the surface of the earth. It was not what is to the full desirable that a nation should be, but all that it can be, when it does not govern itself. The consequences, however, of that fundamental defect soon became evident. The government which the imperfect constitution of our representative assembly threw into the hands of a few aristocrats improved the method of anticipating the taxes by loans, invented by the ministers of William III, until an enormous debt had been created. In the war against the Republic of France, this policy was followed up, until now, the *mere interest* of the public debt amounts to more than twice as much as the lavish expenditure of the public treasure for maintaining the standing army, and the royal family, and the pensioners, and the placemen. The effect of this debt is to produce such an unequal distribution of the means of living as saps the foundation of social union and civilized life. It creates a double aristocracy, instead of one which was sufficiently burdensome before, and gives twice as many people the liberty of living in luxury and idleness on the produce of the industrious and the poor. And it does not give them this because they are more wise and meritorious than the rest, or because their leisure is spent in schemes of public good, or in those exercises of the intellect and the imagination whose creations ennoble or adorn a country. They are not like the old aristocracy men of pride and honour, *sans peur et sans tache*, but petty piddling slaves who have gained a right to the title of public creditors, either by gambling in the funds, or by subserviency to government, or some other villainous trade. They are not the 'Corinthian capital of polished society', but the petty and creeping weeds which deface the rich tracery of its sculpture. The effect of this system is that the day-labourer gains no more now by working sixteen hours a day than he gained before by working eight. I put the thing in its simplest and most intelligible shape. The labourer, he that tills the ground and manufactures cloth,

160

170

180

190

is the man who had to provide, out of what he would bring home
to his wife and children, for the luxuries and comforts of those whose
claims are represented by an annuity of forty-four millions a year
levied upon the English nation. Before, he supported the army and
the pensioners, and the royal family, and the landholders; and this
is a hard necessity to which it was well that he should submit. Many
and various are the mischiefs flowing from oppression, but this is the 200
representative of them all; namely, that one man is forced to labour
for another in a degree not only not necessary to the support of the
subsisting distinctions among mankind, but so as by the excess of the
injustice to endanger the very foundations of all that is valuable in
social order, and to provoke that anarchy which is at once the enemy
of freedom and the child and the chastiser of misrule. The nation,
tottering on the brink of two chasms, began to be weary of a
continuance of such dangers and degradations and the miseries which
are the consequence of them; the public voice loudly demanded a free
representation of the people. It began to be felt that no other con- 210
stituted body of men could meet the difficulties which impend.
Nothing but the nation itself dares to touch the question as to
whether there is any remedy or no to the annual payment of forty-
four millions a year, beyond the necessary expenses of state, forever
and forever. A nobler spirit also went abroad, and the love of liberty,
and patriotism, and the self-respect attendant on those glorious
emotions, revived in the bosoms of men. The government had a
desperate game to play.

IX. In the manufacturing districts of England discontent and
disaffection had prevailed for many years; this was the consequence 220
of that system of double aristocracy produced by the causes before
mentioned. The manufacturers, the helots of luxury, are left by this
system famished, without affections, without health, without leisure
or opportunity for such instruction as might counteract those habits
of turbulence and dissipation, produced by the precariousness and
insecurity of poverty. Here was a ready field for any adventurer who
should wish for whatever purpose to incite a few ignorant men to
acts of illegal outrage. So soon as it was plainly seen that the demands
of the people for a free representation must be conceded, if some
intimidation and prejudice were not conjured up, a conspiracy of the 230
most horrible atrocity was laid in train. It is impossible to know how
far the higher members of the government are involved in the guilt

187

of their infernal agents. It is impossible to know how numerous or how active they have been, or by what false hopes they are yet inflaming the untutored multitude to put their necks under the axe and into the halter. But thus much is known, that so soon as the whole nation lifted up its voice for parliamentary reform, spies were sent forth. These were selected from the most worthless and infamous of mankind and dispersed among the multitude of famished and illiterate labourers. It was their business, if they found no discontent, 240 to create it. It was their business to find victims, no matter whether right or wrong. It was their business to produce upon the public an impression that, if any attempt to attain national freedom, or to diminish the burdens of debt and taxation under which we groan, were successful, the starving multitude would rush in and confound all orders and distinctions, and institutions and laws in common ruin. The inference with which they were required to arm the ministers was that despotic power ought to be eternal. To produce this salutary impression, they betrayed some innocent and unsuspecting rustics into a crime whose penalty is a hideous death. A few 250 hungry and ignorant manufacturers, seduced by the splendid promises of these remorseless blood-conspirators, collected together in what is called rebellion against the state. All was prepared, and the eighteen dragoons assembled in readiness, no doubt, conducted their astonished victims to that dungeon which they left only to be mangled by the executioner's hand. The cruel instigators of their ruin retired to enjoy the great revenues which they had earned by a life of villainy. The public voice was overpowered by the timid and the selfish, who threw the weight of fear into the scale of public opinion, and parliament confided anew to the executive government those 260 extraordinary powers which may never be laid down, or which may be laid down in blood, or which the regularly constituted assembly of the nation must wrest out of their hands. Our alternatives are a despotism, a revolution, or reform.

X. On the 7th November, Brandreth, Turner, and Ludlam ascended the scaffold. We feel for Brandreth the less, because it seems he killed a man. But recollect who instigated him to the proceedings which led to murder. On the word of a dying man, Brandreth tells us, that 'OLIVER *brought him to this*' – that, '*but for* OLIVER, *he would not have been there*.' See, too, Ludlam and Turner, with their sons and 270 brothers and sisters, how they kneel together in a dreadful agony of

prayer. Hell is before their eyes, and they shudder and feel sick with fear lest some unrepented or some wilful sin should seal their doom in everlasting fire. With that dreadful penalty before their eyes – with that tremendous sanction for the truth of all he spoke, Turner exclaimed loudly and distinctly *while the executioner was putting the rope round his neck*, 'This is all Oliver and the Government.' What more he might have said we know not, because the chaplain prevented any further observations. Troops of horse, with keen and glittering swords, hemmed in the multitudes collected to witness this abo-   280
minable exhibition. 'When the stroke of the axe was heard, there was a burst of horror from the crowd. The instant the head was exhibited, there was a tremendous shriek set up, and the multitude ran violently in all directions, as if under the impulse of sudden frenzy. Those who resumed their stations, groaned and hooted.' It is a national calamity that we endure men to rule over us who sanction for whatever ends a conspiracy which is to arrive at its purpose through such a frightful pouring forth of human blood and agony. But when that purpose is to trample upon our rights and liberties forever, to present to us the alternative of anarchy and oppression, and triumph when the   290
astonished nation accepts the latter at their hands, to maintain a vast standing army, and add year by year to a public debt, which, already they know, cannot be discharged, and which, when the delusion that supports it fails, will produce as much misery and confusion through all classes of society as it has continued to produce of famine and degradation to the undefended poor; to imprison and calumniate those who may offend them, at will; when this, if not the purpose, is the effect of that conspiracy, how ought we not to mourn?

XI. Mourn then, People of England. Clothe yourselves in solemn black. Let the bells be tolled. Think of mortality and change. Shroud   300
yourselves in solitude and the gloom of sacred sorrow. Spare no symbol of universal grief. Weep – mourn – lament. Fill the great City – fill the boundless fields with lamentation and the echo of groans. A beautiful Princess is dead; she who should have been the Queen of her beloved nation and whose posterity should have ruled it forever. She loved the domestic affections, and cherished arts which adorn, and valour which defends. She was amiable and would have become wise, but she was young, and in the flower of youth the despoiler came. LIBERTY is dead. Slave! I charge thee, disturb not the depth and solemnity of our grief by any meaner sorrow. If One has   310

died who was like her that should have ruled over this land, like
Liberty, young, innocent, and lovely, know that the power through
which that one perished was God, and that it was a private grief. But
man has murdered Liberty, and whilst the life was ebbing from its
wound, there descended on the heads and on the hearts of every
human thing the sympathy of an universal blast and curse. Fetters
heavier than iron weigh upon us, because they bind our souls. We
move about in a dungeon more pestilential than damp and narrow
walls, because the earth is its floor and the heavens are its roof. Let
us follow the corpse of British Liberty slowly and reverentially to its   320
tomb; and if some glorious Phantom should appear and make its
throne of broken swords and sceptres and royal crowns trampled in
the dust, let us say that the Spirit of Liberty has arisen from its grave
and left all that was gross and mortal there, and kneel down and
worship it as our Queen.

Composed 1817
First published 1843

ON LOVE

What is Love? Ask him who lives, what is life? Ask him who adores,
what is God?

I know not the internal constitution of other men, nor even thine
whom I now address. I see that in some external attributes they
resemble me, but when misled by that appearance I have thought to
appeal to something in common and unburden my inmost soul to
them, I have found my language misunderstood like one in a distant
and savage land. The more opportunities they have afforded me for
experience, the wider has appeared the interval between us, and to
a greater distance have the points of sympathy been withdrawn. With   10
a spirit ill fitted to sustain such proof, trembling and feeble through
its tenderness, I have everywhere sought sympathy and found only
repulse and disappointment.

Thou demandest, What is Love? It is that powerful attraction
towards all that we conceive, or fear, or hope beyond ourselves, when
we find within our own thoughts the chasm of an insufficient void
and seek to awaken in all things that are, a community with what
we experience within ourselves. If we reason, we would be

understood; if we imagine, we would that the airy children of our
brain were born anew within another's; if we feel, we would that   20
another's nerves should vibrate to our own, that the beams of their
eyes should kindle at once and mix and melt into our own, that lips
of motionless ice should not reply to lips quivering and burning with
the heart's best blood. This is Love. This is the bond and the sanction
which connects not only man with man, but with everything which
exists. We are born into the world, and there is something within
us which, from the instant that we live, more and more thirsts after
its likeness. It is probably in correspondence with this law that the
infant drains milk from the bosom of its mother; this propensity
develops itself with the development of our nature. We dimly see   30
within our intellectual nature a miniature as it were of our entire self,
yet deprived of all that we condemn or despise, the ideal prototype
of everything excellent or lovely that we are capable of conceiving
as belonging to the nature of man. Not only the portrait of our
external being, but an assemblage of the minutest particles of which
our nature is composed; a mirror whose surface reflects only the forms
of purity and brightness; a soul within our soul that describes a circle
around its proper Paradise which pain and sorrow and evil dare not
overleap. To this we eagerly refer all sensations, thirsting that they
should resemble or correspond with it. The discovery of its anti-type: 40
the meeting with an understanding capable of clearly estimating our
own; an imagination which should enter into and seize upon the
subtle and delicate peculiarities which we have delighted to cherish
and unfold in secret; with a frame whose nerves, like the chords of
two exquisite lyres, strung to the accompaniment of one delightful
voice, vibrate with the vibrations of our own; and of a combination
of all these in such proportion as the type within demands; this is the
invisible and unattainable point to which Love tends; and to attain
which, it urges forth the powers of man to arrest the faintest shadow
of that without the possession of which there is no rest nor respite   50
to the heart over which it rules. Hence in solitude, or in that deserted
state when we are surrounded by human beings and yet they
sympathize not with us, we love the flowers, the grass, and the
waters, and the sky. In the motion of the very leaves of spring in the
blue air there is then found a secret correspondence with our heart.
There is eloquence in the tongueless wind, and a melody in the
flowing brooks and the rustling of the reeds beside them, which by

their inconceivable relation to something within the soul, awaken the
spirits to a dance of breathless rapture, and bring tears of mysterious
tenderness to the eyes, like the enthusiasm of patriotic success, or the   60
voice of one beloved singing to you alone. Sterne says that, if he were
in a desert, he would love some cypress. So soon as this want or power
is dead, man becomes the living sepulchre of himself, and what yet
survives is the mere husk of what once he was.

Composed 1818
First published 1828

from A PHILOSOPHICAL VIEW OF REFORM

Chapter III
Probable Means

That Commons should reform itself, uninfluenced by any fear that
the people would, on their refusal, assume to itself that office, seems
a contradiction. What need of reform if it expresses the will and
watches over the interests of the public? And if, as is sufficiently
evident, it despises that will and neglects that interest, what motives
would incite it to institute a reform which the aspect of the times
renders indeed sufficiently perilous, but without which there will
speedily be no longer anything in England to distinguish it from the
basest and most abject community of slaves that ever existed.

The great principle of reform consists in every individual of mature   10
age and perfect understanding giving his consent to the institution
and the continued existence of the social system which is instituted
for his advantage and for the advantage of others in his situation. As
in a great nation this is practically impossible, masses of individuals
consent to qualify other individuals, whom they delegate to super-
intend their concerns. These delegates have constitutional authority
to exercise the functions of sovereignty; they unite in the highest
degree the legislative and executive functions. A government that is
founded on any other basis is a government of fraud or force, and
ought on the first convenient occasion to be overthrown. The broad   20
principle of political reform is the natural equality of men, not with
relation to their property but to their rights. That equality in
possessions which Jesus Christ so passionately taught is a moral rather

than political truth and is such as social institutions cannot without mischief inflexibly secure. Morals and politics can only be considered as portions of the same science, with relation to a system of such absolute perfection as Christ and Plato and Rousseau and other reasoners have asserted, and as Godwin has, with irresistible eloquence, systematized and developed. Equality in possessions must be the last result of the utmost refinements of civilization; it is one of the conditions of that system of society towards which, with whatever hope of ultimate success, it is our duty to tend. We may and ought to advert to it as to the elementary principle, as to the goal, unattainable perhaps by us, but which, as it were, we revive in our posterity to pursue. We derive tranquillity and courage and grandeur of soul from contemplating an object which is, because we will it; and may be, because we hope and desire it; and must be, if succeeding generations of the enlightened sincerely and earnestly seek it.

But our present business is with the difficult and unbending realities of actual life, and when we have drawn inspiration from the great object of our hopes it becomes us with patience and resolution to apply ourselves to accommodating our theories to immediate practice.

That representative assembly called the House of Commons ought questionless to be *immediately* nominated by the great mass of the people. The aristocracy and those who unite in their own persons the vast privileges conferred by the possession of inordinate wealth are sufficiently represented by the House of Peers and by the King. Those theorists who admire and would put into action the mechanism of what is called the British Constitution would acquiesce in this view of the question. For if the House of Peers be a permanent representative of the privileged classes, if the regal power be no more than another form and a form still more jealously to be regarded, of the same representation, while the House of Commons be not chosen by the mass of the population, what becomes of that democratic element, upon the presence of which it had been supposed that the waning superiority of England over the surrounding nations has depended?

Any sudden attempt at universal suffrage would produce an immature attempt at a republic. It [is better] that [an] object so inexpressibly great and sacred should never have been attempted than that it should be attempted and fail. It is no prejudice to the ultimate establishment of the boldest political innovations that we temporize so as, when they shall be accomplished, they may be rendered permanent.

Considering the population of Great Britain and Ireland as twenty millions and the representative assembly as five hundred, each member ought to be the expression of the will of 40,000 persons; of these two-thirds would [consist of] women and children and persons under age; the actual number of voters therefore for each member would be 13,333. The whole extent of the empire might be divided into five hundred electoral departments or parishes, and the inhabitants assemble on a certain day to exercise their rights of suffrage.

Mr Bentham and other writers have urged the admission of females to the right of suffrage; this attempt seems somewhat immature. Should my opinion be the result of despondency, the writer of these pages would be the last to withhold his vote from any system which might tend to an equal and full development of the capacities of all living beings.

The system of voting by ballot which some reasoners have recommended is attended with obvious inconveniences. [It withdraws the elector from the regard of his country, and] his neighbours, and permits him to conceal the motives of his vote, which, if concealed, cannot but be dishonourable; when, if he had known that he had to render a public account of his conduct, he would have never permitted them to guide him. There is in this system of voting by ballot and of electing a member of the *Representative Assembly* as a church-warden is elected something too mechanical. The elector and the elected ought to meet one another face to face and interchange the meanings of actual presence and share some common impulses and, in a degree, understand each other. There ought to be the common sympathy of the excitements of a popular assembly among the electors themselves. The imagination would thus be strongly excited, and a mass of generous and enlarged and popular sentiments be awakened, which would give the vitality of [. . .].

That republican boldness of censuring and judging one another, which has indeed [been] exerted in England under the title of 'public opinion', though perverted from its true uses into an instrument of prejudice and calumny, would then be applied to its genuine purposes. Year by year the people would become more susceptible of assuming forms of government more simple and beneficial.

It is in this publicity of the exercise of sovereignty that the difference between the republics of Greece and the monarchies of Asia consisted. The actions of the times [. . .].

If the existing government shall compel the nation to take the task of reform into its own hands, one of the most obvious consequences of such a circumstance would be the abolition of monarchy and aristocracy. Why, it will then be argued, if the subsisting condition of social forms is to be thrown into confusion, should these things be endured? Then why do we now endure them? Is it because we think that an hereditary King is cheaper and wiser than an elected President, or a House of Lords and a Bench of Bishops are institutions modelled by the wisdom of the most refined and civilized periods, beyond which the wit of mortal man can furnish nothing more perfect? In case the subsisting government should compel the people to revolt to establish a representative assembly in defiance of them and to assume in that assembly an attitude of resistance and defence, this question would probably be answered in a very summary manner. No friend of mankind and of his country can desire that such a crisis should suddenly arrive; but still less, once having arrived, can he hesitate under what banner to array his person and his power. At the peace, the people would have been contented with strict economy and severe retrenchment, and some direct and intelligible plan for producing that equilibrium between the capitalists and the land-holders which is delusively styled the payment of the national debt; had this system been adopted, they probably would have refrained from exacting Parliamentary reform, the only secure guarantee that it would have been pursued. Two years ago it might still have been possible to have commenced a system of gradual reform. The people were then insulted, tempted, and betrayed, and *the petitions of a million* of men rejected with disdain. Now they are more miserable, more hopeless, more impatient of their misery. Above all, they have become more universally aware of the true sources of their misery. It is possible that the period of conciliation is past, and that after having played with the confidence and cheated the expectations of the people, their passions will be too little under discipline to allow them to wait the slow, gradual, and certain operation of such a reform as we can imagine the constituted authorities to concede.

Upon the issue of this question depends the species of reform which a philosophical mind should regard with approbation. If reform shall be begun by the existing government, let us be content with a limited *beginning*, with any whatsoever opening; let the rotten boroughs be disfranchised and their rights transferred to the unrepresented cities and districts of the nation; it is no matter how slow, gradual, and cautious be the change; we shall demand more and more with firmness and moderation, never anticipating, but never deferring the moment of successful opposition, so that the people may become habituated [to] exercising the functions of sovereignty, in proportion as they acquire the possession of it. If reform could begin from within the Houses of Parliament, as constituted at present, it appears to me 150 that what is called moderate reform, that is a suffrage whose qualification should be the possession of a certain small property, and triennial parliaments, would be principles – a system in which, for the sake of obtaining without bloodshed or confusion ulterior improvements of a more important character, all reformers ought to acquiesce. Not that such are first principles, or that they would produce a system of perfect social institutions or one approaching to [such]. But nothing is more idle than to reject a limited benefit because we cannot without great sacrifices obtain an unlimited one. We might thus reject a representative republic, if it were obtainable, 160 on the plea that the imagination of man can conceive of something more absolutely perfect. Towards whatsoever we regard as perfect, undoubtedly it is no less our duty than it is our nature to press forward; this is the generous enthusiasm which accomplishes not indeed the consummation after which it aspires, but one which approaches it in a degree far nearer than if the whole powers had not been developed by a delusion. It is in politics rather than in religion that faith is meritorious.

If the Houses of Parliament obstinately and perpetually refuse to concede any reform of the people, my vote is for universal suffrage 170 and equal representation. My vote is – but, it is asked, how shall this be accomplished, in defiance of and in opposition to the constituted authorities of the nation, they who possess whether with or without its consent the command of a standing army and of a legion of spies and police officers and hold all the strings of that complicated mechanism with which the hopes and fears of men are moved like puppets? They would disperse any assembly really chosen by the people; they would shoot and hew down any multitude without regard to sex or age as the Jews did the Canaanites, which might be

collected in its defence; they would calumniate, imprison, starve,   180
ruin, and expatriate every person who wrote or acted, or thought,
or might be suspected to think against them; misery and extermi-
nation would fill the country from one end to another [. . .].

This question I would answer by another.

Will you endure to pay the half of your earnings to maintain in
luxury and idleness the confederation of your tyrants as the reward
of a successful conspiracy to defraud and oppress you? Will you make
your tame cowardice and the branding record of it the everlasting
inheritance of your posterity? Not only this: will you render by your
torpid endurance this condition of things as permanent as the system   190
of castes in India by which the same horrible injustice is perpetrated
under another form?

Assuredly no Englishmen by whom these propositions are
understood will answer in the affirmative; and the opposite side of
the alternative remains.

When the majority in any nation arrive at a conviction that it is
their duty and their interest to divest the minority of a power
employed to their disadvantage, and the minority are sufficiently
mistaken as to believe that their superiority is tenable, a struggle must
ensue.   200

If the majority are enlightened, united, impelled by a uniform
enthusiasm and animated by a distinct and powerful apprehension of
their object – and full confidence in their undoubted power – the
struggle is merely nominal. The minority perceive the approaches of
the development of an irresistible force by the influence of the public
opinion of their weakness of those political forms of which no
government but an absolute despotism is devoid. They divest
themselves of their usurped distinctions; the public tranquillity is not
disturbed by the revolution.

But these conditions may only be imperfectly fulfilled by the state   210
of a people grossly oppressed and impotent to cast off the load. Their
enthusiasm may have been subdued by the killing weight of toil
and suffering; they may be panic-stricken and disunited by their
oppressors and the demagogues, the influence of fraud may have been
sufficient to weaken the union of classes which compose them by
suggesting jealousies, and the position of the conspirators, although
it is to be forced by repeated assaults, may be tenable until the siege
can be vigorously urged. The true patriot will endeavour to enlighten

and to unite the nation and animate it with enthusiasm and confidence. For this purpose he will be indefatigable in promulgating political truth. He will endeavour to rally round one standard the divided friends of liberty and make them forget the subordinate objects with regard to which they differ by appealing to that respecting which they are all agreed. He will promote such open confederations among men of principle and spirit as may tend to make their intentions and their efforts converge to a common centre. He will discourage all secret associations which have a tendency, by making national will develop itself in a partial and premature manner, to cause tumult and confusion. He will urge the necessity of exciting the people frequently to exercise their right of assembling in such limited numbers as that all present may be actual parties to the proceedings of the day. Lastly, if circumstances had collected a more considerable number as at Manchester on the memorable 16th August, if the tyrants command their troops to fire upon them or cut them down unless they disperse, he will exhort them peaceably to risk the danger, and to expect without resistance the onset of the cavalry, and wait with folded arms the event of the fire of the artillery and receive with unshrinking bosoms the bayonets of the charging battalions. Men are every day persuaded to incur greater perils for a less manifest advantage. And this, not because active resistance is not justifiable when all other means shall have failed, but because in this instance temperance and courage would produce greater advantages than the most decisive victory. In the first place the soldiers are men and Englishmen, and it is not to be believed that they would massacre an unresisting multitude of their countrymen drawn up in unarmed array before them and bearing in their looks the calm, deliberate resolution to perish rather than abandon the assertion of their rights. In the confusion of flight the ideas of the soldier become confused and he massacres those who fly from him by the instinct of his trade. In the struggle of conflict and resistance he is irritated by a sense of his own danger; he is flattered by an apprehension of his magnanimity in incurring it; he considers the blood of his countrymen at once the price of his valour, the pledge of his security. He applauds himself by reflecting that these base and dishonourable motives will gain him credit among his comrades and his officers, who are animated by the same as if they were something the same. But if he should observe neither resistance nor flight he would be reduced to impotence and

indecision. Thus far, his ideas were governed by the same law as those of a dog who chases a flock of sheep to the corner of a field and keeps aloof when they make the firm parade of resistance. But the soldier   260
is a man and an Englishman. This unexpected reception would probably throw him back upon a recollection of the true nature of the measures of which he was made the instrument, and the enemy might be converted into the ally.

The patriot will be foremost to publish the boldest truths in the most fearless manner, yet without the slightest tincture of personal malignity. He would encourage all others to the same efforts and assist them to the utmost of his power with the resources both of his intellect and fortune. He would call upon them to despise imprisonment and persecution and lose no opportunity of bringing   270
public opinion and the power of the tyrants into circumstances of perpetual contest and opposition.

All might, however, be ineffectual to produce so uniform an impulse of the national will as to preclude a further struggle. The strongest argument, perhaps, for the necessity of reform is the inoperative and unconscious abjectness to which the purposes of a considerable mass of the people are reduced. They neither know nor care. They are sinking into a resemblance with the Hindus and the Chinese, who were once men as they are. Unless the cause which renders them passive subjects instead of active citizens be removed,   280
they will sink with accelerated gradations into that barbaric and unnatural civilization which destroys all the differences among men. It is in vain to exhort us to wait until all men shall desire freedom whose real interest will consist in its establishment. It is in vain to hope to enlighten them while their tyrants employ the utmost artifices of all their complicated engine to perpetuate the infection of every species of fanaticism and error from generation to generation. The advocates of reform ought indeed to leave no effort unexerted, and they ought to be indefatigable in exciting all men to examine [. . .].   290

But if they wait until those neutral politicians, a class whose opinions represent the actions of this class, are persuaded that as soon [as] effectual reform is necessary, the occasion will have passed or will never arrive, and the people will have exhausted their strength in ineffectual expectation and will have sunk into incurable supineness. It was principally the [effect of] a similar quietism that the populous and extensive nations of Asia have fallen into their existing decrepitude; and that anarchy, insecurity, ignorance, and barbarism, the symptoms of the confirmed disease of monarchy, have reduced nations of the most delicate physical and intellectual organization and 300 under the most fortunate climates of the globe to a blank in the history of man. The manufacturers to a man are persuaded of the necessity of reform; an immense majority of the inhabitants of London [. . .].

The reasoners who incline to the opinion that it is not sufficient that the innovators should produce a majority in the nation, but that we ought to expect such an unanimity as would preclude anything amounting to a serious dispute, are prompted to this view of the question by the dread of anarchy and massacre. Infinite and inestimable calamities belong to oppression, but the most fatal of them all 310 is that mine of unexploded mischief which it has practised beneath the foundations of society, and with which, 'pernicious to one touch', it threatens to involve the ruin of the entire building together with its own. But delay merely renders these mischiefs more tremendous, not the less inevitable. For the utmost may now be the crisis of the social disease [which] is rendered thus periodical, chronic, and incurable.

The savage brutality of the populace is proportioned to the arbitrary character of their government, and tumults and insurrections soon, as in Constantinople, become consistent with the 320 permanence of the causing evil, of which they might have been the critical determination.

The public opinion in England ought first to [be] excited to action, and the durability of those forms within which the oppressors intrench themselves brought perpetually to the test of its operation. No law or institution can last if this opinion be distinctly pronounced against it. For this purpose government ought to be defied, in cases of questionable result, to prosecute for political libel. All questions relating to the jurisdiction of magistrates and courts of law respecting which any doubt could be raised ought to be agitated with indefa- 330 tigable pertinacity. Some two or three of the popular leaders have shown the best spirit in this respect; they only want system and co-operation. The tax-gatherer ought to be compelled in every practicable instance to distrain while the right to impose taxes, as was the case in the beginning of the resistance to the tyranny of Charles the 1st, is formally contested by an overwhelming multitude of defendants before the courts of common law. Confound the subtlety of lawyers with the subtlety of the law. All of the nation would thus be excited to develop itself and to declare whether it acquiesced in the existing forms of government. The manner in which all questions of this nature might be decided would develop the occasions and afford a prognostic as to the success of more decisive measures. Simultaneously with this active and vigilant system of opposition means ought to be taken of solemnly conveying the sense of large bodies and various denominations of the people in a manner the most explicit to the existing depositaries of power. Petitions, couched in the actual language of the petitioners, and emanating from distinct assemblies ought to load the tables of the House of Commons. The poets, philosophers, and artists ought to remonstrate, and the memorials entitled their petitions might show the diversity [of] convictions they entertain of the inevitable connection between national prosperity and freedom, and the cultivation of the imagination and the cultivation of scientific truth, and the profound development of moral and metaphysical enquiry. Suppose these memorials to be severally written by Godwin, Hazlitt, Bentham, and Hunt, they would be worthy of the age and of the cause; these, radiant and irresistible like the meridian sun, would strike all but the eagles who dared to gaze upon its beams, with blindness and confusion. These appeals of solemn and emphatic argument from those who have already a predestined existence among posterity would appal the enemies of mankind by their echoes from every corner of the world in which the majestic literature of England is cultivated; it would be like a voice from beyond the dead of those who will live in the memories of men, when they must be forgotten; it would be Eternity warning Time.

Let us hope that at this stage of the progress of reform, the oppressors would feel their impotence and reluctantly and imperfectly concede some limited portion of the rights of the people and disgorge some morsels of their undigested prey. In this case the people ought to be exhorted by everything ultimately dear to them to pause until by the exercise of those rights which they have regained they become fitted to demand more. It is better that we gain what we demand by a process of negotiation which would occupy twenty years than that by communicating a sudden shock to the interests of those who are the depositaries and dependants of power we should incur the calamity which their revenge might inflict upon us by giving the signal of civil war. If, after all, they consider the chance of personal ruin and the infamy of figuring on the page of history as the promoters of civil war preferable to resigning any portion how small soever of their usurped authority, we are to recollect that we possess 380 a right beyond remonstrance. It has been acknowledged by the most approved writers on the English constitution, which is in this instance merely [a] declaration of the superior decisions of eternal justice, that we possess a right of resistance. The claim of the [reigning] family is founded upon a memorable exertion of this solemnly recorded right.

The last resort of resistance is undoubtedly insurrection. The right of insurrection is derived from the employment of armed force to counteract the will of the nation. Let the government disband the standing army, and the purpose of resistance would be sufficiently 390 fulfilled by the incessant agitation of the points of dispute before the courts of common law and by an unwarlike display of the irresistible number and union of the people.

Before we enter into a consideration of the measures which might terminate in civil war, let us for a moment consider the nature and the consequences of war. This is the alternative which the unprincipled cunning of the tyrants has presented to us from which we must not sh[rink]. There is secret sympathy between destruction and power, between monarchy and war; and the long experience of the history of all recorded time teaches us with what success they have 400 played into each other's hands. War is a kind of superstition; the pageantry of arms and badges corrupts the imagination of men. How far more appropriate would be the symbols of an inconsolable grief – muffled drums, and melancholy music, and arms reversed, and the livery of sorrow rather than of blood. When men mourn at funerals, for what do they mourn in comparison with the calamities which they hasten with all circumstances of festivity to suffer and to inflict! Visit in imagination the scene of a field of battle or a city taken by assault, collect into one group the groans and the distortions of the innumerable dying, the inconsolable grief and horror of their sur- 410 viving friends, the hellish exultation, and unnatural drunkenness of destruction of the conquerors, the burning of the harvests and the obliteration of the traces of cultivation. To this, in civil war is to be added the sudden disruption of the bonds of social life, and 'father against son'.

If there had never been war, there could never have been tyranny in the world; tyrants take advantage of the mechanical organization of armies to establish and defend their encroachments. It is thus that the mighty advantages of the French Revolution have been almost compensated by a succession of tyrants (for demagogues, oligarchies,   420
usurpers, and legitimate kings are merely varieties of the same class) from Robespierre to Louis 18. War, waged from whatever motive, extinguishes the sentiment of reason and justice in the mind. The motive is forgotten, or only adverted to in a mechanical and habitual manner. A sentiment of confidence in brute force and in a contempt of death and danger is considered as the highest virtue, when in truth, and however indispensable, they are merely the means and the instruments, highly capable of being perverted to destroy the cause they were assumed to promote. It is a foppery the most intolerable to an amiable and philosophical mind. It is like what some reasoners   430
have observed of religious faith; no false and indirect motive to action can subsist in the mind without weakening the effect of those which are genuine and true. The person who thinks it virtuous to believe will think a less degree of virtue attaches to good actions than if he had considered it as indifferent. The person who has been accustomed to subdue men by force will be less inclined to the trouble of convincing or persuading them.

These brief considerations suffice to show that the true friend of mankind and of his country would hesitate before he recommended measures which tend to bring down so heavy a calamity as war.   440

I imagine, however, that before the English nation shall arrive at that point of moral and political degradation now occupied by the Chinese, it will be necessary to appeal to an exertion of physical strength. If the madness of parties admits no other mode of determining the question at issue [. . .].

When the people shall have obtained, by whatever means, the victory over their oppressors and when persons appointed by them shall have taken their seats in the Representative Assembly of the nation and assumed the control of public affairs according to constitutional rules, there will remain the great task of accommo-   450
dating all that can be preserved of ancient forms with the improvements of the knowledge of a more enlightened age in legislation,

jurisprudence, government, and religious and academical institutions. The settlement of the national debt is on the principles before elucidated merely circumstance of form, and however necessary and important is an affair of mere arithmetical proportions readily determined; nor can I see how those, who being deprived of their unjust advantages will probably inwardly murmur, can oppose one word of open expostulation to a measure of such inescapable justice.

There is one thing which certain vulgar agitators endeavour to   460
flatter the most uneducated part of the people by assiduously proposing, which they ought not to do nor to require: and that is, Retribution. Men having been injured desire to injure in return. This is falsely called an universal law of human nature; it is a law from which many are exempt, and all in proportion to their virtue and cultivation. The savage is more revengeful than the civilized man, the ignorant and uneducated than the person of a refined and cultivated intellect; the generous and [. . .] [The work was left incomplete.]

Composed 1819–20
First published 1920

A DEFENCE OF POETRY

According to one mode of regarding those two classes of mental action which are called reason and imagination, the former may be considered as mind contemplating the relations borne by one thought to another, however produced, and the latter, as mind acting upon those thoughts so as to colour them with its own light and composing from them, as from elements, other thoughts, each containing within itself the principle of its own integrity. The one is the το ποιειν, or the principle of synthesis, and has for its objects those forms which are common to universal nature and existence itself; the other is the το λογιζειν, or principle of analysis, and its   10
action regards the relations of things simply as relations; considering thoughts, not in their integral unity, but as the algebraical representations which conduct to certain general results. Reason is the enumeration of quantities already known; imagination is the perception of the value of those quantities, both separately and as a whole. Reason respects the differences, and imagination the

similitudes of things. Reason is to imagination as the instrument to
the agent; as the body to the spirit; as the shadow to the substance.

Poetry, in a general sense, may be defined to be 'the expression of
the imagination'; and poetry is connate with the origin of man.   20
Man is an instrument over which a series of external and internal
impressions are driven like the alternations of an ever-changing wind
over an Aeolian lyre which move it by their motion to ever-changing
melody. But there is a principle within the human being, and perhaps
within all sentient beings, which acts otherwise than in a lyre, and
produces not melody alone but harmony, by an internal adjustment
of the sounds and motions thus excited to the impressions which
excite them. It is as if the lyre could accommodate its chords to the
motions of that which strikes them in a determined proportion of
sound, even as the musician can accommodate his voice to the sound   30
of the lyre. A child at play by itself will express its delight by its
voice and motions; and every inflection of tone and every gesture
will bear exact relation to a corresponding antitype in the pleasurable
impressions which awakened it; it will be the reflected image of that
impression; and as the lyre trembles and sounds after the wind has
died away, so the child seeks, by prolonging in its voice and motions
the duration of the effect, to prolong also a consciousness of the
cause. In relation to the objects which delight a child, these
expressions are, what poetry is to higher objects. The savage (for
the savage is to ages what the child is to years) expresses the emotions   40
produced in him by surrounding objects in a similar manner; and
language and gesture, together with plastic or pictorial imitation,
become the image of the combined effect of those objects and of his
apprehension of them. Man in society, with all his passions and his
pleasures, next becomes the object of the passions and pleasures of
man; an additional class of emotions produces an augmented treasure
of expressions; and language, gesture, and the imitative arts become
at once the representation and the medium, the pencil and the
picture, the chisel and the statue, the chord and the harmony. The
social sympathies, or those laws from which as from its elements   50
society results, begin to develop themselves from the moment that
two human beings coexist; the future is contained within the present
as the plant within the seed; and equality, diversity, unity, contrast,
mutual dependence become the principles alone capable of affording
the motives according to which the will of a social being is

205

determined to action inasmuch as he is social; and constitute pleasure in sensation, virtue in sentiment, beauty in art, truth in reasoning, and love in the intercourse of kind. Hence men, even in the infancy of society, observe a certain order in their words and actions, distinct from that of the objects and the impressions represented by them, all expression being subject to the laws of that from which it proceeds. But let us dismiss those more general considerations which might involve an inquiry into the principles of society itself, and restrict our view to the manner in which the imagination is expressed upon its forms.

In the youth of the world, men dance and sing and imitate natural objects, observing in these actions, as in all others, a certain rhythm or order. And, although all men observe a similar, they observe not the same order, in the motions of the dance, in the melody of the song, in the combinations of language, in the series of their imitations of natural objects. For there is a certain order or rhythm belonging to each of these classes of mimetic representation, from which the hearer and the spectator receive an intenser and purer pleasure than from any other. The sense of an approximation to this order has been called taste by modern writers. Every man in the infancy of art, observes an order which approximates more or less closely to that from which this highest delight results; but the diversity is not sufficiently marked, as that its gradations should be sensible, except in those instances where the predominance of this faculty of approximation to the beautiful (for so we may be permitted to name the relation between this highest pleasure and its cause) is very great. Those in whom it exists in excess are poets, in the most universal sense of the word; and the pleasure resulting from the manner in which they express the influence of society or nature upon their own minds, communicates itself to others and gathers a sort of reduplication from that community. Their language is vitally metaphorical; that is, it marks the before unapprehended relations of things, and perpetuates their apprehension until the words which represent them become, through time, signs for portions or classes of thoughts instead of pictures of integral thoughts; and then, if no new poets should arise to create afresh the associations which have been thus disorganized, language will be dead to all the nobler purposes of human intercourse. These similitudes or relations are finely said by Lord Bacon to be 'the same footsteps of nature

impressed upon the various subjects of the world', and he considers the faculty which perceives them as the storehouse of axioms common to all knowledge. In the infancy of society every author is necessarily a poet, because language itself is poetry; and to be a poet is to apprehend the true and the beautiful – in a word, the good which exists in the relation subsisting, first between existence and   100
perception, and secondly between perception and expression. Every original language near to its source is in itself the chaos of a cyclic poem; the copiousness of lexicography and the distinctions of grammar are the works of a later age and are merely the catalogue and the form of the creations of poetry.

But poets, or those who imagine and express this indestructible order, are not only the authors of language and of music, of the dance, and architecture, and statuary and painting: they are the institutors of laws and the founders of civil society and the inventors of the arts of life and the teachers, who draw into a certain   110
propinquity with the beautiful and the true that partial apprehension of the agencies of the invisible world which is called religion. Hence all original religions are allegorical, or susceptible of allegory, and like Janus have a double face of false and true. Poets, according to the circumstances of the age and nation in which they appeared, were called in the earlier epochs of the world legislators or prophets; a poet essentially comprises and unites both these characters. For he not only beholds intensely the present as it is and discovers those laws according to which present things ought to be ordered, but he beholds the future in the present, and his thoughts are the germs   120
of the flower and the fruit of latest time. Not that I assert poets to be prophets in the gross sense of the word, or that they can foretell the form as surely as they foreknow the spirit of events: such is the pretence of superstition which would make poetry an attribute of prophecy rather than prophecy an attribute of poetry. A poet participates in the eternal, the infinite, and the one; as far as relates to his conceptions, time and place and number are not. The grammatical forms which express the moods of time, and the difference of persons, and the distinction of place are convertible with respect to the highest poetry without injuring it as poetry; and the   130
choruses of Aeschylus, and the book of Job, and Dante's *Paradiso* would afford, more than any other writings, examples of this fact, if the limits of this essay did not forbid citation. The creations of

sculpture, painting, and music are illustrations still more decisive.

Language, colour, form, and religious and civil habits of action are all the instruments and materials of poetry; they may be called poetry by that figure of speech which considers the effect as a synonym of the cause. But poetry in a more restricted sense expresses those arrangements of language, and especially metrical language, which are created by that imperial faculty whose throne is curtained   140 within the invisible nature of man. And this springs from the nature itself of language, which is a more direct representation of the actions and passions of our internal being, and is susceptible of more various and delicate combinations than colour, form, or motion, and is more plastic and obedient to the control of that faculty of which it is the creation. For language is arbitrarily produced by the imagination and has relation to thoughts alone; but all other materials, instruments, and conditions of art have relations among each other which limit and interpose between conception and expression. The former is as a mirror which reflects, the latter as a cloud which enfeebles, the   150 light of which both are mediums of communication. Hence the fame of sculptors, painters, and musicians, although the intrinsic powers of the great masters of these arts may yield in no degree to that of those who have employed language as the hieroglyphic of their thoughts, has never equalled that of poets in the restricted sense of the term; as two performers of equal skill will produce unequal effects from a guitar and a harp. The fame of legislators and founders of religion, so long as their institutions last, alone seems to exceed that of poets in the restricted sense; but it can scarcely be a question whether, if we deduct the celebrity which their flattery of the gross   160 opinions of the vulgar usually conciliates, together with that which belonged to them in their higher character of poets, any excess will remain.

We have thus circumscribed the meaning of the word *poetry* within the limits of that art which is the most familiar and the most perfect expression of the faculty itself. It is necessary, however, to make the circle still narrower, and to determine the distinction between measured and unmeasured language; for the popular division into prose and verse is inadmissible in accurate philosophy.

Sounds as well as thoughts have relation both between each other   170 and towards that which they represent, and a perception of the order of those relations has always been found connected with a perception

of the order of the relations of thoughts. Hence the language of poets has ever affected a certain uniform and harmonious recurrence of sound, without which it were not poetry, and which is scarcely less indispensable to the communication of its influence than the words themselves, without reference to that peculiar order. Hence the vanity of translation; it were as wise to cast a violet into a crucible that you might discover the formal principle of its colour and odour, as seek to transfuse from one language into another the creations of   180
a poet. The plant must spring again from its seed, or it will bear no flower – and this is the burthen of the curse of Babel.

An observation of the regular mode of the recurrence of this harmony in the language of poetical minds, together with its relation to music, produced metre, or a certain system of traditional forms of harmony of language. Yet it is by no means essential that a poet should accommodate his language to this traditional form so that the harmony, which is its spirit, be observed. The practice is indeed convenient and popular and to be preferred, especially in such composition as includes much form and action; but every great poet   190
must inevitably innovate upon the example of his predecessors in the exact structure of his peculiar versification. The distinction between poets and prose writers is a vulgar error. The distinction between philosophers and poets has been anticipated. Plato was essentially a poet – the truth and splendour of his imagery and the melody of his language are the most intense that it is possible to conceive. He rejected the harmony of the epic, dramatic, and lyrical forms, because he sought to kindle a harmony in thoughts divested of shape and action, and he forbore to invent any regular plan of rhythm which would include under determinate forms the varied pauses of his style.   200
Cicero sought to imitate the cadence of his periods, but with little success. Lord Bacon was a poet. His language has a sweet and majestic rhythm which satisfies the sense, no less than the almost superhuman wisdom of his philosophy satisfies the intellect; it is a strain which distends and then bursts the circumference of the hearer's mind and pours itself forth together with it into the universal element with which it has perpetual sympathy. All the authors of revolutions in opinion are not only necessarily poets as they are inventors, nor even as their words unveil the permanent analogy of things by images which participate in the life of truth,   210
but as their periods are harmonious and rhythmical and contain in

209

themselves the elements of verse, being the echo of the eternal music. Nor are those supreme poets, who have employed traditional forms of rhythm on account of the form and action of their subjects, less capable of perceiving and teaching the truth of things than those who have omitted that form. Shakespeare, Dante, and Milton (to confine ourselves to modern writers) are philosophers of the very loftiest power.

A poem is the very image of life expressed in its eternal truth. There is this difference between a story and a poem, that a story is a   220 catalogue of detached facts which have no other bond of connection than time, place, circumstance, cause, and effect; the other is the creation of actions according to the unchangeable forms of human nature as existing in the mind of the creator, which is itself the image of all other minds. The one is partial and applies only to a definite period of time and a certain combination of events which can never again recur; the other is universal and contains within itself the germ of a relation to whatever motives or actions have place in the possible varieties of human nature. Time, which destroys the beauty and the use of the story of particular facts stripped of the poetry which should   230 invest them, augments that of poetry, and forever develops new and wonderful applications of the eternal truth which it contains. Hence epitomes have been called the moths of just history; they eat out the poetry of it. A story of particular facts is a mirror which obscures and distorts that which should be beautiful; poetry is a mirror which makes beautiful that which is distorted.

The parts of a composition may be poetical, without the composition as a whole being a poem. A single sentence may be considered as a whole, though it may be found in the midst of a series of unassimilated portions; a single word even may be a spark of inextin-   240 guishable thought. And thus all the great historians, Herodotus, Plutarch, Livy were poets; and although the plan of these writers, especially that of Livy, restrained them from developing this faculty in its highest degree, they make copious and ample amends for their subjection by filling all the interstices of their subjects with living images.

Having determined what is poetry, and who are poets, let us proceed to estimate its effects upon society.

Poetry is ever accompanied with pleasure: all spirits on which it falls, open themselves to receive the wisdom which is mingled with   250

its delight. In the infancy of the world, neither poets themselves nor their auditors are fully aware of the excellence of poetry, for it acts in a divine and unapprehended manner, beyond and above consciousness; and it is reserved for future generations to contemplate and measure the mighty cause and effect in all the strength and splendour of their union. Even in modern times, no living poet ever arrived at the fullness of his fame; the jury which sits in judgement upon a poet, belonging as he does to all time, must be composed of his peers; it must be impanelled by Time from the selectest of the wise of many generations. A poet is a nightingale, who sits in darkness and sings   260
to cheer its own solitude with sweet sounds; his auditors are as men entranced by the melody of an unseen musician, who feel that they are moved and softened, yet know not whence or why. The poems of Homer and his contemporaries were the delight of infant Greece; they were the elements of that social system which is the column upon which all succeeding civilization has reposed. Homer embodied the ideal perfection of his age in human character; nor can we doubt that those who read his verses were awakened to an ambition of becoming like to Achilles, Hector, and Ulysses; the truth and beauty of friendship, patriotism, and persevering devotion to an object, were   270
unveiled to their depths in these immortal creations; the sentiments of the auditors must have been refined and enlarged by a sympathy with such great and lovely impersonations, until from admiring they imitated, and from imitation they identified themselves with, the objects of their admiration. Nor let it be objected that these characters are remote from moral perfection and that they can by no means be considered as edifying patterns for general imitation. Every epoch, under names more or less specious, has deified its peculiar errors; revenge is the naked idol of the worship of a semi-barbarous age; and self-deceit is the veiled image of unknown evil, before which luxury   280
and satiety lie prostrate. But a poet considers the vices of his contemporaries as the temporary dress in which his creations must be arrayed, and which cover without concealing the eternal proportions of their beauty. An epic or dramatic personage is understood to wear them around his soul, as he may the ancient armour or modern uniform around his body while it is easy to conceive a dress more graceful than either. The beauty of the internal nature cannot be so far concealed by its accidental vesture, but that the spirit of its form shall communicate itself to the very disguise, and indicate the

shape it hides from the manner in which it is worn. A majestic form   290
and graceful motions will express themselves through the most
barbarous and tasteless costume. Few poets of the highest class
have chosen to exhibit the beauty of their conceptions in its naked
truth and splendour; and it is doubtful whether the alloy of costume,
habit, etc., be not necessary to temper this planetary music for mortal
ears.

The whole objection, however, of the immorality of poetry rests
upon a misconception of the manner in which poetry acts to produce
the moral improvement of man. Ethical science arranges the elements
which poetry has created and propounds schemes and proposes   300
examples of civil and domestic life; nor is it for want of admirable
doctrines that men hate, and despise, and censure, and deceive, and
subjugate one another. But poetry acts in another and diviner
manner. It awakens and enlarges the mind itself by rendering it the
receptacle of a thousand unapprehended combinations of thought.
Poetry lifts the veil from the hidden beauty of the world and makes
familiar objects be as if they were not familiar; it re-produces all that
it represents, and the impersonations clothed in its Elysian light stand
thenceforward in the minds of those who have once contemplated
them as memorials of that gentle and exalted content which extends   310
itself over all thoughts and actions with which it coexists. The great
secret of morals is love; or a going out of our own nature, and an
identification of ourselves with the beautiful which exists in thought,
action, or person, not our own. A man, to be greatly good, must
imagine intensely and comprehensively; he must put himself in the
place of another and of many others; the pains and pleasures of his
species must become his own. The great instrument of moral good
is the imagination; and poetry administers to the effect by acting upon
the cause. Poetry enlarges the circumference of the imagination by
replenishing it with thoughts of ever new delight, which have the   320
power of attracting and assimilating to their own nature all other
thoughts, and which form new intervals and interstices whose void
forever craves fresh food. Poetry strengthens that faculty which is the
organ of the moral nature of man in the same manner as exercise
strengthens a limb. A poet therefore would do ill to embody his own
conceptions of right and wrong, which are usually those of his place
and time, in his poetical creations which participate in neither. By
this assumption of the inferior office of interpreting the effect, in

which perhaps after all he might acquit himself but imperfectly, he would resign the glory in a participation in the cause. There was little 330 danger that Homer, or any of the eternal poets, should have so far misunderstood themselves as to have abdicated this throne of their widest dominion. Those in whom the poetical faculty, though great, is less intense, as Euripides, Lucan, Tasso, Spenser, have frequently affected a moral aim, and the effect of their poetry is diminished in exact proportion to the degree in which they compel us to advert to this purpose.

Homer and the cyclic poets were followed at a certain interval by the dramatic and lyrical poets of Athens, who flourished contemporaneously with all that is most perfect in the kindred expressions 340 of the poetical faculty: architecture, painting, music, the dance, sculpture, philosophy and – we may add – the forms of civil life. For although the scheme of Athenian society was deformed by many imperfections which the poetry existing in Chivalry and Christianity has erased from the habits and institutions of modern Europe, yet never at any other period has so much energy, beauty, and virtue been developed; never was blind strength and stubborn form so disciplined and rendered subject to the will of man, or that will less repugnant to the dictates of the beautiful and the true, as during the century which preceded the death of Socrates. Of no other epoch in the 350 history of our species have we records and fragments stamped so visibly with the image of the divinity in man. But it is poetry alone, in form, in action, or in language, which has rendered this epoch memorable above all others and the storehouse of examples to everlasting time. For written poetry existed at that epoch simultaneously with the other arts, and it is an idle inquiry to demand which gave and which received the light which all, as from a common focus, have scattered over the darkest periods of succeeding time. We know no more of cause and effect than a constant conjunction of events; poetry is ever found to coexist with whatever other arts 360 contribute to the happiness and perfection of man. I appeal to what has already been established to distinguish between the cause and the effect.

It was at the period here adverted to that the drama had its birth; and however a succeeding writer may have equalled or surpassed those few great specimens of the Athenian drama which have been preserved to us, it is indisputable that the art itself never was

understood or practised according to the true philosophy of it, as at
Athens. For the Athenians employed language, action, music,
painting, the dance, and religious institutions to produce a common   370
effect in the representation of the highest idealisms of passion and of
power; each division in the art was made perfect in its kind by artists
of the most consummate skill and was disciplined into a beautiful
proportion and unity one towards another. On the modern stage a
few only of the elements capable of expressing the image of the poet's
conception are employed at once. We have tragedy without music
and dancing; and music and dancing without the highest imperso-
nations of which they are the fit accompaniment, and both without
religion and solemnity. Religious institution has indeed been usually
banished from the stage. Our system of divesting the actor's face of   380
a mask, on which the many expressions appropriate to his dramatic
character might be moulded into one permanent and unchanging
expression, is favourable only to a partial and inharmonious effect;
it is fit for nothing but a monologue, where all the attention may
be directed to some great master of ideal mimicry. The modern
practice of blending comedy with tragedy, though liable to great
abuse in point of practice, is undoubtedly an extension of the dramatic
circle; but the comedy should be as in *King Lear* universal, ideal, and
sublime. It is perhaps the intervention of this principle which
determines the balance in favour of *King Lear* against the *Oedipus*   390
Tyrannus, or the *Agamemnon*, or, if you will, the trilogies with which
they are connected, unless the intense power of the choral poetry,
especially that of the latter, should be considered as restoring the
equilibrium. *King Lear*, if it can sustain this comparison, may be
judged to be the most perfect specimen of the dramatic art existing
in the world, in spite of the narrow conditions to which the poet was
subjected by the ignorance of the philosophy of the drama which has
prevailed in modern Europe. Calderon in his religious *Autos* has
attempted to fulfil some of the high conditions of dramatic repre-
sentation neglected by Shakespeare, such as the establishing a relation   400
between the drama and religion, and the accommodating them to
music and dancing; but he omits the observation of conditions still
more important, and more is lost than gained by a substitution of
the rigidly defined and ever-repeated idealisms of a distorted super-
stition for the living impersonations of the truth of human passion.

But I digress. – The author of the *Four Ages of Poetry* has prudently omitted to dispute on the effect of the drama upon life and manners. For, if I know the knight by the device of his shield, I have only to inscribe Philoctetes or Agamemnon or Othello upon mine to put to flight the giant sophisms which have enchanted him, as the mirror of intolerable light, though on the arm of one of the weakest of the Paladins, could blind and scatter whole armies of necromancers and pagans. The connection of scenic exhibitions with the improvement or corruption of the manners of men has been universally recognized; in other words, the presence or absence of poetry, in its most perfect and universal form, has been found to be connected with good and evil in conduct and habit. The corruption which has been imputed to the drama as an effect begins when the poetry employed in its constitution ends; I appeal to the history of manners whether the periods of the growth of the one and the decline of the other have not corresponded with an exactness equal to any other example of moral cause and effect.

The drama at Athens, or wheresoever else it may have approached to its perfection, ever coexisted with the moral and intellectual greatness of the age. The tragedies of the Athenian poets are as mirrors in which the spectator beholds himself, under a thin disguise of circumstance, stript of all but that ideal perfection and energy which everyone feels to be the internal type of all that he loves, admires, and would become. The imagination is enlarged by a sympathy with pains and passions so mighty that they distend in their conception the capacity of that by which they are conceived; the good affections are strengthened by pity, indignation, terror, and sorrow; and an exalted calm is prolonged from the satiety of this high exercise of them into the tumult of familiar life; even crime is disarmed of half its horror and all its contagion by being represented as the fatal consequence of the unfathomable agencies of nature; error is thus divested of its wilfulness; men can no longer cherish it as the creation of their choice. In a drama of the highest order there is little food for censure or hatred; it teaches rather self-knowledge and self-respect. Neither the eye nor the mind can see itself unless reflected upon that which it resembles. The drama, so long as it continues to express poetry, is as a prismatic and many-sided mirror, which collects the brightest rays of human nature and divides and reproduces them from the simplicity of these elementary forms, and touches them with majesty and beauty, and multiplies all that it reflects, and

410

420

430

440

215

endows it with the power of propagating its like wherever it may fall.

But in periods of the decay of social life, the drama sympathizes with that decay. Tragedy becomes a cold imitation of the form of the great masterpieces of antiquity, divested of all harmonious accompaniment of the kindred arts, and often the very form misunderstood, or a weak attempt to teach certain doctrines which the writer considers as moral truths and which are usually no more than specious flatteries of some gross vice or weakness with which the author, in common with his auditors, are infected. Hence what has been called the classical and domestic drama. Addison's *Cato* is a specimen of the one; and would it were not superfluous to cite examples of the other! To such purposes poetry cannot be made subservient. Poetry is a sword of lightning, ever unsheathed, which consumes the scabbard that would contain it. And thus we observe that all dramatic writings of this nature are unimaginative in a singular degree; they affect sentiment and passion which, divested of imagination, are other names for caprice and appetite. The period in our own history of the grossest degradation of the drama is the reign of Charles II, when all forms in which poetry had been accustomed to be expressed became hymns to the triumph of kingly power over liberty and virtue. Milton stood alone illuminating an age unworthy of him. At such periods the calculating principle pervades all the forms of dramatic exhibition, and poetry ceases to be expressed upon them. Comedy loses its ideal universality; wit succeeds to humour; we laugh from self-complacency and triumph, instead of pleasure; malignity, sarcasm, and contempt succeed to sympathetic merriment; we hardly laugh, but we smile. Obscenity, which is ever blasphemy against the divine beauty in life, becomes, from the very veil which it assumes, more active if less disgusting; it is a monster for which the corruption of society forever brings forth new food, which it devours in secret.

The drama being that form under which a greater number of modes of expression of poetry are susceptible of being combined than any other, the connection of poetry and social good is more observable in the drama than in whatever other form. And it is indisputable that the highest perfection of human society has ever corresponded with the highest dramatic excellence; and that the corruption or the extinction of the drama in a nation where it has once flourished is a mark of a corruption of manners and an extinction of the energies which

450

460

470

480

216

sustain the soul of social life. But, as Machiavelli says of political institutions, that life may be preserved and renewed if men should arise capable of bringing back the drama to its principles. And this is true with respect to poetry in its most extended sense; all language, institution, and form require not only to be produced but to be sustained; the office and character of a poet participates in the divine 490
nature as regards providence, no less than as regards creation.

Civil war, the spoils of Asia, and the fatal predominance first of the Macedonian and then of the Roman arms, were so many symbols of the extinction or suspension of the creative faculty in Greece. The bucolic writers, who found patronage under the lettered tyrants of Sicily and Egypt, were the latest representatives of its most glorious reign. Their poetry is intensely melodious; like the odour of the tuberose, it overcomes and sickens the spirit with excess of sweetness, while the poetry of the preceding age was as a meadow-gale of June which mingles the fragrance of all the flowers of the field and adds 500
a quickening and harmonizing spirit of its own which endows the sense with a power of sustaining its extreme delight. The bucolic and erotic delicacy in written poetry is correlative with that softness in statuary, music, and the kindred arts, and even in manners and institutions which distinguished the epoch to which we now refer. Nor is it the poetical faculty itself, or any misapplication of it, to which this want of harmony is to be imputed. An equal sensibility to the influence of the senses and the affections is to be found in the writings of Homer and Sophocles; the former, especially, has clothed sensual and pathetic images with irresistible attractions. Their 510
superiority over these succeeding writers consists in the presence of those thoughts which belong to the inner faculties of our nature, not in the absence of those which are connected with the external; their incomparable perfection consists in a harmony of the union of all. It is not what the erotic writers have, but what they have not, in which their imperfection consists. It is not inasmuch as they were poets, but inasmuch as they were not poets, that they can be considered with any plausibility as connected with the corruption of their age. Had that corruption availed so as to extinguish in them the sensibility to pleasure, passion and natural scenery which is imputed to them as an 520
imperfection, the last triumph of evil would have been achieved. For the end of social corruption is to destroy all sensibility to pleasure; and, therefore, it is corruption. It begins at the imagination and the

intellect as at the core and distributes itself thence as a paralysing venom through the affections into the very appetites, until all become a torpid mass in which sense hardly survives. At the approach of such a period, poetry ever addresses itself to those faculties which are the last to be destroyed, and its voice is heard, like the footsteps of Astraea, departing from the world. Poetry ever communicates all the pleasure which men are capable of receiving; it is ever still the light 530 of life – the source of whatever of beautiful or generous or true can have place in an evil time. It will readily be confessed that those among the luxurious citizens of Syracuse and Alexandria who were delighted with the poems of Theocritus, were less cold, cruel, and sensual than the remnant of their tribe. But corruption must utterly have destroyed the fabric of human society before poetry can ever cease. The sacred links of that chain have never been entirely disjoined, which descending through the minds of many men is attached to those great minds, whence as from a magnet the invisible effluence is sent forth, which at once connects, animates, and sustains 540 the life of all. It is the faculty which contains within itself the seeds at once of its own and of social renovation. And let us not circumscribe the effects of the bucolic and erotic poetry within the limits of the sensibility of those to whom it was addressed. They may have perceived the beauty of those immortal compositions simply as fragments and isolated portions; those who are more finely organized, or born in a happier age, may recognize them as episodes to that great poem which all poets, like the co-operating thoughts of one great mind, have built up since the beginning of the world.

The same revolutions within a narrower sphere had place in ancient 550 Rome; but the actions and forms of its social life never seem to have been perfectly saturated with the poetical element. The Romans appear to have considered the Greeks as the selectest treasuries of the selectest forms of manners and of nature, and to have abstained from creating in measured language, sculpture, music, or architecture, anything which might bear a particular relation to their own condition, whilst it should bear a general one to the universal constitution of the world. But we judge from partial evidence, and we judge perhaps partially. Ennius, Varro, Pacuvius, and Accius, all great poets, have been lost. Lucretius is in the highest, and Virgil in 560 a very high sense, a creator. The chosen delicacy of the expressions of the latter is as a mist of light which conceals from us the intense and exceeding truth of his conceptions of nature. Livy is instinct with poetry. Yet Horace, Catullus, Ovid, and generally the other great writers of the Virgilian age, saw man and nature in the mirror of Greece. The institutions also, and the religion of Rome were less poetical than those of Greece, as the shadow is less vivid than the substance. Hence poetry in Rome seemed to follow rather than accompany the perfection of political and domestic society. The true poetry of Rome lived in its institutions; for whatever of beautiful, true, and majestic they contained could have sprung only from the faculty which creates the order in which they consist. The life of Camillus, the death of Regulus; the expectation of the senators, in their godlike state, of the victorious Gauls; the refusal of the Republic to make peace with Hannibal after the battle of Cannae, were not the consequences of a refined calculation of the probable personal advantage to result from such a rhythm and order in the shows of life to those who were at once the poets and the actors of these immortal dramas. The imagination, beholding the beauty of this order, created it out of itself according to its own idea; the consequence was empire, and the reward everliving fame. These things are not the less poetry, *quia carent vate sacro*. They are episodes of that cyclic poem written by Time upon the memories of men. The Past, like an inspired rhapsodist, fills the theatre of everlasting generations with their harmony.

At length the ancient system of religion and manners had fulfilled the circle of its revolutions. And the world would have fallen into utter anarchy and darkness but that there were found poets among the authors of the Christian and Chivalric systems of manners and religion who created forms of opinion and action never before conceived, which, copied into the imaginations of men, became as generals to the bewildered armies of their thoughts. It is foreign to the present purpose to touch upon the evil produced by these systems, except that we protest on the ground of the principles already established that no portion of it can be imputed to the poetry they contain.

It is probable that the astonishing poetry of Moses, Job, David, Solomon, and Isaiah had produced a great effect upon the mind of Jesus and his disciples. The scattered fragments preserved to us by the biographers of this extraordinary person are all instinct with the most vivid poetry. But his doctrines seem to have been quickly distorted.

219

At a certain period after the prevalence of a system of opinions founded upon those promulgated by him, the three forms into which Plato had distributed the faculties of mind underwent a sort of apotheosis and became the object of the worship of the civilized world. Here it is to be confessed that 'Light seems to thicken', and

> The crow makes wing to the rooky wood,
> Good things of day begin to droop and drowse,
> And night's black agents to their preys do rouse.

But mark how beautiful an order has sprung from the dust and blood   610
of this fierce chaos! How the world, as from a resurrection, balancing itself on the golden wings of knowledge and of hope, has reassumed its yet unwearied flight into the heaven of time. Listen to the music, unheard by outward ears, which is as a ceaseless and invisible wind nourishing its everlasting course with strength and swiftness.

The poetry in the doctrines of Jesus Christ, and the mythology and institutions of the Celtic conquerors of the Roman empire, outlived the darkness and the convulsions connected with their growth and victory and blended themselves into a new fabric of manners and opinion. It is an error to impute the ignorance of the Dark Ages to   620
the Christian doctrines or the predominance of the Celtic nations. Whatever of evil their agencies may have contained sprang from the extinction of the poetical principle, connected with the progress of despotism and superstition. Men, from causes too intricate to be here discussed, had become insensible and selfish; their own will had become feeble, and yet they were its slaves, and thence the slaves of the will of others; lust, fear, avarice, cruelty, and fraud characterized a race among whom no one was to be found capable of *creating* in form, language, or institution. The moral anomalies of such a state of society are not justly to be charged upon any class of events   630
immediately connected with them, and those events are most entitled to our approbation which could dissolve it most expeditiously. It is unfortunate for those who cannot distinguish words from thoughts that many of these anomalies have been incorporated into our popular religion.

It was not until the eleventh century that the effects of the poetry of the Christian and Chivalric systems began to manifest themselves. The principle of equality had been discovered and applied by Plato in his *Republic* as the theoretical rule of the mode in which the

materials of pleasure and of power produced by the common skill and   640
labour of human beings ought to be distributed among them. The
limitations of this rule were asserted by him to be determined only
by the sensibility of each, or the utility to result to all. Plato,
following the doctrines of Timaeus and Pythagoras, taught also a
moral and intellectual system of doctrine, comprehending at once the
past, the present, and the future condition of man. Jesus Christ
divulged the sacred and eternal truths contained in these views to
mankind, and Christianity in its abstract purity became the exoteric
expression of the esoteric doctrines of the poetry and wisdom of
antiquity. The incorporation of the Celtic nations with the exhausted   650
population of the south, impressed upon it the figure of the poetry
existing in their mythology and institutions. The result was a sum
of the action and reaction of all the causes included in it; for it may
be assumed as a maxim that no nation or religion can supersede any
other without incorporating into itself a portion of that which it
supersedes. The abolition of personal and domestic slavery and the
emancipation of women from a great part of the degrading restraints
of antiquity were among the consequences of these events.

The abolition of personal slavery is the basis of the highest political
hope that it can enter into the mind of man to conceive. The freedom   660
of women produced the poetry of sexual love. Love became a religion,
the idols of whose worship were ever present. It was as if the statues
of Apollo and the Muses had been endowed with life and motion and
had walked forth among their worshippers; so that earth became
peopled by the inhabitants of a diviner world. The familiar appearance
and proceedings of life became wonderful and heavenly, and a paradise
was created as out of the wrecks of Eden. And as this creation itself
is poetry, so its creators were poets; and language was the instrument
of their art: 'Galeotto fu il libro, e chi lo scrisse.' The Provençal
Trouveurs, or inventors, preceded Petrarch, whose verses are as spells   670
which unseal the inmost enchanted fountains of the delight which
is in the grief of love. It is impossible to feel them without becoming
a portion of that beauty which we contemplate; it were superfluous
to explain how the gentleness and the elevation of mind connected
with these sacred emotions can render men more amiable, more
generous, and wise, and lift them out of the dull vapours of the little
world of self. Dante understood the secret things of love even more
than Petrarch. His *Vita Nuova* is an inexhaustible fountain of purity

221

of sentiment and language; it is the idealized history of that period, and those intervals of his life which were dedicated to love. His 680 apotheosis of Beatrice in Paradise, and the gradations of his own love and her loveliness, by which as by steps he feigns himself to have ascended to the throne of the Supreme Cause, is that most glorious imagination of modern poetry. The acutest critics have justly reversed the judgement of the vulgar and the order of the great acts of the *Divine Drama* in the measure of the admiration which they accord to the Hell, Purgatory, and Paradise. The latter is a perpetual hymn of everlasting love. Love, which found a worthy poet in Plato alone of all the ancients, has been celebrated by a chorus of the greatest writers of the renovated world; and the music has penetrated the caverns of 690 society and its echoes still drown the dissonance of arms and super-stition. At successive intervals Ariosto, Tasso, Shakespeare, Spenser, Calderon, Rousseau, and the great writers of our own age, have celebrated the dominion of love, planting as it were trophies in the human mind of that sublimest victory over sensuality and force. The true relation borne to each other by the sexes into which human kind is distributed has become less misunderstood; and if the error which confounded diversity with inequality of the powers of the two sexes has been partially recognized in the opinions and institutions of modern Europe, we owe this great benefit to the worship of which 700 Chivalry was the law, and poets the prophets.

The poetry of Dante may be considered as the bridge thrown over the stream of time, which unites the modern and ancient world. The distorted notions of invisible things which Dante and his rival Milton have idealized are merely the mask and the mantle in which these great poets walk through eternity enveloped and disguised. It is a difficult question to determine how far they were conscious of the distinction which must have subsisted in their minds between their own creeds and that of the people. Dante at least appears to wish to mark the full extent of it by placing Riphaeus, whom Virgil calls 710 *justissimus unus*, in Paradise, and observing a most heretical caprice in his distribution of rewards and punishments. And Milton's poem contains within itself a philosophical refutation of that system of which, by a strange and natural antithesis, it has been a chief popular support. Nothing can exceed the energy and magnificence of the character of Satan as expressed in *Paradise Lost*. It is a mistake to suppose that he could ever have been intended for the popular personification of evil. Implacable hate, patient cunning, and a sleepless refinement of device to inflict the extremest anguish on an enemy – these things are evil; and, although venial in a slave, are not 720 to be forgiven in a tyrant; although redeemed by much that ennobles his defeat in one subdued, are marked by all that dishonours his conquest in the victor. Milton's Devil as a moral being is as far superior to his God as one who perseveres in some purpose which he has conceived to be excellent in spite of adversity and torture, is to one who in the cold security of undoubted triumph inflicts the most horrible revenge upon his enemy, not from any mistaken notion of inducing him to repent of a perseverance in enmity, but with the alleged design of exasperating him to deserve new torments. Milton has so far violated the popular creed (if this shall be judged to be a 730 violation) as to have alleged no superiority of moral virtue to his God over his Devil. And this bold neglect of a direct moral purpose is the most decisive proof of the supremacy of Milton's genius. He mingled, as it were, the elements of human nature as colours upon a single palette and arranged them in the composition of his great picture according to the laws of epic truth; that is, according to the laws of that principle by which a series of actions of the external universe and of intelligent and ethical beings is calculated to excite the sympathy of succeeding generations of mankind. The *Divina Commedia* and *Paradise Lost* have conferred upon modern mythology a systematic 740 form; and when change and time shall have added one more superstition to the mass of those which have arisen and decayed upon the earth, commentators will be learnedly employed in elucidating the religion of ancestral Europe, only not utterly forgotten because it will have been stamped with the eternity of genius.

Homer was the first, and Dante the second epic poet; that is, the second poet, the series of whose creations bore a defined and intelligible relation to the knowledge and sentiment and religion and political conditions of the age in which he lived, and of the ages which followed it, developing itself in correspondence with their 750 development. For Lucretius had limed the wings of his swift spirit in the dregs of the sensible world; and Virgil, with a modesty which ill became his genius, had affected the fame of an imitator, even whilst he created anew all that he copied; and none among the flock of mockbirds, though their notes were sweet, Apollonius Rhodius, Quintus Calaber Smyrnaeus, Nonnus, Lucan, Statius, or Claudian have sought even to fulfil a single condition of epic truth. Milton was the third epic poet. For if the title of epic in its highest sense be refused to the *Aeneid*, still less can it be conceded to the *Orlando Furioso*, the *Gerusalemme Liberata*, the *Lusiad*, or the *Fairy Queen*. 760

Dante and Milton were both deeply penetrated with the ancient religion of the civilized world, and its spirit exists in their poetry probably in the same proportion as its forms survived in the unreformed worship of modern Europe. The one preceded and the other followed the Reformation at almost equal intervals. Dante was the first religious reformer, and Luther surpassed him rather in the rudeness and acrimony than in the boldness of his censures of papal usurpation. Dante was the first awakener of entranced Europe; he created a language, in itself music and persuasion, out of a chaos of inharmonious barbarisms. He was the congregator of those great 770 spirits who presided over the resurrection of learning, the Lucifer of that starry flock which in the thirteenth century shone forth from republican Italy, as from a heaven, into the darkness of the benighted world. His very words are instinct with spirit; each is as a spark, a burning atom of inextinguishable thought; and many yet lie covered in the ashes of their birth, and pregnant with a lightning which has yet found no conductor. All high poetry is infinite; it is as the first acorn, which contained all oaks potentially. Veil after veil may be undrawn and the inmost naked beauty of the meaning never exposed. A great poem is a fountain forever overflowing with the waters of 780 wisdom and delight; and after one person and one age has exhausted all of its divine effluence which their peculiar relations enable them to share, another and yet another succeeds, and new relations are ever developed, the source of an unforeseen and an unconceived delight.

The age immediately succeeding to that of Dante, Petrarch, and Boccaccio was characterized by a revival of painting, sculpture, music, and architecture. Chaucer caught the sacred inspiration, and the superstructure of English literature is based upon the materials of Italian invention.

But let us not be betrayed from a defence into a critical history of 790 poetry and its influence on society. Be it enough to have pointed out the effects of poets, in the large and true sense of the word, upon their own and all succeeding times, and to revert to the partial instances cited as illustrations of an opinion the reverse of that attempted to be established by the author of *The Four Ages of Poetry*.

But poets have been challenged to resign the civic crown to reasoners and mechanists, on another plea. It is admitted that the exercise of the imagination is most delightful, but it is alleged that that of reason is more useful. Let us examine as the grounds of this distinction what is here meant by utility. Pleasure or good, in a 800 general sense, is that which the consciousness of a sensitive and intelligent being seeks and in which, when found, it acquiesces. There are two kinds of pleasure, one durable, universal, and permanent; the other transitory and particular. Utility may either express the means of producing the former or the latter. In the former sense, whatever strengthens and purifies the affections, enlarges the imagination, and adds spirit to sense is useful. But the meaning in which the author of *The Four Ages of Poetry* seems to have employed the word *Utility* is the narrower one of banishing the importunity of the wants of our animal nature, the surrounding men with security 810 of life, the dispersing the grosser delusions of superstition, and the conciliating such a degree of mutual forbearance among men as may consist with the motives of personal advantage.

Undoubtedly the promoters of utility, in the limited sense, have their appointed office in society. They follow the footsteps of poets and copy the sketches of their creations into the book of common life. They make space and give time. Their exertions are of the highest value so long as they confine their administration of the concerns of the inferior powers of our nature within the limits due to the superior ones. But whilst the sceptic destroys gross superstitions, let him spare 820 to deface, as some of the French writers have defaced, the eternal truths charactered upon the imaginations of men. Whilst the mechanist abridges, and the political economist combines labour, let them beware that their speculations, for want of correspondence with those first principles which belong to the imagination, do not tend, as they have in modern England, to exasperate at once the extremes of luxury and want. They have exemplified the saying, 'To him that hath, more shall be given; and from him that hath not, the little that he hath shall be taken away.' The rich have become richer, and the poor have become poorer; and the vessel of the state is driven between 830 the Scylla and Charybdis of anarchy and despotism. Such are the effects which must ever flow from an unmitigated exercise of the calculating faculty.

It is difficult to define pleasure in its highest sense – the definition involving a number of apparent paradoxes. For, from an inexplicable defect of harmony in the constitution of human nature, the pain of the inferior is frequently connected with the pleasures of the superior portions of our being. Sorrow, terror, anguish, despair itself are often the chosen expressions of an approximation to the highest good. Our sympathy in tragic fiction depends on this principle: tragedy delights   840 by affording a shadow of the pleasure which exists in pain. This is the source also of the melancholy which is inseparable from the sweetest melody. The pleasure that is in sorrow is sweeter than the pleasure of pleasure itself. And hence the saying, 'It is better to go to the house of mourning than to the house of mirth.' Not that this highest species of pleasure is necessarily linked with pain. The delight of love and friendship, the ecstasy of the admiration of nature, the joy of the perception and still more of the creation of poetry, is often wholly unalloyed.

The production and assurance of pleasure in this highest sense is true   850 utility. Those who produce and preserve this pleasure are poets or poetical philosophers.

The exertions of Locke, Hume, Gibbon, Voltaire, Rousseau, and their disciples in favour of oppressed and deluded humanity are entitled to the gratitude of mankind. Yet it is easy to calculate the degree of moral and intellectual improvement which the world would have exhibited had they never lived. A little more nonsense would have been talked for a century or two; and perhaps a few more men, women, and children burnt as heretics. We might not at this moment have been congratulating each other on the abolition of the Inquisition   860 in Spain. But it exceeds all imagination to conceive what would have been the moral condition of the world if neither Dante, Petrarch, Boccaccio, Chaucer, Shakespeare, Calderon, Lord Bacon, nor Milton had ever existed; if Raphael and Michael Angelo had never been born; if the Hebrew poetry had never been translated; if a revival of the study of Greek literature had never taken place; if no monuments of ancient sculpture had been handed down to us; and if the poetry of the religion of the ancient world had been extinguished together with its belief. The human mind could never, except by the intervention of these excitements, have been awakened to the invention of the grosser   870 sciences and that application of analytical reasoning to the aberrations of society which it is now attempted to exalt over the direct expression of the inventive and creative faculty itself.

We have more moral, political, and historical wisdom than we know how to reduce into practice; we have more scientific and economic knowledge than can be accommodated to the just distribution of the produce which it multiplies. The poetry in these systems of thought is concealed by the accumulation of facts and calculating processes. There is no want of knowledge respecting what is wisest and best in morals, government, and political economy, or 880 at least, what is wiser and better than what men now practise and endure. But we let '*I dare not* wait upon *I would*, like the poor cat i' the adage.' We want the creative faculty to imagine that which we know; we want the generous impulse to act that which we imagine; we want the poetry of life; our calculations have outrun our conception; we have eaten more than we can digest. The cultivation of those sciences which have enlarged the limits of the empire of man over the external world has, for want of the poetical faculty, proportionally circumscribed those of the internal world; and man, having enslaved the elements, remains himself a slave. To what but 890 a cultivation of the mechanical arts in a degree disproportioned to the presence of the creative faculty, which is the basis of all knowledge, is to be attributed the abuse of all invention for abridging and combining labour to the exasperation of the inequality of mankind? From what other cause has it arisen that the discoveries which should have lightened, have added a weight to the curse imposed on Adam? Poetry and the principle of self, of which money is the visible incarnation, are the God and Mammon of the world.

The functions of the poetical faculty are twofold: by one it creates new materials of knowledge, and power, and the pleasure; by the 900 other it engenders in the mind a desire to reproduce and arrange them according to a certain rhythm and order, which may be called the beautiful and the good. The cultivation of poetry is never more to be desired than at periods when, from an excess of the selfish and calculating principle, the accumulation of the materials of external life exceed the quantity of the power of assimilating them to the internal laws of human nature. The body has then become too unwieldy for that which animates it.

Poetry is indeed something divine. It is at once the centre and circumference of knowledge; it is that which comprehends all science, 910 and that to which all science must be referred. It is at the same time the root and blossom of all other systems of thought; it is that from

227

which all spring and that which adorns all; and that which, if blighted, denies the fruit and the seed, and withholds from the barren world the nourishment and the succession of the scions of the tree of life. It is the perfect and consummate surface and bloom of things; it is as the odour and the colour of the rose to the texture of the elements which compose it, as the form and the splendour of unfaded beauty to the secrets of anatomy and corruption. What were virtue, love, patriotism, friendship; what were the scenery of this beautiful   920
universe which we inhabit; what were our consolations on this side of the grave and what were our aspirations beyond it, if poetry did not ascend to bring light and fire from those eternal regions where the owl-winged faculty of calculation dare not ever soar? Poetry is not like reasoning, a power to be exerted according to the determination of the will. A man cannot say, 'I will compose poetry.' The greatest poet even cannot say it; for the mind in creation is as a fading coal which some invisible influence, like an inconstant wind, awakens to transitory brightness; this power arises from within like the colour of a flower which fades and changes as it is developed, and the   930
conscious portions of our natures are unprophetic either of its approach or its departure. Could this influence be durable in its original purity and force, it is impossible to predict the greatness of the results; but when composition begins, inspiration is already on the decline, and the most glorious poetry that has ever been communicated to the world is probably a feeble shadow of the original conceptions of the poet. I appeal to the great poets of the present day, whether it be not an error to assert that the finest passages of poetry are produced by labour and study. The toil and the delay recommended by critics can be justly interpreted to mean   940
no more than a careful observation of the inspired moments and an artificial connection of the spaces between their suggestions by the intertexture of conventional expressions – a necessity only imposed by the limitedness of the poetical faculty itself. For Milton conceived the *Paradise Lost* as a whole before he executed it in portions. We have his own authority also for the muse having 'dictated' to him the 'unpremeditated song'. And let this be an answer to those who would allege the fifty-six various readings of the first line of the *Orlando Furioso*. Compositions so produced are to poetry what mosaic is to painting. This instinct and intuition of the poetical faculty is still   950
more observable in the plastic and pictorial arts: a great statue or

picture grows under the power of the artist as a child in the mother's womb; and the very mind which directs the hands in formation is incapable of accounting to itself for the origin, the gradations, or the media of the process.

Poetry is the record of the best and happiest moments of the happiest and best minds. We are aware of evanescent visitations of thought and feeling, sometimes associated with place or person, sometimes regarding our own mind alone, and always arising unforeseen and departing unbidden, but elevating and delightful beyond all 960 expression; so that even in the desire and the regret they leave, there cannot but be pleasure, participating as it does in the nature of its object. It is as it were the interpenetration of a diviner nature through our own; but its footsteps are like those of a wind over the sea, which the coming calm erases, and whose traces remain only as on the wrinkled sand which paves it. These and corresponding conditions of being are experienced principally by those of the most delicate sensibility and the most enlarged imagination; and the state of mind produced by them is at war with every base desire. The enthusiasm of virtue, love, patriotism, and friendship is essentially linked with 970 such emotions; and whilst they last, self appears as what it is, an atom to a universe. Poets are not only subject to these experiences as spirits of the most refined organization, but they can colour all that they combine with the evanescent hues of this ethereal world; a word, a trait in the representation of a scene or a passion, will touch the enchanted chord and reanimate in those who have ever experienced these emotions the sleeping, the cold, the buried image of the past. Poetry thus makes immortal all that is best and most beautiful in the world; it arrests the vanishing apparitions which haunt the interlunations of life and, veiling them, or in language or in form, sends 980 them forth among mankind, bearing sweet news of kindred joy to those with whom their sisters abide – abide, because there is no portal of expression from the caverns of the spirit which they inhabit into the universe of things. Poetry redeems from decay the visitations of the divinity in man.

Poetry turns all things to loveliness; it exalts the beauty of that which is most beautiful and it adds beauty to that which is most deformed; it marries exultation and horror, grief and pleasure, eternity and change; it subdues to union, under its light yoke, all irreconcilable things. It transmutes all that it touches, and every form 990

229

moving within the radiance of its presence is changed by wondrous sympathy to an incarnation of the spirit which it breathes; its secret alchemy turns to potable gold the poisonous waters which flow from death through life; it strips the veil of familiarity from the world and lays bare the naked and sleeping beauty, which is the spirit of its forms.

All things exist as they are perceived – at least in relation to the percipient. 'The mind is its own place, and in itself can make a Heaven of Hell, a Hell of Heaven.' But poetry defeats the curse which binds us to be subjected to the accident of surrounding impressions. And whether it spreads its own figured curtain, or withdraws life's dark veil from before the scene of things, it equally creates for us a being within our being. It makes us the inhabitants of a world to which the familiar world is a chaos. It reproduces the common Universe of which we are portions and percipients, and it purges from our inward sight the film of familiarity which obscures from us the wonder of our being. It compels us to feel that which we perceive, and to imagine that which we know. It creates anew the universe, after it has been annihilated in our minds by the recurrence of impressions blunted by reiteration. It justifies the bold and true word of Tasso: *Non merita nome di creatore, se non Iddio ed il Poeta.*

A poet, as he is the author to others of the highest wisdom, pleasure, virtue, and glory, so he ought personally to be the happiest, the best, the wisest, and the most illustrious of men. As to his glory, let time be challenged to declare whether the fame of any other institutor of human life be comparable to that of a poet. That he is the wisest, the happiest, and the best, inasmuch as he is a poet, is equally incontrovertible; the greatest poets have been men of the most spotless virtue, of the most consummate prudence, and, if we could look into the interior of their lives, the most fortunate of men; and the exceptions, as they regard those who possessed the imaginative faculty in a high yet inferior degree, will be found on consideration to confirm rather than destroy the rule. Let us for a moment stoop to the arbitration of popular breath, and usurping and uniting in our own persons the incompatible characters of accuser, witness, judge, and executioner, let us without trial, testimony, or form, decide that certain motives of those who are 'there sitting where we dare not soar', are reprehensible. Let us assume that Homer was a drunkard, that Virgil was a flatterer, that Horace was a coward, that Tasso was

230

a madman, that Lord Bacon was a peculator, that Raphael was a   1030
libertine, that Spenser was a poet laureate. It is inconsistent with this
division of our subject to cite living poets, but posterity has done
ample justice to the great names now referred to. Their errors have
been weighed and found to have been dust in the balance; if their sins
were as scarlet, they are now white as snow: they have been washed
in the blood of the mediator and the redeemer, Time. Observe in
what a ludicrous chaos the imputations of real or fictitious crime have
been confused in the contemporary calumnies against poetry and
poets; consider how little is, as it appears – or appears, as it is; look
to your own motives, and judge not, lest ye be judged.   1040

Poetry, as has been said, in this respect differs from logic, that it
is not subject to the control of the active powers of the mind, and
that its birth and recurrence have no necessary connection with
consciousness or will. It is presumptuous to determine that these are
the necessary conditions of all mental causation, when mental effects
are experienced insusceptible of being referred to them. The frequent
recurrence of the poetical power, it is obvious to suppose, may
produce in the mind a habit of order and harmony correlative with
its own nature and with its effects upon other minds. But in the
intervals of inspiration, and they may be frequent without being   1050
durable, a poet becomes a man and is abandoned to the sudden reflux
of the influences under which others habitually live. But as he is more
delicately organized than other men and sensible to pain and pleasure,
both his own and that of others, in a degree unknown to them, he
will avoid the one and pursue the other with an ardour proportioned
to this difference. And he renders himself obnoxious to calumny
when he neglects to observe the circumstances under which these
objects of universal pursuit and flight have disguised themselves in
one another's garments.

But there is nothing necessarily evil in this error, and thus cruelty, 1060
envy, revenge, avarice, and the passions purely evil, have never
formed any portion of the popular imputations on the lives of poets.

I have thought it most favourable to the cause of truth to set down
these remarks according to the order in which they were suggested
to my mind, by a consideration of the subject itself, instead of
following that of the treatise that excited me to make them public.
Thus although devoid of the formality of a polemical reply, if the
view which they contain be just, they will be found to involve a

refutation of the doctrines of *The Four Ages of Poetry*, so far at least as regards the first division of the subject. I can readily conjecture 1070 what should have moved the gall of the learned and intelligent author of that paper; I confess myself like him unwilling to be stunned by the Theseids of the hoarse Codri of the day. Bavius and Maevius undoubtedly are, as they ever were, insufferable persons. But it belongs to a philosophical critic to distinguish rather than confound.

The first part of these remarks has related to poetry in its elements and principles; and it has been shown, as well as the narrow limits assigned them would permit, that what is called poetry, in a restricted sense, has a common source with all other forms of order and of beauty, according to which the materials of human life are susceptible 1080 of being arranged, and which is poetry in an universal sense.

The second part will have for its object an application of these principles to the present state of the cultivation of poetry and a defence of the attempt to idealize the modern forms of manners and opinions, and compel them into a subordination to the imaginative and creative faculty. For the literature of England, an energetic development of which has ever preceded or accompanied a great and free development of the national will, has arisen as it were from a new birth. In spite of the low-thoughted envy which would undervalue contemporary merit, our own will be a memorable age 1090 in intellectual achievements, and we live among such philosophers and poets as surpass beyond comparison any who have appeared since the last national struggle for civil and religious liberty. The most unfailing herald, companion, and follower of the awakening of a great people to work a beneficial change in opinion or institution, is poetry. At such periods there is an accumulation of the power of communicating and receiving intense and impassioned conceptions respecting man and nature. The persons in whom this power resides may often, as far as regards many portions of their nature, have little apparent correspondence with that spirit of good of which they are 1100 the ministers. But even while they deny and abjure, they are yet compelled to serve, the power which is seated upon the throne of their own soul. It is impossible to read the compositions of the most celebrated writers of the present day without being startled with the electric life which burns within their words. They measure the circumference and sound the depths of human nature with a comprehensive and all-penetrating spirit, and they are themselves

232

perhaps the most sincerely astonished at its manifestations; for it is less their spirit than the spirit of the age. Poets are the hierophants of an unapprehended inspiration; the mirrors of the gigantic shadows   1110 which futurity casts upon the present; the words which express what they understand not; the trumpets which sing to battle and feel not what they inspire; the influence which is moved not, but moves. Poets are the unacknowledged legislators of the world.

Composed 1821
First published 1840

Critical commentary

Shelley's reputation has undergone major alterations in the period between his lifetime and now. While he was alive he was judged as much on the notoriety of his way of life and rumours about him as on the evidence provided by his then published work (only a proportion of what is available to us). His literary notoriety was provoked by three works: *The Necessity of Atheism*, *Queen Mab* and *The Cenci*. In 1811 Shelley with his collaborator T. J. Hogg was sent down from Oxford for issuing his pamphlet, *The Necessity of Atheism*, which challenged the authorities in the university and the bishops of the Church of England to prove the existence of God. In 1813 *Queen Mab* was printed without his name on the title page and distributed to sympathetic persons; Shelley realised that the poem, with its long prose notes attacking the monarchy, armies, the social order, religion and meat-eating, was dangerously radical. Later, in 1821, when a pirated edition appeared without his consent, he denounced the quality of the writing and its didactic weakness: 'It is villainous trash; and I dare say much better fitted to injure than to serve the cause which it advocates.' None the less, the poem came to enjoy enormous success in radical political circles and was reprinted at least fourteen times before 1840, by which time it had attained its status as 'the Chartists' Bible'. Shelley hoped that his play, *The Cenci*, would be produced at the Theatre Royal, Covent Garden in 1820 but it was to remain unperformed until 1886. Throughout the nineteenth century it could not have eluded the censorship laws; it challenged too many taboo subjects in its handling of incest and its identification of evil and corruption in Count Cenci with the father, the Pope and the Christian God: a triumvirate of paternal authorities. After its 'private' performance in 1886 organized by the Shelley Society for an audience of 2,400 in Islington, the play was staged in France, Germany, Russia and Czechoslovakia and London (1922) before Antonin Artaud's historic production in Paris in 1935 to launch his Theatre of Cruelty.

Alongside his moral reputation as, to quote the anonymous reviewer of *Adonais* in 1821, one of the 'notorious libellers, exiled adulterers and avowed atheists', Shelley was credited with a considerable lyric gift and it was probably this aspect that led Wordsworth to opine, 'Shelley was one of the best *artists* of us all: I mean in workmanship of style.' In 1861, Palgrave's *Golden Treasury*, the most influential and reprinted anthology over the following century, granted Shelley a special prominence for his short poems; concurrently he emerged as a prime example of the Romantic genius – inspired, impassioned, rhapsodic, impractical. In a lecture in 1865, Matthew Arnold pronounced, 'It always seemed to me that the right medium for Shelley's genius would be the sphere of music, not of poetry; the medium of sounds he can master, but to master the more difficult medium of words he has neither intellectual force enough nor sanity enough.' Many readers, and the habit still continues, did not bother to read through the body of poetry and prose, accepting instead Arnold's description of him as 'a beautiful and ineffectual angel, beating in the void his luminous wings in vain'. Between the 1930s and 1950s this concentration on the short lyrics persisted in the New Critics, who devalued them for what they saw as a lack of complexity, an embarrassing blurting quality, a lack of ironic self-awareness. T. S. Eliot, despite his declaring a growing admiration for *The Triumph of Life*, deemed Shelley to be a poet suited to juvenile tastes; F. R. Leavis in 1936 savaged him in an intellectually unscrupulous way, and, for a generation, Shelley was dismissed by many British academics as poetically vulgar and inadequate.

For Shelley himself his short lyrics were often occasional or even private pieces, often left in an unfinished condition, and he and Mary Shelley over and over again stressed his view of himself as a poet of ideas whose ambitions can best be seen in his longer poems. In an essay in 1856, Walter Bagehot identified 'the peculiarity of his style' as its 'intellectuality' and he contrasted him with Byron: 'As it was the instinct of Byron to give in glaring words the gross phenomena of evident objects, so it was that of Shelley to refine the most inscrutable with the curious nicety of an attenuating metaphysician.' It was Yeats, however, with his interest in myth and symbolism, who at the turn of the century discussed Shelley most openly in terms of his recurring images, his symbology and his whole scheme of thought. For Yeats, *Prometheus Unbound* was one of the world's sacred books and in his regard for *Alastor*, *The Witch of Atlas* and *The Triumph of Life* he anticipated the notion of quest which is so central to more recent commentators such as Harold Bloom, Peter Butter, M. H. Abrams and Earl Wasserman. Since the Second World War, critics have taken Shelley's reading in philosophers and scientists much more seriously and even Donald Davie, so negative to much of the poetry, allowed in a hugely influential essay 'Shelley's Urbanity' (1952) that the poet had a sophisticated mind, trained in thinking and literary modes.

Karl Marx saw Shelley as one of the main inspirations to the Chartist movement and through that to the development of socialist thinking in Britain. George Bernard Shaw, who was a founding member of the Fabian Society, in 1884 acknowledged Shelley's influence (to the extent, among other things, of becoming a vegetarian). Notwithstanding this tradition of reading Shelley among radical politicians, the political content of his poetry (and prose) was not given much prominence in the writings of academic critics until fairly recently. Leavis did praise *The Mask of Anarchy*, and gradually the satirical and comical as well as the solemn poems have come to be properly appreciated. Although Paul Foot in his very partial *Red Shelley* (1980) exaggerates his own newness of approach, his book is certainly part of an attempt to see Shelley whole. Since the publication of *Shelley's Prose*, edited by David Lee Clark, in 1954 and *The Letters of Percy Bysshe Shelley*, edited by Frederic L. Jones, in 1964, and considerable work on the text over the past twenty years, it has been easier to have a fuller view of him.

Possibly the very assertiveness and didacticism which earlier appealed to some readers and repelled others have now attracted the attention of some deconstructionist critics who have detected an ambivalence in Shelley's rhetoric. The poems, under their examination, emerge as less categorical and more subtle processes of thought; aspects of Shelley's own thinking about language support this approach where words lack a stability and leave themselves available to a variety of responses. Language, according to Shelley, is endlessly coloured by the assumptions and training of the user. In a letter to Leigh Hunt in 1819 he writes about his choice of language in his poem *Julian and Maddalo*:

I have employed a certain familiar style of language to express the actual way in which people talk with each other whom education and a certain refinement of sentiment have placed above the use of vulgar idioms. I use the word *vulgar* in its most extensive sense; the vulgarity of rank and

237

fashion is as gross in its way as that of Poverty, and its cant terms equally expressive of bare conceptions, and therefore equally unfit for Poetry.

SHELLEY'S VIEW OF THE POET

The foundation of Shelley's ambition as a poet was moral. In the Dedication to *The Revolt of Islam* he writes of his spiritual coming-of-age:

> I do remember well the hour which burst
>   My spirit's sleep: a fresh May-dawn it was,
>   When I walked forth upon the glittering grass,
> And wept, I knew not why; until there rose
>   From the near schoolroom, voices, that, alas!
> Were but one echo from a world of woes –
> The harsh and grating strife of tyrants and of foes.
>
> And then I clasped my hands and looked around –
>   – But none was near to mock my streaming eyes,
> Which poured their warm drops on the sunny ground –
>   So, without shame, I spake: – 'I will be wise,
>   And just, and free, and mild, if in me lies
> Such power, for I grow weary to behold
>   The selfish and the strong still tyrannise
> Without reproach or check.' I then controlled
> My tears, my heart grew calm, and I was meek and bold.
>
> And from that hour did I with earnest thought
>   Heap knowledge from forbidden mines of lore,
> Yet nothing that my tyrants knew or taught
>   I cared to learn, but from that secret store
>   Wrought linked armour to my soul, before
> It might walk forth to war among mankind.

Notwithstanding the extravagant religious tone of this conversion and his commitment to a holy war, the experience he had at Eton announced a programme he was to set himself and for which poetry was to be his chosen instrument. In the Preface to the same poem he explains his use of poetry:

I have sought to enlist the harmony of metrical language, the ethereal combinations of the fancy, the rapid and subtle transitions of human passion, all those elements which essentially compose a Poem, in the cause of a liberal and comprehensive morality; and in the view of kindling within the bosoms of my readers a virtuous enthusiasm for those doctrines of liberty and justice, that faith and hope in something good, which neither violence nor misrepresentation nor prejudice can ever totally extinguish among mankind.

Of course, this is not to say that all of his poetry is programmatic, designed to persuade the reader to accept a scheme of thought. In the Preface to *Prometheus Unbound* he appears to contradict himself within four sentences when he acknowledges that he has 'a passion for reforming the world' but declares that 'Didactic poetry is my abhorrence; nothing can be equally well expressed in prose that is not tedious and supererogatory in verse.'

So what, for Shelley, is the particular moral force of poetry? His central attempt to answer the question is 'A Defence of Poetry', and one of the strongest statements in the essay declares:

The great secret of morals is love; or a going out of our own nature, and an identification of ourselves with the beautiful which exists in thought, action, or person, not our own. A man, to be greatly good, must imagine intensely and comprehensively; he must put himself in the place of another and of many others; the pains and pleasures of his species must become his own. The great instrument of moral good is the imagination; and poetry administers to the effect by acting upon the cause. Poetry enlarges the circumference of the imagination by replenishing it with thoughts of ever new delight, which have the power of attracting and assimilating to their own nature all other thoughts, and which form new intervals and interstices whose void forever craves fresh food.

These sentences have a syllogistic linkage which makes them sound plausible, but how persuasive is the line of argument? As is often the case with Shelley, we are asked to take on trust some very large words – 'love', 'imagination' and 'poetry', for example – although, to be fair to him, he does expand on these notions throughout his essay. Even though he mentions 'pains', he seems to see poetry more in terms of delight. Would a test of his argument be to compare the conduct of regular readers of poetry with the conduct of people who do not read poetry? Shelley does not suggest that poetry (or the reading of poetry) is the only means to moral behaviour. What he is trying to do is defend poetry against a charge that it is irrelevant to morality or even inimical to it. He argues that we can behave well to other people only by imagining their situation and feelings and differences from ourselves, and acting on that knowledge of other people. He does not seek to limit poetry to the fictional presentation of human situations with which the reader can sympathize; rather, he wants poetry to enlarge the reader's capacity to feel and think beyond his or her immediate circumstances. To see a stone, to feel the stirrings of the spring in a landscape through words, can, he believed, 'strengthen that faculty' of the imagination in the reader as well as can stories of human behaviour.

In 'A Defence of Poetry' and elsewhere, a connection is argued between periods of political and moral maturity and phases of artistic activity in the history of societies. Shelley's evidence, unfortunately, is somewhat partial, although he does succeed in showing an interconnectedness between some of the Greek writers, Dante, Shakespeare and Milton and some aspects of their respective societies. His intention to demonstrate the greatness of contemporary writing was not fulfilled, and the 'Defence' remained unfinished at his death; nevertheless, the final paragraph does triumphantly extol the power of writers in progressive change. His claim that 'Poets are the unacknowledged legislators of the world', a claim dismissed by W. H. Auden as nonsensical, rests on his view that the imaginative mind has a barometric sensitivity to incipient changes in its society, such that it appears to anticipate or even create these changes.

The old question whether poets are born or made Shelley sees as a vexed one. In the Preface to *The Revolt of Islam* he writes about his own training, remarking that 'There is an education peculiarly fitted for a Poet, without which genius and sensibility hardly fill the circle of their capacities.' However, after itemizing his own educative processes, he declares: 'Yet the experience and the feelings to which I refer do not in themselves constitute men Poets', for which they must 'possess that more essential attribute of Poetry, the power of awakening in others sensations like those which animate my own bosom'. This power is a linguistic one but, again, Shelley is not altogether confident of language's ability to convey sensations from one person to another. His doubts go deeper in that he is unsure of the stability of the person as an entity:

The words *I*, *you*, *they*, are not signs of any actual difference subsisting between the assemblage of thoughts thus indicated, but are merely marks employed to denote the different modifications of the one mind . . . grammatical devices invented simply for arrangement, and totally devoid of the intense and exclusive sense usually attached to them. . . . We are on that verge where words abandon us, and what wonder if we grow dizzy to look down the dark abyss of how little we know.

These sentiments in the essay 'On Life' are echoed in Demogorgon's statement in *Prometheus Unbound*: 'The deep truth is imageless.' None the less, for Shelley language has an advantage over other instruments of expression in that it is a 'more direct representation of the actions and passions of our internal being . . . for language is arbitrarily produced by the imagination and has relation to thoughts alone.' How this 'internal being' and the 'thoughts' relate to the world outside the mind is a difficult and ultimately, for Shelley, unanswerable question.

What is meant by 'inspiration' is also a mystery, but of its occurrence Shelley has no doubts. The terms he uses to describe the creative process are of a vehicle or instrument for a superior force; he speaks of a coal being set alight, of seeds being propagated, of musical instruments being played on, of mirrors being filled with images. Often, for example in 'Mont Blanc', 'Hymn to Intellectual Beauty', 'Ode to the West Wind', 'To a Skylark', *The Witch of Atlas* and *Adonais*, inspiration is associated with the divine and the language used by Shelley is derived from religion. In fact, poetry for him seems to operate as a substitute for a discredited religion; the snag is that this divinity touches mankind, including the poet, in an inconstant way and it cannot be summoned. His claim that the poet is the main channel for this enlightenment and beneficence again emphasizes the central, prophetic role of the poet in society. At the same time, this singular quality sets the poet apart from his society, 'a nightingale who sits in darkness and sings to cheer his own solitude with sweet sounds', and, as happened with the prophets in the Old Testament, he may be disregarded or treated as a madman or outcast by the society. Certainly, in the reactionary climate of his time, Shelley saw the true poet as antagonistic and seditious to the orthodoxies of the establishment.

STYLE IN THE POETRY

In 'A Defence of Poetry', while arguing that 'the distinction between poets and prose writers is a vulgar error', Shelley insists on the inseparability of form and content, sound and sense:

241

Sounds as well as thoughts have relation both between each other and towards that which they represent, and a perception of the order of those relations has always been found connected with a perception of the order of the relation of thoughts. Hence the language of poets has ever affected a certain uniform and harmonious recurrence of sound, without which it were not poetry, and which is scarcely less indispensable to the communication of its influence than the words themselves, without reference to that peculiar order.

In his ordering of metre and verse forms, he is one of the most versatile of all English poets, and a listing of his poetic types would include narratives, dramas, lyrics, satires, parodies, elegies, sonnets, odes, allegories, verse letters, meditative poems and ballads.

Too often critics have categorized the voice of Shelley's poetry as shrilly rhapsodic and nothing else. It is true, of course, that he has a facility for a high-flown rhetoric which can sound like the 'harmonious madness' he longs for in 'To a Skylark'. Characteristic of this rhetoric are images of height and light and an exclamatory excitement. One example from *Prometheus Unbound* will suffice:

> Thou art folded, thou art lying
> In the light which is undying
> Of thine own joy, and heaven's smile divine;
> All suns and constellations shower
> On thee a light, a life, a power
> Which doth array thy sphere; thou pourest thine
> On mine, on mine!

(Act IV, ll. 437–43)

There is something in the accumulation of undefined abstract terms which is, particularly to late twentieth-century ears, deeply suspect and even meretricious. The New Critics certainly felt that they had succeeded in discrediting such poetry, but it may be that the reader has to learn to apprehend it not as irrational or meaningless but as a fierce striving at the very edge of comprehensibility to say something very difficult. Shelley was well aware that language has to be endlessly renewed and that his own writing could seem, in T. S. Eliot's phrase, 'A periphrastic study in a worn-out poetical fashion'. He did experiment with very different voices, very different registers.

Some of his most extreme experiments are not included in this selection, and his attempts at stageable plays are not represented. The dramatis personae of *Oedipus Tyrannus or Swellfoot the Tyrant* includes a Gadfly, a Leech and a Rat, and a rabble of Pigs who are transformed into Bulls in the final scene; these characters speak a language appropriate to their animal nature. Mimicking the structure of a Greek tragedy, it is a painful farce based on contemporary political events and written with an extravagance worthy of Monty Python. In the Preface to *The Cenci*, Shelley outlines his ambition to devise a dramatically appropriate language:

> I have avoided with great care in writing this play the introduction of what is commonly called mere poetry. . . . In a dramatic composition the imagery and the passion should interpenetrate one another, the former being reserved simply for the full development and illustration of the latter. . . . In other respects, I have written more carelessly; that is, without an over-fastidious and learned choice of words. In this respect I entirely agree with those modern critics who assert that in order to move men to true sympathy we must use the familiar language of men. . . . But it must be the real language of men in general and not that of any particular class to whose society the writer happens to belong.

This extension of Wordsworth's pronouncement on language in the Preface to *Lyrical Ballads* is demonstrated in a significant number of Shelley's poems.

The opening forty lines of *Julian and Maddalo* and the whole of 'Letter to Maria Gisborne' are two of the best examples of his plain style. In *Peter Bell the Third* there are sudden and shocking shifts of register; the first excerpt from the poem included in this selection shows Shelley's ability to use colloquialism and the terms of a specific time to give sharpness to his satirical attack. Many of the lyrics written in his final two years have a casual, unforced poise indicative of his ability to adopt different voices. 'The Boat on the Serchio' accommodates description, narration and dialogue with apparent ease:

> 'Ay, heave the ballast overboard,
> And stow the eatables in the aft locker.'
> 'Would not this keg be best a little lowered?'
> 'No, now all's right.' 'Those bottles of warm tea –
> (Give me some straw) – must be stowed tenderly;
> Such as we used, in summer after six,

To cram in greatcoat pockets, and to mix
Hard eggs and radishes and rolls at Eton,
And couched on stolen hay in those green harbours
Farmers called gaps, and we schoolboys arbours,
Would feast till eight.'

These lines could be mistaken for a passage from Browning, the great master of colloquial speech in poetry.

Much of the poetry, of course, is not markedly rhapsodic or markedly plain: these are extremes of style; the point argued above is that Shelley developed a plain style to a degree often ignored by commentators on his work. A similar serviceable mode of writing is apparent in his political pieces. What, however, in the variety of his poetry are the striking characteristics of his style?

In a letter to Shelley in August 1820, Keats urged him to 'curb your magnanimity, and be more of an artist, and load every rift of your subject with ore'; he felt that Shelley lacked 'self-concentration'. What Keats (and many later critics) took exception to is precisely what has given pleasure to other readers: a rushing, metrical prodigality of phrase and image, sweeping readers on but leaving them dizzy and unsure of their own or the poet's control. From the juvenilia to *The Triumph of Life* this hectic tendency is apparent, although the poet's mastery in the later poetry is much more obvious. It is quite possible to analyse the ingredients of this speed and see how in particular passages he exploits verse forms, syntax, repetitions of sound, linkings of imagery, enjambment and words suggesting movement; the opening stanza of 'Ode to the West Wind' provides an example. Often the rapidity in the verse has been taken as indicative of the way in which, according to reports, Shelley composed. In *Records of Shelley, Byron and the Author*, Trelawny quotes the poet: 'When my brain gets heated with thought, it soon boils and throws off images and words faster than I can skim them off. In the morning, when cooled down, out of the rude sketch, as you justly call it, I shall attempt a drawing.' If the manuscripts of the first drafts, the 'rude sketch', are examined, it does, indeed, appear as if he composed at great speed, as if there was a tune already in his head but he could not immediately find words to fit all the notes. However, as he suggests, he revised carefully and the poems he sent for publication often had gone through many drafts. Therefore, in poems as different as *Prometheus Unbound* and 'To a Skylark', if we sense an impetuous flow or 'profuse strains of unpremeditated art', we can be sure that Shelley worked hard to achieve that effect.

The frequency of a sensation of speed is related to other aspects of his style which in turn indicate Shelley's modes of thinking. His style is seldom aphoristic and his lines do lack the 'self-concentration' advocated by Keats. He favours simile rather than metaphor for the most part and offers likenesses rather than assertions. Often a single simile seems inadequate and he uses a series of resemblances, as in the opening stanza of 'Hymn to Intellectual Beauty' and in lines 31–55 of 'Ode to a Skylark'. What he is trying to do is to define an obscure or difficult entity in terms of approximations, stabs from different angles, sweeps which overlap with each other, and in the area of overlap lies the entity. Everything of importance to him resists a simple or single formulation. Furthermore, the distinction commonly granted to our different senses is unacceptable to him and, according to him, the world is apprehended synaesthetically. Sensations gained through the senses mingle, blur, overlap with one another so that a colour is heard and a sound is tasted. Lines 86–93 of 'The Sensitive Plant' illustrate the phenomenon:

> The unseen clouds of the dew, which lie
> Like fire in the flowers till the sun rides high,
> Then wander like spirits among the spheres,
> Each cloud faint with the fragrance it bears;
>
> The quivering vapours of dim noontide,
> Which like a sea o'er the warm earth glide,
> In which every sound, and odour, and beam,
> Move, as reeds in a single stream.

Although the senses are so involved in such a description, there is, as so often in Shelley, an intangible quality which makes us unsure of the physicality of what is described. It is not just that the senses blur, but also that the ordinary dividing line between the physical and the mental melts or proves unreliable:

> I saw not, heard not, moved not, only felt
> His presence flow and mingle through my blood
> Till it became his life, and his grew mine,
> And I was thus absorbed, until it passed,
> And like the vapours when the sun sinks down,
> Gathering again in drops upon the pines,
> And tremulous as they, in the deep night

My being was condensed; and as the rays
Of thought were slowly gathered, I could hear
His voice, whose accents lingered ere they died
Like footsteps of weak melody: thy name
Among the many sounds alone I heard
Of what might be articulate; though still
I listened through the night when sound was none.

(Prometheus Unbound, II.i.79–92)

Admittedly, this passage describes a dream, a vision of illumination, but the poetic method is very typical of Shelley, in whose mind the earthly and the spiritual, the negative and the positive, the articulate and the inarticulate coexist and jostle with each other.

It would be wrong to suggest that he is incapable of writing straight-forwardly about the physical world. There are, throughout the poems, wonderful passages of observation. Carl Grabo's *A Newton among Poets* (1930) and *Shelley: His Thought and Work* (1960) by Desmond King-Hele, himself a scientist, are only two of the books which emphasize the scientific accuracy of many of Shelley's descriptions of meteorological and chemical events. Even 'The Cloud', with all its verbal dexterity and mischievous fancy is, for its time, a reliable description of the behaviour of clouds. The main source of his imagery is the natural world and, particularly in the late lyrics and *The Triumph of Life*, there are striking evocations of place and weather and natural life.

THOUGHT IN SHELLEY

Throughout his adult life, Shelley detested organized religion. He saw the gods of religion as created by societies, as reflections of the worst aspects of humankind:

Barbarous and uncivilized nations have uniformly adored under various names a god of which themselves were the model: revengeful, blood-thirsty, grovelling and capricious. The idol of a savage is a demon that delights in carnage. The steam of slaughter, the dissonance of groans, the flames of a desolated land are the offerings which he deems acceptable, and his innumerable votaries throughout the world have made it a point of duty to worship him to his taste. The Phoenicians, the Druids, and the Mexicans have immolated hundreds at the shrines of their divinity, and the high and holy name of God has been in all ages the watchword of the most unsparing massacres, the sanction of the most atrocious perfidies.

This denunciation by Theosophus in *A Refutation of Deism* (printed 1814) voices Shelley's own view, and modern societies have not shown much improvement. On the other hand, the poet did not deny the probable existence of a force, a spirit, beyond or behind the material universe; but such a force may not be comprehended or characterized by human beings. In a rather Nietzschean affirmation, Shelley even suggests that we can become the God:

> Whosoever is no deceiver or destroyer of his fellow men – no liar, no flatterer, no murderer – may walk among his species, deriving from the communion with all which they contain of beautiful or majestic, some intercourse with the Universal God. Whoever has maintained with his own heart the strictest correspondence of confidence, who dares to examine and to estimate every imagination which suggests itself to his mind, who is that which he designs to become, and only aspires to that which the divinity of his own nature shall consider and approve – he has already seen God. We live and move and think, but we are not the creators of our own origin and existence; we are not the arbiters of every notion of our own complicated nature; we are not the masters of our own imaginations and moods of mental being. There is a Power by which we are surrounded. . . . This Power is God.
>
> ('Essay on Christianity' undated)

The most sustained attack on religion in his poetry is in sections VI and VII of *Queen Mab*.

It has often been claimed that Shelley had an inadequate theory of evil. Certainly, evidence can be found in the earlier works to support the view that he saw evil as an illusion or delusion or mistake which could be rectified by rational thought and that he supported Godwin's belief in the perfectibility of mankind. In her 'Note on *Prometheus Unbound*' (written 1839), Mary Shelley claims:

> The prominent feature of Shelley's theory of the destiny of the human species was that evil is not inherent in the system of the creation, but an accident that might be expelled . . . mankind had only to will that there should be no evil, and there would be none. That man could be

perfectionized as to be able to expel evil from his own nature, and from the greater part of the creation, was the cardinal point of his system.

Corroboration for this claim can be found in the words of Julian (usually taken to represent Shelley) in lines 161–91 of *Julian and Maddalo*. However, what actually happens in *Julian and Maddalo* and *Prometheus Unbound* does not allow the acceptance of such a tidy and glib procedure. In neither case is evil, the source of suffering, shown as something so easy to identify or so easy to eradicate. In the former poem, the ending and the madman's utterance are densely enigmatic and there is no happy conclusion. In the latter poem, Asia's attempt in Act II (see extract) to ascertain the basis of evil is not clearly answered, and Prometheus's victory over what Jupiter represents is presented in Demogorgon's concluding speech as an example hedged about with conditions for the future. Shelley concedes in a note to *Hellas*, written in the year before his death: 'Let it not be supposed that I mean to dogmatize upon a subject, concerning which all men are equally ignorant, or that I think the Gordian knot of the origin of evil can be disentangled by that or any similar assertions.' He was aware that beyond the schemes and devices of individuals and societies there are constraining forces. Sometimes his term for these forces is Necessity, and Demogorgon in *Prometheus Unbound* appears to be its agent; in his final, incomplete poem he bleakly suggests that only Socrates and Jesus have been able to withstand the crushing power of Life.

The interplay of the personal and the impersonal, the internal and the external, the conscious and the unconscious, runs through most of his poetry. Dreams feature prominently and it is not surprising that poems as different from each other as *The Mask of Anarchy* and *The Triumph of Life* should both take the form of visions. The opening section of 'Mont Blanc' is symptomatic of Shelley's perplexity, and the poem opens up the problem:

> and when I gaze on thee [the Ravine of Arve]
> I seem as in a trance sublime and strange
> To muse on my own separate phantasy,
> My own, my human mind, which passively
> Now renders and receives fast influencings,
> Holding an unremitting interchange
> With the clear universe of things around.

The maziness of these lines compounds rather than resolves a problem which has been one of the main subjects of poets between Wordsworth and Wallace Stevens. Operating with an elaborate symbology of caverns, rivers, journeys, natural and cosmic cycles, Shelley explores the nature of the self. Often this symbolic pattern allows for several interpretations of a poem such as *Alastor*; and *Prometheus Unbound* or the 'Ode to the West Wind' can be read in a psychological, a political and a metaphysical way. The ability to create and manipulate symbols is a manifestation of the faculty of the imagination to which he gives such a significance. It is through the imagination, according to Shelley, that we achieve our humanity and our liberation: it allows us to envisage possibilities and aspire beyond the limitations of our present situation.

For Shelley as an individual, the principal means by which the self is transcended is love for another person, and, in his case, a woman. The poet figure in *Alastor* is visited in a dream by a woman who talks to him, and 'Her voice was like the voice of his own soul / Heard in the calm of thought.' This paragon of his imagination is unattainable in actual life, as she is in the poem, where the poet figure dies in self-pitying misery. There is a deep ambivalence in Shelley towards the female characters he creates in poems. Women figure prominently in most of his major poems. In *The Revolt of Islam*, *Prometheus Unbound*, *The Mask of Anarchy* and *The Cenci* they feature as leaders or instigators and he appears to grant them a special role in effecting change in society. None the less, he also shows a tendency to devise women so extraordinary that they can be admired only from afar and thus remain safely out of reach of the male. Is this a devious mechanism of self-defence? In a letter to John Gisborne written one month before he drowned, he writes dismissively about his autobiographical poem, *Epipsychidion*, and concludes: 'It is an idealized history of my life and feelings. I think one is always in love with something or other; the error, and I confess it is not easy for spirits cased in flesh and blood to avoid it, consists in seeking in a mortal image the likeness of what is perhaps eternal.' Although his poetry reveals a painful understanding of the dangers of narcissism, his imagination continued to contrive women who were projections of the very self he hoped to transcend.

Although he died young, he was in no way an inexperienced or ignorant man. He had seen the ravages of war, he followed with interest the public events of his time, he had seen poverty and brutality and prejudice, and he had experienced love and happiness. As he grew older, the world came to appear more tragically paradoxical, and in a letter to Mary in August 1821 he confesses that 'good far more than evil impulses – love far more than hatred – has been to me, except as you have been its object, the source of all sorts of mischief.' The climax of the Furies' assault on Prometheus comes in these lines:

> The good want power, but to weep barren tears;
> The powerful goodness want: worse need for them.
> The wise want love; and those who love want wisdom;
> And all best things are thus confused to ill.
> Many are strong and rich, – and would be just –
> But live among their suffering fellow men
> As if none felt: they know not what they do.

> (Act I, ll. 625–31)

The words in the final line derive from Jesus' forgiveness of his crucifiers, and the whole passage was borrowed by Yeats in his poem 'The Second Coming': it is a classic statement of the impotence felt by a progressive liberal who lacks a doctrinaire policy of action. For Shelley, the problem was specially burdensome because he could not see life in compartments. With an ambition which anticipates Gramsci's notion of hegemony, he saw as inadequate or even dangerous anything less than a total realignment of the mentality of a whole people. He chose to write visionary poems in which a process of transformation is imaged but which he knew could not be realised in the actuality of his own time. *Prometheus Unbound* serves as a model of, and inspiration towards, the regeneration of humanity. *The Revolt of Islam* and *Adonais* are both elegies for the sacrifice involved in trying to better the world, and both end with a consolatory concept that the struggle is not in vain but feeds cumulatively into a spiritual reservoir (like Blake's Golgonooza) on which future generations can draw.

What about the sharp end of political action? No writer of his time denounced corruption, inequality, hypocrisy and cruelty more fiercely than Shelley and, in the short term, he felt that much could be improved immediately if there was a will for change:

> We have more moral, political, and historical wisdom than we know how to reduce into practice; we have more scientific and economic knowledge than can be accommodated to the just distribution of the produce which it multiplies. . . . The cultivation of those sciences which have enlarged the limits of the empire of man over the external world has, for want of the poetical faculty, proportionally circumscribed those

of the internal world; and man, having enslaved the elements, remains himself a slave.

These thoughts in 'A Defence of Poetry' are repeated elsewhere, but he saw two major obstacles to quick and peaceful reform. First, those with power and inherited privilege would agree to share their wealth only if such a redistribution was to their advantage or if they had no choice. Second, the unprivileged who had been exploited and brutalized for so long could not drop their habits of bitterness, envy and a wish for revenge at the mere declaration of reform. What Shelley analysed was a deepening class antagonism and he had to face the probability that real reform could happen only through violent revolution:

> This is the age of the war of the oppressed against the oppressors, and every one of those ringleaders of the privileged gangs of murderers and swindlers, called Sovereigns, look to each other for aid against the common enemy, and suspend their mutual jealousies in the presence of a mightier fear. . . . But a new race has arisen throughout Europe, nursed in the abhorrence of the opinions which are its chains, and she will continue to produce fresh generations to accomplish that destiny which tyrants foresee and dread.

His publisher suppressed this paragraph from the Preface to *Hellas* when the poem was printed in 1822. In the final paragraphs of *A Philosophical View of Reform*, Shelley reluctantly concedes that 'The last resort of resistance is undoubtedly insurrection', but for a passionate vegetarian and a pacifist this was not a prospect that he could welcome. However, in his poems most specifically concerned with political revolution, *The Revolt of Islam* and *The Mask of Anarchy*, there is a measure of violence on the side of the oppressed and the imagery often suggests violence: 'Rise like lions after slumber.'

Despite his early campaigning in Ireland, some behaviour and associations deemed provocative by the authorities in England, and the shocking effect of some of his publications, Shelley did not see his involvement in revolutionary politics as that of an activist but in terms of raising consciousness and in pushing back the limits of ignorance, prejudice and custom that we unimaginatively accept as fixed. The deepest subservience, he claims, is when the slave accepts the master's definition as natural. In the play *The Cenci* Beatrice, an idealistic girl, is broken by her father's brutal rape into using violence against him. Beatrice, according to Shelley, is a tragic figure not because she is degraded by an incestuous rape but because she resorts, against her ideals, to deceit and violence: she accepts her father's corruption as the way the world is. With the Pope and God (according to the Church) on her father's side, what chance does she have? Shelley felt that some hope has to be rescued from the direst circumstances; otherwise, there is no possibility of change and progress.

Bibliography

BIOGRAPHY AND BACKGROUND

Brailsford, H. N., *Shelley, Godwin and their Circle*, London, Oxford University Press, 1913.

Holmes, R., *Shelley: The Pursuit*, London, Weidenfeld & Nicolson, 1974.

St Clair, W., *The Godwins and the Shelleys*, London, Faber, 1989.

Thompson, E. P., *The Making of the English Working Class*, London, Gollancz, 1963.

Tomalin, C., *Shelley and his World*, London, Thames & Hudson, 1980.

Trelawny, E. J., *Records of Shelley, Byron and the Author* (1878), ed. David Wright, Harmondsworth, Penguin, 1973.

White, N. I., *Shelley*, 2 vols, New York, Knopf, 1940.

CRITICISM

Abrams, M. H., *Natural Supernaturalism: Tradition and Revolution in Romantic Literature*, London, Oxford University Press, 1971.

Baker, C., *Shelley's Major Poetry: The Fabric of a Vision*, Princeton, NJ, Princeton University Press, 1948.

Barcus, J. E., *Shelley: The Critical Heritage*, London, Routledge & Kegan Paul, 1975.

Bloom, H., *Shelley's Mythmaking*, New Haven, Conn., Yale University Press, 1959.

Bloom, H. (ed.), *Deconstruction and Criticism*, London, Routledge & Kegan Paul, 1979.

Butter, P., *Shelley's Idols of the Cave*, Edinburgh, Edinburgh University Press, 1954.

Cameron, K. N., *The Young Shelley: Genesis of a Radical*, New York, Collier, 1962.

——*Shelley: The Golden Years*, Cambridge, Mass., Harvard University Press, 1974.

Chernaik, J., *The Lyrics of Shelley*, Cleveland, Ohio, Case Western Reserve University Press, 1972.

Cronin, R., *Shelley's Poetic Thoughts*, London, Macmillan, 1981.

Dawson, P. M. S., *The Unacknowledged Legislator: Shelley and Politics*, Oxford, Clarendon Press, 1980.

Everest, K. (ed.), *Shelley Revalued: Essays from the Gregynog Conference*, Leicester, Leicester University Press, 1983.

Foot, P., *Red Shelley*, London, Sidgwick & Jackson, 1980.

Grabo, C., *A Newton among Poets*, Chapel Hill, University of North Carolina Press, 1930.

Hodgart, P., *A Preface to Shelley*, London, Longman, 1985.

Keach, W., *Shelley's Style*, London, Methuen, 1984.

King-Hele, D., *Shelley: His Thought and Work*, London, Macmillan, 1960.

Leighton, A., *Shelley and the Sublime*, Cambridge, Cambridge University Press, 1984.

Notopoulos, J. A., *The Platonism of Shelley: A Study of Platonism and the Poetic Mind*, Durham, NC, Duke University Press, 1949.

Pulos, C. E., *The Deep Truth: A Study of Shelley's Scepticism*, Lincoln, University of Nebraska Press, 1954.

Ridenour, G. M. (ed.), *Shelley: A Collection of Critical Essays*, Englewood Cliffs, NJ, Prentice-Hall, 1965.

Swinden, P. (ed.), *Shelley: Shorter Poems and Lyrics*, London, Macmillan, 1976.

Wasserman, E. R., *Shelley: A Critical Reading*, Baltimore, Md, Johns Hopkins University Press, 1971.

Webb, T., *Shelley: A Voice Not Understood*, Manchester, Manchester University Press, 1977.

Woodings, R. B. (ed.), *Shelley: Modern Judgements*, London, Macmillan, 1968.

Yeats, W. B., *Essays and Introductions*, London, Macmillan, 1961.

Notes

MUTABILITY

Published with *Alastor*, this is an early treatment by Shelley of one of the most persistent, conventional subjects in poetry. For human beings, according to the poem, everything is changeable, subject to the forces of Necessity.

5–8   The Aeolian lyre (or harp or lute) is a stringed instrument which, when placed in a position exposed to the wind, emits sounds which can be interpreted as the random harmonies of Nature. Aeolus was the Greek god of wind.

TO WORDSWORTH

A sonnet with an unusual rhyme scheme. Shelley felt strong admiration for Wordsworth's earlier poetry but he came to disapprove of Wordsworth's political position, a position reflected in the later poetry. In 1813 Wordsworth accepted a well-paid job from the reactionary government and Shelley saw this acceptance as a betrayal of the principles Wordsworth had held at the beginning of the French Revolution.

HYMN TO INTELLECTUAL BEAUTY

This poem and 'Mont Blanc' were written in Switzerland in the summer of 1816. It is a secular hymn in praise of the spirit which he believes lies behind the visible, temporal world and which he found described in Plato's *The Symposium* (sections 209–12), a work he translated two years later. The emphasis in the poem shifts about between the spiritual, the aesthetic and the moral as if Shelley is possessed by an unfocused idealism.

25–31   Shelley dismisses a religious explanation of his experience. Compare *poisonous names* (l. 53).

84   *fear* have proper respect. Throughout the poem, Shelley subverts the traditional language of Christianity and uses it for his own purposes. In Christian terms 'the fear of the Lord is the beginning of wisdom'.

MONT BLANC

Shelley's concern is with the processes by which we perceive and can make sense of the world. The representative aspect of the geographical descriptions is indicated in the opening line of the second section. Mont Blanc, the highest mountain in Europe and first climbed in 1786, had become a subject for poets and painters, and Shelley is partly following and partly challenging this fashion of seeing the mountain reverentially. The peak (and the actual appearance of the mountain is held back in the poem till l. 61) marks the ultimate bound of human thought; the source of all phenomena and power lies beyond the peak but can the human imagination grasp or comprehend the scheme of the revealed world? See Shelley's letters to Peacock (*The Letters of Percy Bysshe Shelley*, Oxford, Clarendon Press, 1964, vol. 1, pp. 495–502) for the immediate background to the poem, and compare the poem with Coleridge's 'Hymn before Sun-rise in the Vale of Chamouni'.

Subtitle   Chamonix (*Chamouni*) is in south-east France. The River Arve runs through it into Lake Geneva. The River Rhône (see l. 123) has its source in the lake.

5   *tribute* contribution (like a tributary to a river).

27   *unsculptured image* The shape of the rock is suggestive but the image is blurred by the water.

36   *my own separate phantasy* my individual imagination.

43   *that or thou* my individual mind or the ravine representing a human consciousness and the external world.

49   *remoter world* superior dimension (Plato's realm of pure forms).

72   *Earthquake-daemon* a spirit of nature who, when the earth was being created, experimented with wild shapes. In these lines Shelley refers to different theories of how the earth took shape.

76–83   Untamed nature is open to two interpretations: the *awful doubt* (which Shelley appears to favour) emphasizes the puniness of human achievement; the *faith so mild* allows human beings a submissive place in the overall scheme of creation. *In* (l. 79) is a preferred reading over *But*, which occurs in some of the manuscripts and editions. By *the wise, and great, and good* Shelley may mean the philosophers, artists and saints who, respectively, interpret and cause others to feel and are particularly sensitive.

86   *daedal* wonderfully made.

142–4   If the human imagination could not create something out of *Silence and solitude*, the power apparent in Mont Blanc and all the forces in the external world would be meaningless to man.

OZYMANDIAS

Ozymandias was the Greek name of Rameses II (1304–1237 BC), who, according to biblical scholars of Shelley's time, was the pharaoh of Egypt who oppressed the captive Hebrews and opposed Moses' wishes to free them.

8   *hand ... heart* The hand (of the sculptor) imitated or represented the passions for power of Ozymandias and possibly included his scorn for them; the heart (of Ozymandias) encouraged the passions.

JULIAN AND MADDALO

Although the enquiry at the heart of the poem is a recurring subject in his poetry, the immediate provocation for this poem was an argument Shelley had with Byron in Venice on 23 August 1818 and the main characters, Julian and Maddalo, are based on the two poets respectively. According to the Preface, 'Count Maddalo is a Venetian nobleman. . . . He is a person of the most consummate genius. . . . But it is his weakness to be proud: he derives, from a comparison of his own extraordinary mind with the dwarfish intellects which surround him, an intense apprehension of the nothingness of human life.' And Julian 'is an Englishman of good family, passionately attached to those philosophical notions which assert the power of man over his own mind, and the immense improvements of which, by the extinction of certain moral superstitions, human society may be yet susceptible. Without concealing the evil in the world, he is for ever speculating how good may be made superior.' The example of the madman, which the two characters wish to cite in support of their optimistic or pessimistic viewpoints, is inconclusive. Has he been driven into despair and madness by his own obsession or by the cruelty of the woman and the lack of understanding in the world around him? His barely coherent torrent of passions, memories, bitternesses and aspirations makes it difficult for the reader to see his story simplistically or to take sides with Julian or Maddalo. In the end, the reader is denied an explanation and the poem closes with a juxtaposition of the tragic decline of the madman and the delightful promise of Maddalo's daughter.

2–3	*bank . . . Adria*	The Lido is a bank of land between Venice and the Adriatic Sea.
37	*raillery*	banter.
40–2		Milton in *Paradise Lost*, II, 555–61, so describes the fallen angels in Hell.
46	*descanted*	discussed at length.
50–2		The eagle, according to legend, could look into the sun and not be blinded; Maddalo (Byron) is blinded by his own self-regard.
67	*hoar*	ancient, grey.
88	*funereal bark*	Gondolas are painted black.
90	*isles*	Venice is built on a network of small islands.
163	*own*	acknowledge.
164	*teachless*	unteachable.
170–6	*it is . . . desire*	the core of Julian's argument (and a recurring belief in Shelley's poetry).
188–91	*So taught . . . religion*	Julian is in agreement with the Greek philosophers who argued that human beings have a measure of control over their happiness and he opposes the fatalism of organized religion; he distinguishes between religion and Religion.
211		Shelley removed some lines from his manuscript and this is the sole unrhyming line in the poem.
226	*those*	other inmates.
244	*humourist*	person with an unbalanced temperament.
277	*brackish*	salty.
301	*jade*	worn-out horse.
424–5		Like a monk obsessed with chastity he should have torn out his sexual organs (Matthew 18: 8–9).
433	*cearedst*	sealed with wax or wrapped in a winding-sheet.
446	*glance of phantasy*	eye of the imagination.
463	*admire*	be amazed.

496	*for* in return for.
532	*canker* diseased growth (of self-accusation).
536	*nice . . . gentleness* refined behaviour and gentlemanly breeding.
538	*changed* accepted as exchange.
540	*colours of his mind* qualities of his imagination.
542	*measure* verse.
547	*unconnected* without responsibilities.
578	*baseless* without foundation.
589	*doom* fortune.
608–15	(I have altered the usual punctuation of these lines in order to clarify the sense.)

THE TWO SPIRITS: AN ALLEGORY

The different mentalities characterized in Maddalo and Julian are manifested by the two Spirits; the first one urging caution, doubt and foreboding; the second advocating daring, hope and optimism. The final stanza may tip the balance of the poem towards renewal and light. Where the allegory is to be located is not made clear: in the individual psyche or society or both?

42	*death-dews* dew of night.
	morass marsh.

from PROMETHEUS UNBOUND

Written between autumn 1818 and autumn 1819, the poem is in four acts and, of the total poem, more than half is included in this edition. In the Preface, Shelley attempts to explain something of his subject and style, but the poem is extremely difficult to grasp. Even his description of the work as 'a lyrical drama' (compare 'lyrical ballad' as used by Wordsworth and Coleridge) is puzzling and somewhat paradoxical: a drama suggests conflict, action and characters; lyrical suggests the personal, emotional and musical. This friction of modes, one more public, the other more internal, is indicative of the scale of the work.

The action of the poem may be summarized as follows. In Act I, Prometheus, chained in agony to the rocks, considers his suffering and decides to revoke his earlier curse on Jupiter his oppressor. The Phantasm of Jupiter is summoned, he articulates the curse, and Prometheus withdraws his wish for revenge. The Furies arrive with Jupiter's messenger, Mercury, to punish Prometheus further and in the hope of forcing him to reveal his secret knowledge of the fate of Jupiter. The Furies are finally repulsed by Prometheus' pity for them and they are replaced by contrary Spirits of hope. In Act II, Panthea, a female companion of Prometheus in the first act, arrives in a lovely valley to greet Asia, his loved one. Asia deciphers Panthea's dreams and they feel a compulsion to journey through a beautiful landscape eventually to arrive at the cave of Demogorgon. After Asia has questioned him about the nature of the universe and power, Demogorgon announces that the moment of change has come in the form of the Spirit of the Hour. Act III sees the overthrow of Jupiter, the release of Prometheus and the transformation of the world and human society. This transformation is celebrated and manifested in Act IV.

The figure of Prometheus in classical myths is strikingly enigmatic. In different accounts or in different readings of the accounts he emerges as a benefactor to human beings or as a malefactor. That Shelley was aware of this range of interpretations is apparent in his long note to *Queen Mab*, VIII. 211–12, where he holds Prometheus responsible for mankind's loss of innocence and bliss by introducing fire and thereby the eating of cooked meat. According to the myth, Prometheus' gift of fire was counterbalanced by Zeus (Jupiter) releasing into the world Pandora's Box with all its evils. Some commentators even see the Titan as responsible for the tyranny of Zeus, and in the poem it is possible to see Jupiter as a creation or emanation of a corrupt Prometheus; until Prometheus rids himself of the wish for revenge and purges his hatred, he can only sustain Jupiter in his power. The sequence of events supports this interpretation; the protagonist's repentance allows Asia (love) to be directed to Demogorgon (the mechanism of change); Jupiter is destroyed by his own rape of Thetis, the offspring of which is Demogorgon, and harmony is made possible in the world by the earlier wholeness in Prometheus. To say that Demogorgon is the offspring of Jupiter and Thetis seems confusing, in that he appears to exist prior to Jupiter's description of the rape (Act III, scene 1, ll. 33–48); but, if Demogorgon is considered as a general force of Necessity and the visible Demogorgon is the embodiment of that force, the sequence does make sense.

Shelley's Prometheus is very much his own creation. Goethe and Byron had written poems on the Promethean figure but here we encounter an ambition to write a cosmic drama which looks back to Milton's *Paradise Lost* and forward to the epic struggle of Melville's *Moby Dick*. In 1817 Shelley wrote *The Revolt of Islam* (original title, *Laon and Cythna; or, The Revolution of the Golden City: A Vision of the Nineteenth Century*) in which he tried to come

260

to terms with the failure of the French Revolution. In *Prometheus Unbound* he moves from the attempt to achieve revolution by changing the structure of social power to a focus on a regenerative process starting from within the individual. What Demogorgon advocates in the final stanzas stresses endless commitment and struggle on the part of the individual. The lyrical drama is not an allegory, although parts of it can be related to events, people and patterns of experience in an ordinary world. Prometheus does represent elements of fidelity to an ideal, resistance to injustice and aspirations to happiness which reflect Shelley's notions of human betterment, but he emphasizes in the Preface that he has written a poem, not a manifesto. And there is probably no poem in the English language which demonstrates such a versatility in verse forms.

Epigraph   'Do you hear this, Amphiaraus, hidden under the earth?' The line comes from *Epigoni*, a play (now lost) by Aeschylus, quoted by Cicero. Amphiaraus was a seer who was miraculously transformed into an oracle. Here, Shelley is addressing Aeschylus, the authority under the ground, and warning him that he is about to present Prometheus in a different way from the compromising figure in Aeschylus's *Prometheus Unbound* (also now lost).

Preface

21–2   *I was averse . . . mankind* In the Greek plays, the *catastrophe* is the resolution of the plot. Shelley feels that the evil in Jupiter's tyranny is beyond repair, it must be opposed and eliminated.

33–4   *pernicious casuistry* dangerous and dishonest use of argument.

42   *Baths of Caracalla* baths at Rome established by the Emperor Aurelius Antoninus (nicknamed Caracalla) in the third century.

52   *Dante* Dante Alighieri (1265–1321), Italy's greatest poet, author of *The Divine Comedy*.

93–4   *The cloud of mind . . . lightning* a current theory that electricity accumulated in clouds.

120–3   *Homer . . . Pope* Shelley refers to pairs of writers living in the same period and culture: Greece in the eighth century BC; Greece in the fifth century BC; Rome in the first century BC; Italy in the fourteenth century; England in the late sixteenth and early seventeenth centuries; England in the late seventeenth and early eighteenth centuries.

127	*Scotch philosopher* Robert Forsyth, *The Principles of Moral Science*, 1805.
130–1	*Plato and Lord Bacon ... Paley and Malthus* Plato and Francis Bacon (1561–1626) sought to eradicate human error and promote development. William Paley (1743–1805) was a conservative and, according to Shelley, immoral theologian; his book *The Principles of Moral and Political Philosophy* (1785) was popular at the time. Thomas Malthus (1766–1834) wrote *An Essay on the Principle of Population as it Affects the Future Improvements of Society* (1798; revised 1803) in which he argued that population increases faster than natural resources and that war, disease and famine are inevitable as controls on population. In Shelley's eyes, both Paley and Malthus argued against the possibility of reform.
148	*candid* (in its older sense) free from bias or malice.

Main characters who appear in the extracts

Prometheus	In Greek mythology he is one of the Titans, gods who are the children of Uranos (heaven) and Gaia (earth). In the poem he represents what mankind is capable of at its best.
Demogorgon	A figure with this or a similar name occurs in Plato, Lucan, Boccaccio, Spenser, Milton and in Shelley's friend Peacock but it does not have a clear or consistent significance. In the present poem he is deliberately obscure because he is only partly a character; he represents the process of change, the amoral, impersonal pattern which is activated by but precedes individual decisions and actions. In certain political readings of the poem he is taken to represent the inevitable force of the People (Greek *demos*), or historical necessity.
Jupiter	The supreme god (Greek Zeus; Shelley appears to use Roman and Greek names for the gods interchangeably). Here he is a tyrannical figure who enjoys cruelty and the humiliation of others. He is an emblem of religious and political power, entrenched and arbitrary.
The Earth	In mythology, Gaia (Earth) is the mother of the Titans, but it is important to see her in the drama of the poem as identified with the forces and processes of the earth.

Asia	Daughter of Oceanus and the bride of Prometheus. She represents love and regeneration; while Prometheus maintains hatred for Jupiter, these powers cannot operate.
Panthea and Ione	Younger sisters of Asia and supporters of Prometheus. They represent aspects of idealism, and some interpreters have seen them as Faith (Panthea) and Hope (Ione) co-operating with their sister, Love.
Mercury	Messenger of the gods (Roman version of the Greek Hermes). In the poem he sees the injustice done to Prometheus but is not prepared to oppose the tyranny of Jupiter.
The Furies	Avenging spirits who torture the mind. Prometheus has extinguished his wish for revenge; Jupiter persists in his.

Act I

1	*Monarch* Jupiter.
	Daemons beings halfway between gods and men.
2	*One* Prometheus.
7	*hecatombs* mass public sacrifices.
9	*eyeless in hate* blind with hatred.
34	*wingèd hound* Each day an eagle tears at Prometheus.
59	*recall* remember and revoke.
73–111	All nature is frightened by Prometheus' curse.
74	Orthodox opinion considered the earth to be about 6,000 years old. Shelley sides with recent scientists who realised that it was much older.
121	*frore* frozen.
123	*Asia* see note above.
124	*informs* fills.
135	*inorganic* incoherent, without shape.
138	*language of the dead* Prometheus, being immortal, cannot understand the terms of mortal creatures.
140	*fell* dreadful.
141	*wheel of pain* In mythology, Ixion was bound to a revolving wheel of fire for challenging the authority of Zeus.
191	*Babylon* The ancient kingdom of Babylon (in what is now Iraq) survived in one form or another for more than a thousand years before the final destruction of the city of Babylon in 539 BC.

192	*Magus Zoroaster* ancient Persian sage, according to whom a power of good (light) struggles with a power of evil (darkness) for control of the world. A source has not been discovered for the story that he met his double; such a phenomenon is widely supposed to be an intimation of death.
212	*Hades, or Typhon* Pluto, brother of Jupiter, and king of the Underworld (Hades); Typhon, a hundred-headed giant imprisoned by Jupiter under the volcanic Mount Etna.
216	*shades* ghosts in the Underworld.
236	*stay* support.
262–301	The words are those that had been pronounced by Prometheus against Jupiter. The Phantasm or ghost (see ll. 191–218) of Jupiter now repeats them.
270	*legioned* organized like an army.
271	*furies* see note above.
288–92	Jupiter's very immortality and power will add to his suffering. The robe and crown of gold, emblems of kingship, become instruments of torture.
303–5	a crucial declaration by Prometheus, but not understood by those around him.
319–25	Mercury is recognizable by his winged sandals and his staff twined with snakes.
326	*hydra tresses* hair of snakes. Hydra was a many-headed snake in Greek mythology. Also Medusa was cursed by having her hair turned into serpents and her face so terrible that anyone who looked at it was turned to stone.
331	*hounds* the Furies.
342	*Maia* mother by Jupiter of Mercury.
346–7	*Geryon . . . Gorgon . . . Chimaera . . . Sphinx* monsters in Greek mythology. Oedipus' deliverance of Thebes from the power of the Sphinx led unwittingly to his marriage with his own mother, and when later he cursed his sons they killed each other. Mercury threatens to send the Furies back to Hades and summon these monsters instead to torment Prometheus.
371	*secret* that the son born to Thetis by Jupiter would overthrow him. In the poem Jupiter is overthrown by a moral process.
377	*fane* temple.
398	*Sicilian's . . . sword* Damocles, a courtier of King Dionysius of Sicily, envied his master's wealth. Dionysius placed him at a

lavish banquet under a sword suspended by a single hair in order to demonstrate how precarious is the happiness of a king.

437   *child of Heaven*   Mercury departs at the summons from Jupiter.

479   *lidless*   unclosing.

527   *rapt*   carried.

530   *Kingly conclaves*   secret meetings and arrangements between rulers.

539   *Tear the veil!*   The Furies show Prometheus incidents across history in which the innocent and good are persecuted and how goodness itself appears to bring more suffering to human beings. The fate of Jesus is the central example.

546   *One*   Jesus.

548   *His words ... poison*   The teachings of Jesus hardened into intolerant doctrines after his death.

567   *A disenchanted nation*   France released from an evil spell by the Revolution (and as with Christ's original teachings the idealism turns into its opposite).

594   *emblem*   allegory or proverb.

609   *hooded ounces*   hunting leopards.

618–33   The final and hardest temptation to resist is that goodness is self-defeating and despair or apathy is inevitable. Prometheus feels acutely the force of the Fury's taunt but he repulses it by extending his sympathy to those who do not care or are beyond caring for others.

658–63   The Earth summons spirits, the opposite of the Furies, to demonstrate the strength of goodness and hope in human affairs; they inhabit the collective mind of humanity.

688   *unpent*   unconfined.

752   *two shapes*   represent a mixture or struggle of love and despair which in the present world are inseparable.

760   *grain*   dye.

765   *planet-crested Shape*   Venus, the planet of love.

766   *ambrosial*   conferring endless life (like ambrosia, the food of the gods).

793   *elder brake*   thicket of elder trees.

795   *white-thorn ... blow*   hawthorn soon will blossom.

20   *great chain*   the old notion that every aspect of creation is connected in an order (usually referred to as 'The Great Chain of Being').

25   *self-contempt*   the most abject condition, in Shelley's view.

28   *He reigns*   Demogorgon adds nothing to Asia's questions and statements.

33   *Saturn*   god (Greek Kronos = Time) born of Uranos (Heaven) and Gaia (Earth); he was removed by Jupiter with the help of Prometheus.

52   *unseasonable seasons*   In the earlier Golden Age of Saturn there had been no alteration of seasons (and no development).

60   *Elysian*   paradisal.

61   *Nepenthe, Moly, Amaranth*   plants with legendary powers, in this case, to remove anxiety.

72–3   *speech . . . universe*   language shapes thought and it is by means of language that human beings understand and order the world.

74   *Science*   knowledge.

80   *mimicked . . . mocked*   imitated and then created forms more beautiful than those in nature.

83–4   Women, looking at the perfection in statues, conceive children according to that image, but such an intoxication with beauty is fatal.

91   *interlunar*   dark; the time between the old and the new moon.

94   *Celt*   The word was used for any tribe north of the Alps. Shelley is describing a worldwide understanding between races.

107   *adamantine*   unbreakable.

114   *abysm*   (like abyss) unfathomable void or primal chaos below the created world.

120   *eternal Love*   the centre of Shelley's moral thinking; very similar to his idea of Intellectual Beauty (see p. 255). When Asia accepts this truth, the deliverance of Prometheus and the overthrow of Jupiter can take place.

Act III, Scene 4, ll. 124–204

The Spirit of the Hour, who had banished Jupiter and released Prometheus, now describes to Prometheus and Asia how earth has been transformed.

136	Written above the gate of Hell in Dante's *Inferno*.
140	*abject* degraded one.
162	*treasured gall* hoarded bitterness.
163	*nepenthe* a legendary Egyptian drug which could remove grief.
167	*glozed on* commented on, flattered.
170	*obelisks* tapering pillars of stone erected by the pharaohs at the entrance to temples.
180	*foul shapes* effigies or idols.
187	*unreclaiming* futile.
189	*Frown* The subject of *frown* is *shapes*, l. 180.
190	*painted veil* a commonly used image in Shelley for the barrier or false façade, often created by human beings themselves, and standing between them and truth.
202	*clogs* impediments.
204	*intense inane* infinite space.

ACT IV ll. 93–193 and ll. 356–578

The scene is the forest outside the cave of Prometheus. What the various voices celebrate is a reordered universe in which the forces of nature and those of human love and intellect harmonize.

104	*Hours* the Chorus of Hours.
110	*siren wiles* seductive charms.
116	*Science ... wings* knowledge tries out her beautifully made wings. (Daedalus was the legendary craftsman who devised a pair of wings.)
140	*clips* embraces.
184	*unpavilioned* unclouded.
188	*Aeolian* See note to 'Mutability', p. 255.
356	*my lifeless mountains* The Moon and the Earth in this section of the poem are aspects of the universe and parts of the myth of regeneration. The Moon has many of the attributes of the physical moon but it (she) is given a life through its relationship in love with the Earth (male in this part of the poem).
370	*It* Love.
375	*bowers* dwellings.
380	*unremoved for ever* never moved before.
388–93	The reference is to King Bladud, who, a leper outcast, followed an animal and came on the healing springs which are now Bath.

The child who returns cured is first taken for a ghost by its mother before being accepted as miraculous; it is difficult to believe that man can be so wonderfully cured.

392   *Unconscious*   unaware.

408–10   The will is a bad ruler but, under the guidance of love, can be a useful instrument for human conduct.

414   *Bright . . . wear*   Mothers model their children on the examples provided by art.

415   *Orphic*   Orpheus in Greek mythology had the ability to use music to control animals and even stones.

416   *daedal*   skilful.

418–23   Earth's (Shelley's) vision must have seemed merely fanciful in 1820 but many of the prophecies have been fulfilled in our century. Mankind has learned how to harness the forces of nature to provide energy, and space is being explored.

428   *paramours*   lovers.

431   *fold*   embrace.

436   *fleece . . . amethyst*   red- and violet-coloured cloud.

444–9   This is a continuation, after the Moon's interruption, of the Earth's previous stanza.

444   *pyramid*   cone-shaped shadow of the earth cast on the side away from the sun. The sunlight surrounds the cone (see l. 449).

470   *Maniac-like*   like someone mad with love (lunar = lunatic).

471–2   *Gazing . . . side*   The moon in its circling of the earth always keeps the same side towards the earth, like a bride who cannot tire of looking at her lover.

473–5   *Maenad . . . forest*   Agave, the daughter of Cadmus, joined the Maenads, followers of the god Dionysus, and, in her religious intoxication, pulled her own son to pieces.

483   *chameleon*   small reptile with an ability to alter its colouring to match its surroundings.

495–502   The Earth (male) has come to acknowledge that its nature can be rather forceful and that it needs the balancing softness of the Moon (female).

530   *Dominations*   an alternative form of 'Dominions', one of the hierarchy of angels; appears to be a third class of power after Daemons and Gods.

532   *constelled wilderness*   confusion of constellations

539   *elemental Genii*   basic atoms

552	*dim night . . . day* The individual life of man is like a dim night in comparison with the brightness of immortality.
555	*Earth-born's . . . despotism* Prometheus' power has caused the tyranny of Jupiter to disappear.
565	*Eternity* all future time (contains all possibilities).
567	*serpent* evil (which has been banished).
569	*disentangled Doom* released terror, the serpent.
573	*bear* endure.

SONNET: LIFT NOT THE PAINTED VEIL

1	*veil* See note to *Prometheus Unbound*, Act III scene 4, ll. 190–2.
6	*sightless* without anything to see.
7	*one* partly his younger self, partly a fictional figure.
14	*the Preacher* like the biblical Ecclesiastes (the Preacher), who says, 'And I gave my heart to know wisdom, and to know madness and folly: I perceived that this also is vexation of spirit.'

SONNET: TO THE REPUBLIC OF BENEVENTO

Early in 1820 there was a political rising in Spain against a despotic regime and in July there was a similar rising led by the secret society, the Carbonari, around Naples. Benevento was a small papal enclave surrounded by Neapolitan territory. The citizens of Benevento disowned their papal attachment and requested Naples to accept them. When Naples refused, they attempted to set up an independent state. The liberalizing process in southern Italy was crushed in the following year by an Austrian army. This poem is slightly out of chronological order with those around it in this edition, but with the other two sonnets it acts as a bridge between *Prometheus Unbound* and *The Mask of Anarchy*. (It was first published in *Posthumous Poems*, 1824, with Mary Shelley's title for it, 'Political Greatness'.) It is a declaration of congratulation and encouragement to the young republic.

1	The first *nor* means 'neither' and this grammatical construction can be followed by a plural verb, *shepherd*.
3	*Shepherd* accompany or guide.
6	Art refuses to mirror or rushes in shock away from the vulgar show.
7	*fleet* hurry.

8	*Heaven* holy domain of art.
9–10	*What . . . custom?* What value is there in people held together by physical force or habit?
10–14	*Man . . . alone* Compare *Prometheus Unbound*, Act IV, ll. 400–11.

SONNET: ENGLAND IN 1819

The sonnet was written late in 1819 but not published till 1839. For a fuller description of the situation in England, see the Introduction and the notes on *The Mask of Anarchy*. Shelley had the idea of publishing a book of poems on the current political situation but, although he wrote a number of related poems, the book did not take shape and, anyway, the punitive censorship in England would have prevented any sales. In her Note to the poems of 1819, Mary Shelley writes: 'He believed that a clash between the two classes of society was inevitable, and he eagerly ranged himself on the people's side.' The title was given by Mary Shelley.

1	*King* George III was over 80 years old and had been insane for many years. He died in 1820.
2	*Princes* George III had nine sons and they were notorious for their extravagance, corruption and debauchery. The Prince Regent, who became George IV in 1820, was particularly dissolute.
6	*without a blow* The people of England are so debilitated by the demands of their parasitic rulers that they are incapable of opposing them.
7	*field* St Peter's Fields at Manchester (see note on *The Mask of Anarchy*). Although the people are starving, the field is untilled.
8	*liberticide and prey* destroying of freedom and booty.
9	*two-edged sword* sharpened on both edges and therefore more deadly (but with a suggestion that it can operate against those who wield it).
10	*Golden . . . slay* a legal system based on established wealth and power which forces poor people to break the laws and then punishes them.
12	*senate* parliament which, like religion in the previous line, is the antithesis of what it should be.
13–14	A very tentative hope; see the final sentence of 'An Address

to the People on the Death of the Princess Charlotte', and compare with the Shape of Liberty in *The Mask of Anarchy*. Shelley's belief is that corruption breeds its own destruction (*graves*).

SONG: MEN OF ENGLAND

7   *drones* non-worker bees, idle parasites.
9   *Bees* a common image for the workers in political discussion after *The Grumbling Hive* (1705), reissued as *The Fable of the Bees* (1714), by Bernard de Mandeville. This explains the apparent mixed metaphors in the stanza.
25–32   If the workers do not shake off their subservience and stand up for themselves, all their labour will merely facilitate their misery and destruction.
26   *deck* decorate.

THE MASK OF ANARCHY

On 16 August 1819, a huge crowd of 80,000 people gathered in St Peter's Fields in Manchester to support the cause of parliamentary reform and to hear speeches on the subject. Henry 'Orator' Hunt was addressing the crowd when an attempt to arrest him went wrong and a detachment of cavalry was ordered to charge the crowd. Eleven people were killed and hundreds were seriously wounded, many of them women. The incident was immediately nicknamed the Peterloo massacre in ironic comparison with the Battle of Waterloo in 1815.

Although living in Italy, Shelley was well informed on events in Britain and by 9 September he could write to his friend Peacock: 'Many thanks for your attention in sending the papers which contain the terrible and important news of Manchester. These are, as it were, the distant thunders of the terrible storm which is approaching. The tyrants here, as in the French Revolution, have first shed blood. May their execrable lessons not be learnt with equal facility.' His poem was sent to Leigh Hunt (no relation to 'Orator' Hunt) for inclusion in *The Examiner*, but Hunt, who had been prosecuted and imprisoned before for seditious writings, delayed publishing the poem till the Reform Bill was eventually passed in 1832. In his letter accompanying the poem, the poet wrote: 'I fear that in England things will be carried violently by the rulers, and that they will not have learned to yield in time to the spirit of the age. The great thing to do is to hold the balance between popular impatience and tyrannical obstinacy; to inculcate with fervour both the right of resistance and the duty of forbearance.' In a number of poems prompted by public events, he tried to contrive a more popularly accessible idiom and here he adopted an irregular ballad verse form, familiar to many from broadsheets. The style of the first half is a kind of caricature similar to the cartoon technique of William Hogarth (1697–1764) and James Gillray (1757–1815); Gillray's *Presages of the Millennium* (1795) shows the Prime Minister, Pitt, as Death on the white horse of the Apocalypse savaging the radical politicians of the time. The poem does not attempt to describe factually the events which provoked it but rather takes the form of a vision of the whole terrible situation and a possible solution. Based on actual people, the figures in the early part are presented allegorically as characters in a pageant or masque. The title contains a pun on masque and mask as a disguise adopted by Anarchy; 'Anarchy' here is the total abuse of power, the arbitrary immorality which ignores law. Against Anarchy with all the support of the establishment in England, Hope seems frail and helpless. At the crucial moment, Hope is saved by the intervention of a Shape which is paradoxically described in images of power and gentleness. Various interpretations have been offered: enlightenment, nature, the people, England, liberty. Despite the acute analysis of freedom, the stimulating advice to the men of England, there is something unsatisfactory about the miraculous power of the Shape to destroy Anarchy and the ambivalent attitude to violent struggle. Is the Shape (or Shelley) advocating passive resistance to tyranny (ll. 348–51) or armed insurrection ('Rise like Lions after slumber', ll. 151 and 372)? And how exactly does Hope come to be walking 'ankle-deep in blood' (l. 127)?

6 *Castlereagh* Foreign Secretary (1812–22) and leader of the Tory Party in the House of Commons. He had been ruthless in suppressing trouble in Ireland and was totally opposed to the revolutionary movement in France.

8 *Seven bloodhounds* Seven European countries agreed with Britain at the Congress of Vienna in 1815 not to insist on the immediate abolition of the slave-trade. The *human hearts* (l. 12) could be slaves.

10 *plight* condition.

15 *Eldon* Lord Chancellor, notorious for his harsh sentences and for sometimes bursting into tears in court. It was Eldon who

ruled that Shelley could not have charge of his children on the death of his first wife, Harriet.

24   *Sidmouth*   Home Secretary, responsible for repressive measures. He infiltrated his agents into groups of workers in order to identify and deport leaders of agitation. He believed that religion could teach acceptance to poor people and was responsible for spending a million pounds in building churches in wretched areas of the cities. Both his cruelty and the hypocritical nature of his sympathy are conveyed in the emblem of the crocodile which, according to legend, appears to weep while devouring its prey.

30   *Anarchy*   In the Bible (Revelation 6:8) the fourth of the Riders of the Apocalypse is described: 'And I looked, and behold a pale horse: and his name that sat on him was Death, and Hell followed after him. And power was given unto them over the fourth part of the earth, to kill with the sword, and with hunger, and with death, and with the beasts of the field.'

83   *Bank and Tower*   Bank of England; Tower of London, where the Crown Jewels are kept.

85   *pensioned*   bought.

86   *maniac*   distraught.

90   *My father Time*   previous generations.

110   *arrayed in mail*   dressed in armour.

112   *grain*   colour.

115   *planet … Morning's*   Venus, the planet of love.

129   *mien*   expression.

145   *accent unwithstood*   irresistable utterance.

148   *unwritten story*   unrecorded history.

169   *pine and peak*   waste away.

175   *Surfeiting*   suffering from overeating.

176   *Ghost of Gold*   paper money.

197–208 echo of the words of Jesus: 'The foxes have holes, and the birds of the air have nests, but the Son of man hath no where to lay his head' (Matthew 8:20).

220   *Fame*   rumour, speculation.

245   *Leagued … Gaul*   The countries around France, including Britain, united against the Revolution in 1793.

254–7   The enlightened rich fight against the very evils by which they have become wealthy.

260   *cot* cottage.

279   *workhouse* institution paid for by government where poor and unemployed people could receive food and shelter in return for work. The system was harsh and allowed cruel exploitation to take place.

286   *tares* weeds.

305   *targes* shields.

310   *emblazonry* colourful display.

330   *phalanx* defensive military formation.

331–43   Shelley was not an anarchist (in the modern sense) and he believed that notions of fair play and decency can survive behind the corrupt and unjust statutes of formalized law. This idea of a common law, a basic agreement about rights, has a long history in England, going back to Alfred the Great. The *sacred heralds* (l. 341) are the announcers of such a common law.

360–3   The *true warriors* are regular soldiers as distinct from local militia (*base company*) who were raised by employers to quell disturbances and to intimidate their workers.

from PETER BELL THE THIRD

Written in the month following *The Mask of Anarchy*, this 'party squib', as Shelley described it, is similar in style to the political protest but with stronger elements of satire, burlesque and personal vituperation. Wordsworth had written his *Peter Bell* in 1798 but it was not published until April 1819, when it attracted considerable ridicule including a parody by Keats's friend, John Hamilton Reynolds, called *Peter Bell; A Lyrical Ballad*. Shelley's poem on Peter is, therefore, the third. After a mocking Dedication and Prologue, it consists of 772 lines and is in seven parts: 'Death', 'The Devil', 'Hell', 'Sin', 'Grace', 'Damnation' and 'Double Damnation'. It attacks the hypocritical and corrupt world of the establishment in London and tells the miserable story of the decline of Peter (Wordsworth) in his association with the powers of the day.

The first extract (ll. 147–51 and 172–201) is from the third part, 'Hell'.

174   *German soldiers* There were rumours and fears that the Hanoverian George would bring in German soldiers to crush English unrest.

176	*Gin ... methodism* Alcohol abuse in cheap gin shops was common; for methodism see Introduction (p. 4).
183	*amant misere* love to be miserable.
186	*Without ... chastity* 'What would this husk and excuse for a virtue be without its kernel prostitution, or the kernel prostitution without this husk of a virtue' (Shelley's note).
187	*hobnobbers* companions (but with a suggestion of self-seeking).
190	*stock-jobbers* speculators in stocks and shares.
195	*courteous* mechanically polite.
197	*moiling* striving dully.

The second extract (ll. 273–317) is from the fourth part, 'Sin'. Shelley's picture of Peter (Wordsworth) is partly complimentary and partly critical. His main objection here is that Wordsworth does not appreciate the world around him on its own terms but rather converts the world into his own scheme of things and writes of it then in a wonderfully intense way.

285	*trim* nature.
295	*or ... or* either . . . or.
313	*drift* tendency.

The third extract (ll. 378–441) is from the fifth part, 'Grace', and describes Coleridge and his influence on Peter. Again, the portrait of Coleridge contains praise as well as criticism. Coleridge's view of inspiration couched in religious terms can be compared with Shelley's own notion of Intellectual Beauty. The remarks on Wordsworth's poems, despite the ironies, show the range of his poetry and the high regard felt for him by Shelley.

399	*pate* head.
400	*baulk* neglect to give.
425	*quickset* hedge.
431	*saws* sayings, maxims.
437	*augured* announced or offered as a promise (of inspiration).

ODE TO THE WEST WIND

Formally and texturally this poem is extremely complex. Each of the five stanzas is a sonnet written in terza rima, and an intricate interplay of alliteration, assonance and rhyme contributes to the poem's density. In the first three stanzas the imagery related to the wind is centred on leaves–earth, clouds–air and waves–water respectively and all the seasons of the year are included; these main lines of imagery are harnessed to the poet's self at the opening of stanza 4, and the poem comes to its climax on the element of fire in ll. 66–7. The overall structure is similar to that of a traditional religious prayer: in the opening stanzas the power and awesomeness of the divinity (the wind) are proclaimed, each stanza ending with an invocation; in the fourth stanza the weakness of the poet-disciple is confessed, and in the final stanza he begs for a renewal of power and a role as prophet of a wider regenerative process.

Although the imagery is so obviously from the world of nature, the concern of the poem is not with the cycle of the seasons as such. Three chief areas of concern emerge: Shelley's fear that his poetic gift is fading (a loss of inspiration) ; a sense of spiritual inadequacy, of defeat; and a wider wish for political change. The first two are clearly visible, the third becomes apparent gradually. In the opening stanzas the very extravagance of the language points to something beyond the straightforwardly autumnal, and the wind in its destructive aspect is accepted as if violence and death may be necessary stages on the way to transformation. In stanza 3 the wind from the Atlantic (the newly created United States) disturbs the languid and complacent beauty of the Mediterranean, and by the final stanza the revolutionary hope is global ('over the universe', 'among mankind', 'Earth'). The final question checks the rhetorical rush of the poem. Is Shelley voicing a truism, or does the question challenge the central hope of the preceding stanzas that regeneration in human affairs can happen as mechanically as spring follows winter?

Title   Shelley appended a note to the poem: 'This poem was conceived and chiefly written in a wood that skirts the Arno, near Florence, and on a day when that tempestuous wind, whose temperature is at once mild and animating, was collecting the vapours which pour down the autumnal rains. They began, as I foresaw, at sunset with a violent tempest of hail and rain, attended by that magnificent thunder and lightning peculiar to the Cisalpine regions.

The phenomenon alluded to at the conclusion of the third stanza is well known to naturalists. The vegetation at the bottom of the sea, of rivers, and of lakes, sympathizes with that of the land in the change of seasons, and is consequently influenced by the winds which announce it.'

4   *Yellow . . . red* It has been suggested that the colours represent the various races of human beings.
hectic fevered.

9	*azure* clear blue (of the cloudless sky).
18	*Angels* heralds.
21	*Maenad* female devotee of Dionysus, Greek god of wine, revelry and vegetation; when possessed by the god's power, the Maenads acted as if mad.
32	*pumice* porous stone made from volcanic lava.
	Baiae's bay near Naples and the volcanic area including Vesuvius.
33	*old palaces and towers* In the time of the Roman Empire, emperors had built palaces in the bay, and Baiae had become notorious for ostentatious luxury and immorality. A change in the level of the sea submerged the town but Shelley had himself seen the buildings still standing beneath the waves. For him the palaces were symbols of aristocratic and corrupt power.
39	*oozy woods* slimy seaweeds growing upward from the seabed
57	*lyre* See note on ll. 5–8 of 'Mutability' (p. 255) and the second paragraph of Shelley's 'A Defence of Poetry'.
64	*quicken* give life to or speed up.

THE CLOUD

Shelley's fascination with change and permanence is explored, and he catalogues the various cloud formations and meteorological conditions, probably following Luke Howard's 'Essay on Clouds' (1803), which first classified clouds in the terms that we still use and which influenced Constable, Turner, Goethe and Wordsworth. Whether or not the poem is to be read symbolically or allegorically is an open question. For Shelley, flux has to be accepted as a constant in natural and human existence; life and death may be charades or may be seen only partially by our minds at present. His poem 'The Sensitive Plant', written about the same time, can be read as a reverse argument. The Cloud partakes of all elements but is not bound to any.

The persona of the Cloud is like a benevolent Puck from Shakespeare's *A Midsummer Night's Dream* or Ariel from *The Tempest*. The mingling of iambic and anapaestic metres, combined with the intricate but self-advertising rhymes, emphasizes a mischievous, good-humoured and amoral quality in the speaker.

| 7 | *their mother's* the earth's. |
| 9 | *flail* instrument for threshing the grain from the chaff. |

18	*Lightning my pilot* A current theory suggested that electricity (lightning) charged and guided clouds and the electrical balance between clouds and earth was re-established through thunderstorms.
23	*genii* The electrical impulses are presented as compatible spirits.
33	*rack* high, wind-pushed cloud.
51	*woof* fabric.
58	*these* stars (of l. 52).
71	*sphere-fire* sun.
79	*convex* The sunlight is refracted by the atmosphere.
81	*cenotaph* monument erected in honour of a dead person whose body is elsewhere.

TO A SKYLARK

As its name suggests, the skylark seems more of the sky than of the earth and is more heard than seen. Shelley develops this detail and attributes to the creature an unworldly, spiritual, even miraculous quality. The unearthly bird cannot be described directly; what it is can be defined only in terms of the analogues (ll. 36–55) in which something extraordinary is divulged from a hidden source. The very purity and beauty of the song distinguish it from earthbound compositions, but the 'blithe Spirit' can provide an example and inspiration to the poet, who has, by necessity, to write in a world of 'Hate and pride and fear'. Poetry as 'harmonious madness' corresponds with Plato's idea of inspiration.

22	*silver sphere* Venus, the bright morning star.
56	*vernal* spring, fresh.
66	*Hymeneal* celebrating marriage; Hymen was the Greek deity of weddings.
80	*satiety* disgust caused by excess.
100	*Thy skill . . . were* The bird's natural talent is a better inspiration to a poet.

LETTER TO MARIA GISBORNE

This verse epistle, not intended for publication apparently, was written early in the summer of 1820 when the Shelleys were living at Livorno in the house of John and Maria Gisborne who were on a visit to London.

Maria, aged 50, had been a member of liberal circles, a friend of Godwin, and was helping Shelley to learn Spanish. Her son Henry, in whose workshop Shelley is writing, was building a steamship with the excited support of Shelley. The poem, in relaxed couplets, is a delightful blend of the informal and formal, personal and public, lighthearted and serious.

Although the letter was published by Mary Shelley in 1824, modern editions are based on the revised text prepared by H. B. Forman in 1876.

12	*asphodels* flowers in the Elysian Fields symbolic of immortality.
16	*mechanist* mechanic, inventor.
17	*Archimedean* like Archimedes, the Greek mathematician and inventor who lived in Sicily in the third century BC.
19	*gin* engine.
23	*Vulcan* blacksmith to Jove.
24	*Ixion* Ixion was tied to a wheel for trying to seduce Jove's wife.
	Titan Prometheus, who was chained to a mountain.
25	*St Dominic* Spanish founder (1170–1221) of the Dominican Order; he helped to suppress with great cruelty the Albigensian heresy in southern France and was instrumental in establishing the Inquisition which used torture on pagans and heretics.
27	*philanthropic council* ironic reference to the Council under Philip II of Spain which organized the Spanish Armada of 1588 to punish heretic England with torture (see l. 35).
33	*relumes her fire* A new liberal mood in Spain abolished the Inquisition (but it was almost immediately restored).
37–43	The Armada was wrecked in a huge storm on islands round the coast of Britain.
45	*Proteus* Greek sea-god capable of adopting any shape.
51	*Tubal Cain* the first worker in metal, according to the Bible.
55	*knacks and quips* devices and oddments.
59	*swink* can mean either to work hard or drink heavily.
83	*statical* related to weight and balance.
94	*conic … logarithms* mathematical diagrams and equations.
95	*Laplace … Saunderson … Sims* writers of books on mathematics.
98	*Baron de Tott* author of a book about Turkey.
106	*Archimage* great wizard (like Archimago in Spenser's *The*

Faerie Queene). Shelley compares his writing with a devious invention to annoy the staid reviewers.

114	*Libeccio* the south-west wind.
176	*language* Maria Gisborne and Shelley had been reading Spanish literature together, particularly the plays of Calderón (1600–81).
180	*'My name is Legion!'* in Mark 5:9, the answer given by an evil spirit to Jesus. It is difficult to understand what Shelley means by it.
197	*Godwin* See Introduction.
209	*Hunt* Leigh Hunt, poet and radical journalist, was the editor of the *Examiner* and a good friend to Shelley.
213	*cast from Shout* Robert Shout was a maker of plaster copies of famous sculptures.
215	*coronals of bay* garlands of laurel (emblematic of success).
220	*duns* debt collectors.
226	*Hogg* Thomas Jefferson Hogg, one of Shelley's oldest friends, expelled with him from Oxford. Deceitful, he wrote an unreliable biography of Shelley (1858).
233	*Peacock* Thomas Love Peacock, poet and satirical novelist. He included a caricature portrait of Shelley in his novel *Nightmare Abbey* (1818). Always interested in oriental culture, he took a job in the East India House in 1819. He married a Welsh woman, Jane Gryffydh, in 1819.
240	*Cameleopard* giraffe.
250	*Horace Smith* stockbroker and verse satirist, always helpful to Shelley.
265–6	*stand . . . coaches* line of carriages for hire.
272	*Pollonia* Apollonia Ricci, daughter of the landlord in Livorno, was attracted to Henry Gisborne.
286	*Contadino's* Italian peasant's.
302	Shelley was vegetarian and did not like alcohol.
305	*syllabubs* puddings made of cream and wine.
308	*fires . . . wood* The right to gather wood from the Duke of Tuscany's estates was strictly guarded.
316	*laudanum* derived from opium and widely used as a sedative (here used metaphorically).
317	*Helicon or Himeros* the source of poetic inspiration (on Mount Parnassus) or love (according to Shelley's note).
323	the final line of Milton's *Lycidas*.

from THE WITCH OF ATLAS

The whole poem consists of 672 lines in eight-line stanzas (ottava rima) of the sort used by Byron in *Don Juan*. In August 1820, Shelley climbed on his own to a shrine on a mountain in the Apennines. After his journey of three days he took three days to write a poem about a witch, the daughter of Apollo, God of the sun and the arts. She has miraculous power to create and manipulate things according to her whims and represents the power of the imagination to redevise the world. She intervenes in human affairs to frustrate bad rulers and to remove inhibitions, but the bulk of the poem is a flight of fantasy through exotic landscapes accompanied by her created mate, a beautiful hermaphroditic creature.

The two extracts, of six stanzas each, illustrate the powers of the Witch, who seems to operate not from a distinct moral concern but rather from a benign nonchalance.

168	*beck*	command.
171	*Clipt*	enclosed.
174	*vans*	wings.
186	*Saturnian Archimage*	great wizard before the fall of mankind (the Golden Age of Saturn).
189	*native vice*	natural evil or original sin.
199	*prophane*	uninitiated.
541	*code ... law*	pattern of established social order (which ignores rights).
544	*liquid*	alterable.
552	*weltering*	surging.
564–5	*who ... concealment*	who conceal only their contempt for clothes.

from EPIPSYCHIDION

Written and published anonymously at Pisa in 1821. The basis of the poem of 604 lines is largely autobiographical and traces Shelley's quest for an ideal female partner through a partial description of his first wife Harriet Westbrook, Mary Shelley, Claire Clairmont and Teresa Viviani. Teresa was an Italian girl who was badly treated by her father and who aroused longing and a desire for justice in the poet. The poem is addressed to her (renamed as Emilia and represented as the sun) and is very bitter towards

Mary (the moon); Shelley, it seems, later denounced the piece as misguided. The title possibly means 'song of a little soul' and may indicate that in his quest the poet seeks not an actual person but a Platonic ideal or a Muse. The brief extract voices Shelley's refusal to accept monogamy.

160   *True Love*   Originally Shelley wrote 'Free Love'.
168   *worm*   evil serpent or dragon of myths.
189   *Elysian*   paradisal.

ADONAIS

Shelley heard of John Keats's death in Rome some weeks after the event and he decided on scanty evidence that his fellow poet's poor health had been critically aggravated by the hostility of reviewers to his poetry. He determined to write a poem on the precariousness of life and on how artistic genius is thwarted and crushed in a reactionary and uncaring society; what survives of this brief appearance of genius? The pastoral elegies of the Greek poets Bion and Moschus and Milton's *Lycidas* provided a model for such a poem, prompted by the death of a talented contemporary and raising wider issues. The conventions of the pastoral elegy include a distress that a protector was absent at the time of death, a setting in nature (pastoral) with the main figures presented as shepherds, a lament of nature with a procession of mourners, and the transformation of the dead person into something eternal and of sorrow into triumph. The transformation begins in stanza 38. The Spenserian stanza (from Spenser's *Faerie Queene*) used in *Adonais* was employed by Keats in *The Eve of St Agnes* and because of its intricate rhyme scheme can provide a very rich texture, what Shelley himself described as 'a highly wrought piece of art'.

Adonis was a handsome youth loved by Aphrodite, goddess of love. While she was absent he was killed by a wild boar. Aphrodite pleaded with the gods of the Underworld that he be restored to life and he was eventually allowed to live in the world for half of the year. He came to be associated with the cycle of the seasons and was worshipped as a god of fertility who is resurrected each spring. The name 'Adonai' in Hebrew means 'Lord' and Shelley does not feel bound to any one meaning. The name 'Adonais' is pronounced with four syllables.

Epigraph   Lines (originally in Greek) attributed to Plato and translated by Shelley. The planet Venus appears as the morning star (Lucifer) and as the evening star (Hesperus).

10	*mighty Mother* Aphrodite had two identities: Pandemos of physical love and Urania of spiritual love. Here Urania is a combination of spiritual love and a mother figure; she is also the Muse of astronomy and represents (as in Milton's *Paradise Lost*) the inspiration of the highest poetry.
25	*amorous Deep* possessive Underworld.
29–36	John Milton was the father of a line of poets (including Keats). Blind and old, Milton saw the destruction by the restoration of the monarchy (1660) of all his political and moral ideals but he did not despair. With Homer and Dante, Milton was the third great epic poet.
47	*thy widowhood* Urania was widowed by the death of Milton.
52	*nipped ... blew* perished before the blossom could develop.
55	*Capital* Rome.
63	*liquid* pure.
69	*eternal Hunger* decomposition.
73	*Dreams* In stanzas 9–14 Shelley personifies *All he* [Adonais] *had loved, and moulded into thought* as Dreams, Splendours, etc.
94	*anadem* garland.
107	*clips* holds or embraces. The rhyme of *clips* with *eclipse* in the following line makes them sound like opposites.
127	*Echo* a nymph who loved the beautiful Narcissus. Because he loved only himself (see l. 141) and ignored her, Echo pined away till she could only echo the sounds around her. Shelley makes her love Adonais even more intensely and she becomes even more inarticulate.
140	*Hyacinth* a youth loved by Phoebus Apollo (sun god) and accidentally killed by him.
142	*wan ... sere* Hyacinth and Narcissus were turned into flowers bearing their names. In mourning for Adonais they are pale and withered.
144	*ruth* pity.
145	*nightingale* There are echoes in these lines of Keats's 'Ode to a Nightingale'.
147–50	The eagle, according to legend, could restore its youth by flying towards the sun; Keats had attempted an epic flight in *Hyperion* (a name for the sun-god).
151	*Albion* England.
	Cain In the biblical story of Genesis, Cain was punished by

God for the murder of his brother Abel by having to wander the earth as an outcast with a brand mark on his forehead to indicate his crime.

160   *brere*   briar bush.

198   *ambrosial*   divinely fragrant. In Greek mythology ambrosia is the food of the gods.

240   *mirrored shield*   In Greek myth, Perseus, knowing that if he looked directly at the monster Medusa he would be killed, fought against her with the aid of a reflecting shield.

242   *crescent*   growing.

249   *like Apollo*   As Apollo killed the monster Python and so liberated the shrine at Delphi, so Byron demolished the critics (*wolves, ravens, vultures*) with his poem *English Bards and Scotch Reviewers* (1809). *Pythia* was the name given to the oracle at Delphi, the holiest place in Greece.

262   *mountain shepherds*   fellow poets come in their bardic costumes (l. 263).

264   *Pilgrim of Eternity*   Byron.

268–9   *from . . . wrong*   from Ireland (*Ierne*) comes Thomas Moore, who wrote songs about his country's sad condition.

271   *one frail Form*   Shelley (or a Shelleyan figure).

276   *Actaeon-like*   Actaeon came on Diana, goddess of chastity and hunting, when she was bathing; she turned him into a stag and his hounds tore him to pieces.

280   *pardlike*   like a leopard.

283   *superincumbent*   oppressive.

289–95 He is dressed as a devotee of Dionysus with flowers in his hair and a symbol of fertility in his hand.

306   *Cain's or Christ's*   (See note to l. 151) Both were branded and made into outcasts by their societies; in a similar manner the poet is persecuted.

310   *mockery*   imitation.

312   *He*   Leigh Hunt, poet and radical journalist, encouraged and published Keats and Shelley. He cared for Keats during the earlier part of his illness.

381   *plastic stress*   shaping power.

393   *mortal lair*   earthly place or grave.

399   *Unapparent*   unseen realm of the spirit.

        Chatterton   Thomas Chatterton, poet, committed suicide in

1770 at the age of 17. Keats dedicated *Endymion* to him.

401   *Sidney*   Sir Philip Sidney died of his wounds in battle (1586) at the age of 32 while he was helping another soldier.

404   *Lucan*   Roman poet forced by the tyrant Nero to take his own life at the age of 26 after writing against political oppression.

411   *kingless sphere*   the old belief that the famous on earth become stars; Venus is waiting for Adonais.

440   *infant's smile*   possibly a reference to the fact that Shelley's 3-year-old son William was buried there.

444   *pyramid*   tomb of Roman politician, Caius Cestius (first century BC).

460–4   The Neoplatonic One is the absolute perfection, and earthly reality is a distorted semblance of this, even when very beautiful to human eyes. The idea derives less from Plato than from Plotinus (AD 205–70), the later Greek philosopher and mystic.

CHORUS from HELLAS

The lyrical drama was dedicated to Prince Alexandros Mavrokordatos, a Greek exile in Pisa, who became friendly with Shelley and acquainted him with the struggle for independence of the Greeks against the Turks. Mavrokordatos played a major role in the subsequent war (in which Byron was to die) and, after independence was gained, he was chief minister four times between 1833 and 1855. *Hellas* is modelled on *The Persians* by Aeschylus, a play about the defeat by the Greeks of the Persian army under Xerxes. Shelley's drama is set in Constantinople and envisages the defeat of the Turks as the cycle of history moves forward inevitably. The extract is the final Chorus of the play spoken by captive Greek women. In a note, Shelley writes, 'The final chorus is indistinct and obscure . . . Prophecies of wars . . . may safely be made by poet or prophet in any age, but to anticipate however darkly a period of regeneration and happiness is a more hazardous exercise . . . It will remind the reader . . . of Isaiah and Virgil, whose ardent spirits overleaping the actual reign of evil which we endure and bewail, already saw the possible and perhaps approaching state of society in which the "lion shall lie down with the lamb".'

Title   *Hellas*   Greek for 'Greece'.

4   *weeds*   clothes (particularly of mourning). The snake changes its skin each year.

9	*Peneus* river in north-east Greece in the valley Tempe (l. 11).
12	*Cyclads* The Cyclades are islands in the Aegean Sea.
13	*Argo* the ship in which Jason and his Argonauts sailed in search of the Golden Fleece.
	main ocean.
15	*Orpheus* Orpheus could charm nature with his music but he lost his wife Eurydice to the Underworld and was himself torn to pieces by Maenads (wild female devotees of Dionysus).
17	*Ulysses* In the *Odyssey*, Ulysses (Odysseus) lived with Calypso for several years on his way home from Troy to Ithaca.
21–4	By solving the riddle of the Sphinx, Oedipus freed Thebes from plague and became king; but Oedipus had killed his father Laius inadvertently and the fatal consequences of the old curse on the family had to be enacted.
31–4	(Shelley's note) 'Saturn and Love were among the deities of a real or imaginary state of innocence and happiness. All those who fell were the Gods of Greece, Asia and Egypt. The One who rose was Jesus Christ. The many unsubdued are the monstrous objects of the idolatory of China, India, the Antarctic islands, and the native tribes of America.'
35	*dowers* presented as gifts

TO JANE: THE INVITATION

Originally Mary Shelley published a version of this poem and the one following ('To Jane: The Recollection') as a single piece entitled 'The Pine Forest of the Cascine, near Pisa'. The two poems were based on a walk Shelley went on with Jane Williams and Mary on 2 February 1822, but Mary does not feature in the poems. For details about Jane, see note on 'To Edward Williams'.

6	*brake* thicket.
9	*halcyon* calm. (The kingfisher or halcyon was supposed to build its nest on the sea in a special period of tranquil weather.)
38	*stave* verse.
59	*wind-flowers* wood anemones; *anemos* is Greek for 'wind'.

TO EDWARD WILLIAMS

In January 1821, Edward Williams and Jane, his common-law wife, arrived in Pisa with introductions to Shelley and they quickly became good friends. Edward, the same age as Shelley, had been in the navy and the army in India. He sailed with Shelley and was to drown with him in July 1822. Shelley fell in love with Jane, it would appear with Edward's knowledge, and he wrote a number of his late lyrics to her. This poem seems intended for both Edward and Jane.

1	*serpent . . . Paradise* Satan (turned into a serpent) was excluded from Heaven. Shelley's nickname was 'the snake', either because of his quick sinewy movements or as a pun on his name (*bischelli* is Italian for a small snake).
18	*dear friend* This must surely be addressed to Jane.
30	*mean* small.
49	*her* Mary Shelley.

WITH A GUITAR, TO JANE

Behind these late poems addressed to Jane Williams, there is a loneliness and bleakness on Shelley's part. As far as is known, Jane was friendly to him and enjoyed his company but the relationship did not go further. The situation was made more complicated by the fact that Edward and Jane shared a house with the Shelleys and they knew that Mary at the time was deeply unhappy. In this poem Shelley casts Jane, Edward and himself as characters in Shakespeare's *The Tempest*: Jane and Edward are the young lovers Miranda, Prospero's daughter, and Ferdinand, the shipwrecked son of the King of Naples; Shelley is the sprite Ariel on Prospero's island and acts as a guardian angel to Miranda. The poem was written to accompany Shelley's gift of a guitar to Jane.

17	*enchanted cell* In *The Tempest*, Prospero has magical powers. He lives in a cave.
23	*When you die* Ariel is an immortal spirit, whereas Miranda is human. The suggestion is that she has a number of lives.
24	*interlunar* between the old and the new moon.
28	*Star of birth* As in astrological systems, he is her presiding and guiding influence.
37–9	Ariel had been imprisoned in a tree by Sycorax, the witch of the island, and was released by Prospero but had to obey his commands before he would be set completely free.
43	*idol* guitar (an image or shape of nature).

57	*beneath ... star* under the influence of Venus, the planet of love.
64	*sylvan cells* enclosed spaces in the forest.
75	*mysterious sound* like the harmony of the spheres, the pure sound of the universe.
76	*diurnal* daily.
82	*wit* skill.

LINES WRITTEN IN THE BAY OF LERICI

Written in the final month of his life, this poem was probably unfinished. Lerici is a small village on the coast of north-west Italy and it was south of Lerici that Shelley drowned in July.

1	*wanderer* the moon.
7	*She* Jane Williams.
10	*albatross asleep* large oceanic bird with huge wing-span, reputed to sleep while gliding.
22	*vibrations of her touch* Jane practised hypnotism or mesmerism on Shelley to reduce his nervous tension (see his poem 'The Magnetic Lady to her Patient').
41	*ministrations* beneficial things.
42	*Elysian* paradisal.
54	*delusive flame* The fishermen use lights to attract the fish at night and then spear them.
55–8	It is difficult to make sense of lines that appear incomplete. Shelley seems to envy the fish or people who enjoy their pleasure or delusion of pleasure and then die; most people have to suffer regrets and disquiet after their pleasures.

THE TRIUMPH OF LIFE

Shelley's last major poem was left incomplete and unrevised at his death. Various elements of his reading are discernible in the work: the prophetic books and Revelation in the Bible; Petrarch's *Trionfi* where such forces as love, death, time and eternity triumph over each other in a sequence; accounts of Roman military processions where captives were displayed in humiliation and of the car of the juggernaut (Lord of the World in Hindu mythology) under which, it was believed, his devotees sacrificed themselves; Dante; and Rousseau. These final two items require further comment. *The Triumph of Life*, like *The Revolt of Islam* and *The Mask of Anarchy*, is a vision poem in which the poet becomes a narrator, an enquirer, rather than a participant in the action. Dante's *Divine Comedy* is also a vision poem and Shelley derives from it not just a Dante-like fluency and sharpness and the terza rima form but the use of a guide (in Dante's *Inferno* the guide is Virgil, in Shelley's poem the guide is Rousseau). Shelley's admiration for Rousseau was huge but, as he grew older and saw various idealistic schemes and dreams come to nothing or even cause greater unhappiness, he became sceptical of Rousseau's gospel of naturalness and self-expression. In the poem, the 'Shape all light' (l. 352), an embodiment of nature, is ultimately destructive to Rousseau when he drinks from her crystal glass and he, too, is inexorably drawn into the crushing process of the juggernaut. Looking back across history, Shelley seems to find only two people, Socrates and Jesus, strong enough to withstand the corrosive power of life (and they were both executed). Whether or not, if Shelley had continued the poem, a more optimistic view would have emerged is an open question.

7	*orison*	prayer. Note the religious imagery in the introductory section.
8	*tempered . . . lay*	adjusted their morning song (dawn chorus).
11	*censers*	vessels in which incense is burned.
12	*orient*	rich.
23	*cone of night*	shadow made by earth away from the sun.
27	*behind . . . Deep*	He is facing west towards the sea (the Gulf of Genoa).
78	*[blinding]*	Mary Shelley suggested *blinding* to fill the gap.
79–85		The crescent of the new moon holds the dim shape (*ghost*) of the old moon; taken as an omen of an imminent storm.
91	*crape*	black material worn round the hat of a person in mourning.
94	*Janus-visaged*	Janus, the Roman god of doors and turning-points, had faces which looked backwards and forwards and sometimes, as here, to the sides.
100	*banded*	blindfolded.
111	*jubilee*	Originally in Jewish society every fiftieth year saw the cancelling of debts and freeing of slaves. The word came to mean the fiftieth year of a reign or a marriage and the pageant associated with it. George III had such a jubilee in 1809 and Shelley probably uses the word ironically.
121	*age*	later life or period of history.

126	*great winter* death or the end of the world.
134	*they of Athens and Jerusalem* Socrates and Jesus.
145	*fierce spirit* sexual passion (*leisure* is the same word originally as 'licence').
175	*frost . . . those* impotence destroys the old as sensuality destroys the young.
190	*Feature* shape (turns out to be Rousseau).
212	*know themselves* 'Know thyself' was inscribed on the temple of Apollo at Delphi.
214–15	*for the morn . . . evening* because they falsely professed a new knowledge, they lost control before they grew old.
217	*child . . . hour* Napoleon, the product of the Revolution in France.
235–7	*Voltaire . . . sage* Voltaire (see Introduction) is a demagogue because he roused people; Frederick the Great of Prussia, Catherine the Great of Russia and Holy Roman Emperor Leopold, Grand Duke of Tuscany, are anarchs or creatures of chaos; Immanuel Kant, the German philosopher, is the sage.
255–7	Socrates did not succumb to sexual (homosexual) desire as his pupil, Plato, did with a youth called Aster (meaning both a star and a flower).
260	*twain* Aristotle and his pupil, Alexander the Great.
265	*minion* favourite.
269	*Bacon's* Francis Bacon (1561–1626), widely regarded as the founder of modern science and an opponent of scholastic philosophy based on Aristotle.
271	*Proteus* in Greek mythology, the sea-god Neptune's herdsman, who could change his shape at will and so elude capture while awake; Bacon saw Proteus as a metaphor for the natural world.
284	*Caesar's . . . Constantine* from the founding of Roman imperial power with Julius Caesar till the Emperor Constantine established Christianity as the official religion of the empire in 312.
288	*Gregory . . . divine* popes and theologians of the Roman Catholic Church. There were many popes who took the name Gregory or John but Shelley may be referring particularly to Gregory VII (Hildebrand), who in the eleventh century firmly established the political power of the papacy.
290	*eclipse* The darkness of organized Christianity obscures truth.
308	*prime* springtime.

331	*oblivious* inducing forgetfulness; see also l. 341.
357	*Iris* the rainbow.
359	*Mantling ... Nepenthe* colouring with a drug which removes anxiety and induces forgetfulness.
361	*palms* soles of feet.
372	*amethyst* violet-blue colour.
392	*Heaven's ... eyes* stars.
396	*Thou comest ... name* Although the Shape is described in terms of beautiful sights and sounds of the natural world, she is unnatural, dangerous and probably malevolent in her very attractiveness.
414	*Lucifer* Venus as morning star (l. 416) and as evening star (l. 419).
	chrysolite greenish yellow (a gem).
420	*jonquil* flower particularly fragrant in evening.
421–2	*soft notes ... breathes* a popular folk song, 'I am weary of tending the sheep'. Brescia is in northern Italy.
432	*obscure tenor* vague character.
440	*Iris* a rainbow forms a triumphal arch.
446	*atomies* particles of dust.
463	*Lethean* causing forgetfulness (like the river Lethe in Hades).
471–6	*him ... Love* Dante, who in *The Divine Comedy* describes his descent to Hell and his eventual ascent through Purgatory to Paradise guided by Beatrice, his first love and a figure of pure love.
479	*sphere* Venus, planet of love.
496	*tiar* tiara or crown of popes.
500	*anatomies* skeletons.
505	*charnel* building where bones of the dead are kept.

AN ADDRESS TO THE PEOPLE ON THE DEATH OF THE PRINCESS CHARLOTTE

On 6 November 1817, Princess Charlotte, only child of the Prince Regent, later to be king as George IV, died in childbirth aged 21. There was widespread mourning. On the following day, three of the agitators arrested in connection with the Pentridge Rising in Derbyshire in June were executed and beheaded. In his 'Address', Shelley ironically considers the two events in parallel and gradually compels the reader towards a revision of sympathy and priority. The details of the sufferings of the condemned men are factual. The Pentridge Rising was typical of the working-class agitation of the time and the government commonly infiltrated the secret societies with spies and *agents provocateurs* such as Oliver (see paragraphs IX and X).

The original title page reads: ' "We Pity the Plumage, but Forget The Dying Bird"; An address to the People on the Death of the Princess Charlotte, by the Hermit of Marlow.' The quotation is from Thomas Paine's *The Rights of Man* where he rebukes Burke for sympathizing with Marie Antoinette, the executed Queen of France, and for neglecting the misery of the people. Shelley was living at Marlow in Buckinghamshire, and wished to remain half-anonymous; the 'Address' was not published in his lifetime.

44	*'that bourne . . . returns'* misquotation from Shakespeare's *Hamlet* (death).
64	*Horne Tooke* a radical reformer (1736–1812), who supported the Americans in the War of Independence, was charged with high treason and acquitted in 1794.
	Hardy Thomas Hardy (1752–1832), promoter of political reform; charged with treason in 1794 but acquitted.
77–8	*Brandreth . . . Turner* the three agitators (see above) executed for their part in the troubles in Derbyshire. Brandreth was a leader. They were skilled workers and Nonconformists.
90	*Lady Jane Grey* contemporary of Elizabeth I, involved in public life, and finally executed.
116	*hurdle* wooden frame on which traitors were drawn through the streets to execution.
142	*proscriptions* condemnations to execution or banishment.
175	*placemen* appointees of the monarch, hangers-on.
185	*sans peur . . . tache* without fear and without dishonour.
187	*funds* national stocks.
222	*manufacturers* workers in the factories (not the owners).
	helots slaves.
269	OLIVER See above.
281–5	*'When the stroke . . . hooted'* Shelley quotes the report in *The Examiner*, 9 November.
296	*calumniate* slander, falsely incriminate.

There is a considerable problem in dating many of Shelley's shorter pieces of prose. The ideas and images in this essay can be matched with elements in poems written over several years; possibly the most obvious connections are with *Alastor*, written in the second half of 1815, but *Epipsychidion*, finished early in 1821, seems to echo some phrases. Furthermore, it is not known how complete or fragmentary this piece is.

3   *thine*   It is not known whether or not he had a particular addressee in mind.

35–6   *assemblage . . . composed*   Shelley added a note: 'These words are ineffectual and metaphorical – Most words so – No help –'.

37   *soul within our soul*   Some critics have regarded this as the meaning of the title, *Epipsychidion*.

61   *Sterne*   Laurence Sterne (1713–68), author of *Tristram Shandy* and *A Sentimental Journey Through France and Italy*.

64   *mere husk*   This idea appears in *Alastor* and can be related to the image of 'anatomies' in *The Triumph of Life*.

from A PHILOSOPHICAL VIEW OF REFORM

In a letter (dated 6 November 1819) to the Gisbornes Shelley wrote, 'I have deserted the odorous gardens of literature, to journey across the great sandy desert of politics; not, as you may imagine, without the hope of finding some enchanted paradise'. What he was working on is in three chapters; how near completion it is we do not know, but in May 1820 he was making enquiries about a possible publisher. It was eventually published exactly a century later and has remained difficult for readers to find. In chapter I Shelley ranges widely in time and place offering examples of how progressive movements have challenged oppressive regimes. He considers the recent experience of the United States of America as an encouraging model. A link between social progress and artistic achievement is advanced, and the chapter ends with the paragraph he was to use as the conclusion to 'A Defence of Poetry'. In chapter II he analyses what is wrong in contemporary Britain; his analysis is based on what he sees as class divisions, inequalities rooted in class and the lack of representation of the mass of the people. He identifies the national debt as a means whereby the people are obliged to work harder to pay more, with no benefit to themselves, towards a debt which they did not incur. He favours a republic in which the national debt would be abolished, the existing army would be disbanded, all beliefs would be 'equal in the eye of the law', and a tax for the good of all would be levied according to wealth. Chapter III envisages how political reform may take place and enquires whether violent revolution can be avoided or not.

1   *Commons* House of Commons. Shelley's view is that in the present moral climate no individual or group will give up a position of privilege except when under a threat.

45   *questionless* unquestionably.

57   *waning superiority* In the eighteenth century, England was considered by continental intellectuals as a place of tolerance.

66   *Ireland* By the Act of Union (1800) Ireland was joined with Great Britain and, for the first time, Irish Protestants would be represented in Westminster.

74   *Mr Bentham* Jeremy Bentham (1748–1832), radical thinker, theorist of jurisprudence, and exponent of utilitarianism.

75   *immature* premature.

123   *retrenchment* reduction.

128   *Two years ago* before the events of 1819, particularly the Peterloo massacre.

142   *rotten boroughs* parliamentary constituencies where those people eligible to vote were so few or easily bribed as to be totally unrepresentative; Old Sarum, for example, was uninhabited but could 'elect' two members to Parliament.

165   *consummation* satisfactory conclusion.

179   *as the Jews . . . Canaanites* In the Bible (Numbers) the tribes of Israelites are commanded by God to drive out or destroy the inhabitants of Canaan, the Promised Land of the Jews.

191   *castes in India* in Hindu society, a rigid classification of people according to which some people have wonderful privileges and some people have none.

206   *political forms* All political systems rely on co-operation or acquiescence on the part of the populace; if such co-operation is generally removed in, for example, communications or the army, the system will collapse.

214   *demagogues* mob orators.

233–4 *Manchester . . . August* the Peterloo massacre at Manchester in 1819. See introductory note to *The Mask of Anarchy*.

251   *magnanimity* courage (rather than generosity).

294

286	*engine* ingenuity, scheme.
295	*supineness* passivity.
296	*quietism* passivity.
312	*'pernicious . . . touch'* misquoted line from Milton's *Paradise Lost*, VI, 520. The line reads 'Pernicious with one touch to fire' and describes Satan's invention of gunpowder with which he hopes to defeat God. *Pernicious* means 'ready (to explode)' and contains the idea of destructive power.
316	*periodical* (of an illness) having regular, recurring symptoms. *chronic* (of an illness) lingering.
320	*Constantinople* the capital of the repressive Turkish Empire.
334	*distrain* Shelley seems to mean 'restrain' or 'desist'.
335–6	*resistance . . . Charles the 1st* John Hampden (1594–1643) refused to pay a tax imposed by Charles I and he became famous as an advocate of parliamentary representation. Hampden Clubs were set up in 1811 to agitate for reform.
342	*prognostic* pre-indication.
355–6	*Godwin . . . Hunt* respected radical intellectuals.
358	*eagles* Eagles were alleged to be able to look into the sun and renew their youth.
390	*standing army* army maintained in peacetime. The practice began in the late seventeenth century and caused constant argument. The army was used to impose government policies.
405	*livery* costume, uniform.
418	*encroachments* seizures of power.
420	*compensated* balanced.
422	*Robespierre to Louis 18* one of the most vicious of the leaders in the French Revolution and the monarch restored to the French throne after the Napoleonic Wars.
443	*Chinese* Shelley saw the Asiatic countries as suffering under even worse tyrannies than those in Europe. In his opening chapter of *A Philosophical View of Reform* he surveys the prospects for freedom across the world.
455	*circumstance of form* matter of routine.

A DEFENCE OF POETRY

In 1820 Thomas Love Peacock published an essay, 'The Four Ages of Poetry', in which he argued that as civilization advances poetry retreats.

Ingeniously and extravagantly, he classified poetry in four main periods, four types, which he labelled the iron, the golden, the silver and the brass. These types recur in a cycle and, after the silver of the eighteenth-century poets, his contemporary period is a pathetic imitation of heroic, savage qualities; Wordsworth, Scott and Byron are amusingly mocked and poets are dismissed as irrelevant or foolish triflers. For all its wit and satirical exaggeration, the essay makes some telling points and Shelley was stung into making an immediate reply, hence the 'Defence' of the title. The thrust of the argument is not always direct but, after establishing what he means by poetry and a poet, Shelley follows two main lines of defence: love and imagination are central to all morality and poetry can help to develop these; and poetry plays a crucial part in the progressive reformings of society. He intended to add an assessment of the contemporary poets of whom Peacock had been so critical.

8	*το ποιειν* making.
10	*το λογιζειν* reasoning. (Note that Shelley reverses the order of the two mental actions from the first sentence to the second.)
20	*connate* born at the same time.
23	*Aeolian lyre* stringed instrument placed so that it is 'played' by the passing wind.
42	*plastic* shaping.
58	*kind* compatible people.
67	*observing* complying with.
72	*mimetic* imitative.
79	*sensible* noticeable.
90	*integral* whole, general.
102	*chaos* unorganized pieces.
	cyclic vast, epic.
103	*copiousness of lexicography* inclusiveness of dictionaries.
111	*propinquity* close relationship. (Note here how Shelley includes all creative insights as equal to or analogous with poetry.)
114	*Janus* god of doorways and points of transition.
116	*prophets* In Latin, *vates* means 'prophet' and 'poet'.
120	*germs* seeds.
154	*hieroglyphic* emblem or medium.
161	*conciliates* procures.
182	*curse of Babel* According to the Bible, Genesis 2, God cursed early mankind's vanity in attempting to build a tower at Babel

to reach Heaven, and he thwarted the work by causing the people to speak different languages.

201 *Cicero* Roman statesman and writer (first century BC), famous for his speeches to the senate.

periods sentences.

233 *epitomes* abbreviations, bare summaries. Shelley refers to Francis Bacon's sentence 'As for the corruption and moths of history, which are epitomes, the use of them deserveth to be banished.'

269 *Achilles, Hector, and Ulysses* heroic figures in Homer's *Iliad* who respectively manifested the qualities listed.

295 *planetary music* According to tradition, the heavenly music of the spheres, made as the planets spin through space, cannot be heard by fallen human beings.

299 *Ethical science* moral philosophy.

308 *Elysian* glorious, idealized.

310 *content* The stress is on the second syllable.

344 *imperfections* Shelley considered slavery and the subjugation of women as the major defects in Athenian society.

398 *Calderon . . . Autos* Calderón de la Barca (1600–81) was the leading Spanish writer of *autos sacramentales*, religious or allegorical dramas.

409 *Philoctetes or Agamemnon or Othello* the main characters respectively in plays by Sophocles, Aeschylus and Shakespeare.

410 *sophisms* tricks of thought.

410–12 *mirror . . . Paladins* The image is of chivalric knights meeting in combat with their distinctive shields.

412 *necromancers* bogus magicians.

414 *manners* conduct.

417 *corruption . . . imputed* Shelley is probably referring particularly to the denunciation of the theatres by the Puritans in the seventeenth century, but he is always aware of Plato's attack on writers in *The Republic*.

455 *Addison's Cato* Produced in 1713 to popular acclaim, it was written in a dutiful imitation of classical style.

463 *drama . . . Charles II* now usually called Restoration drama.

485 *Machiavelli* statesman, political theorist and dramatist in Renaissance Florence during the period of power of the Medici family. His book *The Prince* (1513) was influential throughout Europe as an analysis of power in the state.

297

Carthaginians, this Roman leader accepted torture and death rather than encourage his fellow Romans to make peace.

573   *senators*   When the Gauls captured Rome, the defeated senators sat in dignified silence.

574–5   *refusal . . . Cannae*   After a major defeat at the hands of Hannibal at the battle of Cannae, the Romans refused to give in and eventually defeated Carthage.

582   *quia . . . sacro*   'because they lack a poet' (quotation from Horace).

597–8   *Moses . . . Isaiah*   The authorship of the books of the Old Testament in the Bible is uncertain. Notwithstanding his own views on religion, Shelley read the Bible repeatedly and with much pleasure.

607–9   *The crow . . . rouse*   Shakespeare, *Macbeth*, III.ii. 50–3.

617   *Celtic*   Shelley uses the term to mean the people to the north of the Mediterranean peoples.

644   *Timaeus and Pythagoras*   earlier Greek philosophers.

648–9   *exoteric . . . esoteric doctrines*   popularly accessible form of secret ideas.

663   *Apollo*   The sun-god was also god of music and poetry.

663   *Muses*   the nine goddesses of arts and sciences.

669   *'Galeotto . . . scrisse'.*   'Galeot (Galahad) was the book, and he who wrote it.' The line comes from Canto V of Dante's *Inferno* but Shelley rather takes the line out of context to mean that the poet is the work and the work is the poet.

669–70   *Provençal Trouveurs*   Troubadours or *trouvères* (from the verb 'to discover') of southern France wrote about love and heroism between the eleventh and fourteenth centuries.

670   *Petrarch*   Italian humanist and love poet (1304–74), spent much of his life in Provence.

678   *Vita Nuova*   early work by Dante exploring his love for Beatrice, who is later to serve as his guide in *Paradiso*.

710   *Riphaeus*   In Virgil's *Aeneid*, Riphaeus is described as the most just man among the Trojans and Dante places him in the Circle of the Just in *Paradiso*.

716   *Satan*   Compare this view of Milton's Satan with that expressed in the Preface to *Prometheus Unbound*.

751   *Lucretius*   Roman philosophical poet, author of *De Rerum Natura*.

751   *limed the wings*   weighed down.

752	*sensible* actual.
755–6	*Apollonius ... Claudian* Greek and Latin poets who each attempted to write an epic.
759–60	*Orlando ... Queen* *Orlando Furioso* (1532) by Ariosto (Italian), *Gerusalemme Liberata* (1580–1) by Tasso (Italian), *The Lusiads* (1572) by Camoens (Portuguese), *Faerie Queene* (1590–6) by Spenser (English), are all long poems with some epic qualities.
768–9	*he created a language* Dante wrote his epic in Italian and is praised as the father of standard literary Italian.
771	*Lucifer* the morning star (means 'light-bearer').
797	*mechanists* exponents of the practical and who have a view of the world as limited and unspiritual.
800	*utility* a term central to the writings of Jeremy Bentham and James Mill in the development of utilitarianism, according to which the aim of morality is the greatest happiness of the greatest number. Shelley uses *utility* here to mean immediate, practical advantage.
826	*exasperate* intensify.
827–9	*'To him ... away.'* a warning of Jesus, Matthew 25: 29.
831	*Scylla and Charybdis* equal dangers based on hazards at sea in Greek mythology, where the two dangers were variously seen as rocks or whirlpools or monsters.
844–5	*'It is better ... mirth.'* Ecclesiastes 7: 2.
860	*Inquisition* In Spain the official system for the persecution of religious unorthodoxy was removed in 1820. However, it was restored, and finally abolished only in 1834.
868	*Hebrew poetry* the Old Testament of the Bible.
882–3	*'I dare not ... adage.'* *Macbeth*, I.vii. 44–5; *adage* means 'proverb'.
883	*want* lack.
893–4	*abridging and combining labour* The new inventions and processes which should make conditions of work better actually allow a greater exploitation of working people (to live by the sweat of his brow was the curse on the fallen Adam).
897–8	*Poetry ... world* Poetry is the true God, greed is the false god of materialism.
848–9	*Orlando Furioso* Ariosto was famous for elaborate revisions in writing his poetry.

979–80   *interlunations*   blank or dark periods (between the old and the new moon).

990–4   *transmutes . . . life*   Shelley uses the image of alchemical change for poetry by which what is base and poisonous can be transformed into something precious and beneficial.

998–9   *'The mind . . . Heaven.'*   Satan's speech, *Paradise Lost*, I.254–5.

1001   *figured*   decorated.

1011   *Non merita . . . Poeta*   'No one deserves the name of creator except God and the Poet.'

1027   *'there sitting . . . soar'*   *Paradise Lost*, IV.829.

1030   *peculator*   embezzler.

1034–6   *sins . . . redeemer*   The imagery is derived from the Bible, and the language at the end of the following sentence is biblical.

1056   *obnoxious to calumny*   exposed to slander.

1071   *gall*   annoyance.

1073   *Theseids . . . Maevius*   Epic poems about Theseus, a legendary hero in ancient Greece, were attempted by mediocre Roman poets such as Codrus, Bavius and Maevius.

1082   *The second part*   Shelley did not write this proposed section.

1093   *last national struggle*   the time of the English Civil War and Milton.

1101   *abjure*   renounce.

1109   *hierophants*   interpreters of sacred mysteries.